Early English Delftware from London and Virginia

Colonial Williamsburg Occasional Papers in Archaeology

Ivor Noël Hume, Editor

Volume II

Early English Delftware from London and Virginia

by

Ivor Noël Hume

Published by
The Colonial Williamsburg
Foundation
Williamsburg, Virginia

Distributed by
The University Press of Virginia
Charlottesville, Virginia

This book was designed by Vernon E. Wooten.
Printed in the United States of America

Library of Congress Cataloging in Publication Data
Noël Hume, Ivor.
Early English delftware from London and Virginia.

(Occasional papers in archaeology ; v. 2)
Bibliography: p. 119
Includes index.
1. Delft ware—England. 2. Delft ware—Virginia.
3. Williamsburg, Va.—Antiquities. I. Title.
II. Series.
NK4295.5.G7N63 738.3'7 76-16560
ISBN 0-87935-034-2

Table of Contents

Foreword

THE study of English delftware has in the past proceeded on two different planes. Connoisseurs have put together collections of mainly intact pieces, whether inspired (like the Hodgkins) by historical curiosity in collecting objects with inscriptions and dates; or by aesthetic quality (collectors like Dr. Glaisher managing to combine both approaches). Archaeologists for their part have interpreted delftwares found in their excavations either by contextual evidence, or by the yardstick of dated pieces in museums or private collections. The supply of collectible intact wares is inevitably strictly limited, but the accumulation of archaeological evidence increases year by year, and since archaeology is an instrument which is honed by the increase of its statistical sample, it is probably to this source of knowledge that ceramic studies will progressively turn in the years ahead. The present book is an important harbinger of that development. Treating as it does a body of excavated material, it relies much for evidence of date on previous archaeological finds, but by no means neglects the *corpus* of material in museums and private collections.

One advantage the author enjoys beyond others. In interpreting material found in England, he has been able to draw on the evidence of comparable material found in excavations in America. By a curious paradox, mainly thanks to the Navigation Acts, there is probably more likelihood that an American-found fragment is of English origin than there is in the case of a fragment excavated in London itself. This added triangulation-point, as it were, gives to the present book a prospect of accuracy denied to its predecessors. It may safely be predicted that it will long remain a landmark in the study of English tin-glazed earthenwares, particularly those of the seventeenth century.

R. J. CHARLESTON
Keeper of Ceramics and Glass
Victoria and Albert Museum

Preface

THE publication in America of a report built around a collection of pottery recovered from a manufacturing site in England might, at first glance, be thought unusual and even inappropriate. Consequently, it is pertinent to outline the remarkable series of coincidences that brought it about.

In 1954 and 1955, while serving as archaeologist for the Corporation of London's Guildhall Museum, I undertook a number of archaeological salvage projects on bombed sites adjacent to Tooley Street in what is now the Borough of Bermondsey, and which were owned and being developed by Hay's Wharf Limited. In the process, I came to know the company's present chairman, Sir David Burnett, Bt., who fortunately possesses a lifelong interest in archaeology and history. Although the sites that I was investigating lay considerably to the west of those to be discussed here, they did yield quantities of broken delftware pottery, some of which had been discarded prior to completion.

Sir David Burnett's interest in the artifacts of the seventeenth and eighteenth centuries was whetted by these early discoveries, and after I left London to join the staff of Colonial Williamsburg, he continued to salvage and record the artifacts found during the rebuilding of other Hay's Wharf properties farther east in the vicinity of Battle Bridge House, Abbot's Lane (formerly Stoney Lane), Vine Lane (formerly Vine Yard), and Pickle Herring Street. On visits to England, I subsequently examined the new discoveries and saw that much of the pottery represented kiln waste and that some of it was decorated in styles that had hitherto been classified as dating from the sixteenth century—a period in which no delftware potting was known to have been going on in London south of the Thames.

In 1966 I undertook the excavation of an extremely important seventeenth-century plantation site at Denbigh near Newport News, Virginia. In the second quarter of the century, that property had been occupied by Captain Samuel Mathews (whose son of the same name became governor of the Virginia colony), a man of accomplishment and substance, best remembered for having been a ringleader in the 1635 revolt against Governor Sir John Harvey. In the course of the digging, foundations assumed to be those of the building once known as Mathews Manor were discovered, along with very large quantities of artifacts of high quality—among them many pieces of decorated delftware of types comparable to those being found by Sir David Burnett in London. Although the Mathews Manor material was being recovered from contexts datable to the mid-seventeenth century, the delftware designs were comparable to examples attributed by previous ceramic historians to earlier dates.

Because the material in the Burnett Collection was not, by and large, recovered from datable archaeological contexts and because it was desirable to learn more about the origins of the Mathews specimens, I decided that the London and the Virginia material should be studied together. Sir David Burnett very generously sent his collection to Williamsburg for that purpose. It later became evident that before the Mathews Manor report could be completed, it would be necessary to prepare an in-depth study of the Southwark evidence.

At the time that this decision was made, no thorough study of the documentary history of the Southwark potting industry had been published, and although the name of the pioneer potter, Christian Wilhelm, figured in many of the books, much still needed to be known about him. Indeed, the precise date of his death was unknown, no one in England being aware that his will had been found and published in the *Virginia Magazine of History and Biography* as long ago as 1906. It is hardly surprising, of course, that no English historian had thought to look there—although it remains so only until one sees the content of the will that was proved on April 9, 1630, and which stated, among other things, that Wilhelm was "a great adventurer to Virginia and other parts beyond the seas, and have a great stocke with Sr. John Harvie Knight and other company touchinge sope-ashes and pott-ashes." Thus the presence of Southwark delftware in Virginia in the early years of the seventeenth century may, in part, be the logical extension of Wilhelm's relationship with Harvey—although it is ironical that the connection should be suggested by the study of the home site of one of the men whom the governor most detested and who was ultimately responsible for his dismissal.

The definitive historical study of the history of the St. Olave Parish potters in the seventeenth century was written by Miss Isabel Davies in 1968, a major research contribution published in the *Surrey Archaeological Collections* in 1969. The arm of coincidence linking these Anglo-American delftware studies was lengthened even further when, in the same year, Miss Davies joined the staff of Colonial Williamsburg's Department of Archaeology, and generously made her then unpublished information available to me.

Although Wilhelm's name has long figured in studies of the origins of English delftware, recent research by Miss Rhoda Edwards, assistant archivist for the Bermondsey Public Library, has shown that two London merchants, Edmund Bradshawe and Hugh Cressey, established a delftware manufactory at Montague Close in the Southwark parish of St. Saviour in about 1613, and in that year were granted a patent that predated Wilhelm's by fifteen years. Furthermore, the firm was joined in 1613–1614 by a new business partner, Sir Thomas Smith, who, among other duties, was the first treasurer of the Virginia Company of London, a post that he held until 1619. One may reasonably assume, therefore, that Sir Thomas was as interested in finding a Virginia market for Montague Close products as Wilhelm must have been for his Pickleherring wares. It is highly likely that both are included among the fragments found in Virginia excavations, and equally likely that it may be a long time before anyone can confidently distinguish between them.

By no means all the examples in the Burnett Collection are yet paralleled by fragments excavated in Virginia. Nevertheless, there is reason to suppose that as more and more seventeenth-century sites are studied, the number of items *not* paralleled will become relatively small. Dr. William M. Kelso, working on behalf of the Virginia Research Center for Archaeology on several sites above and below Jamestown, has indicated that a broad—and perhaps full—spectrum of London delftware was to be found in contemporary Virginia homes. In several instances fragments unearthed on Dr. Kelso's sites match examples in the Burnett Collection but are so far without parallel in published sources. Unquestionably the most dramatic parallel was provided, not by a professional archaeologist, but by a resident of Lee Hall, Virginia, Mrs. Nancy Sweeney, who habitually picked up whatever artifacts came to the surface of her plowed farmland. Although her discoveries were generally of fairly late date, she recovered several fragments indicative of occupation on the property at least as early as the third quarter of the seventeenth century. She eventually found three small but joining fragments of a delftware plate that almost exactly paralleled the design of a stack of such plates that had fused in a firing accident, and which represent the single most important item in the Burnett Collection. Until Mrs. Sweeney's fragments were found there was no evidence that this design was shipped to Virginia; indeed, parallels in English museum and private collections were less close than were these sherds.

Only rarely does an archaeological excavation yield a group of artifacts that can unequivocally be claimed to have been in use at a specific moment in history. Documented shipwrecks can sometimes provide precise dating, and so, occasionally, can land sites when buildings are known to have been destroyed by fire at a recorded time. But more often than not the terrestrial archaeologist must date his features within relatively broad brackets. His clues are derived from the presence or absence of certain artifacts, the recognition of stylistic and technological features, and on that indefinable (and often unreliable) factor—his own experience. Consequently, there remains a pressing need for detailed studies of every category of domestic artifacts, particularly in the seventeenth century, whose documentary records are far less full and informative than are those of the eighteenth or nineteenth centuries. To get such research moving, a catalyst is required, something around which to build and off which to bounce theories and questions. The availability of the Burnett Collection provided just such an opportunity, offering, as it did, not only a corpus of its own information about manufacturing processes, but also a reason to look beyond it to reexamine many of the overly familiar (and thus not carefully considered) pieces in major collections. The publication that follows is the product of this new look at old problems and concepts. The results are by no means flawless; many questions remain unanswered, many dates untidily imprecise, and many attributions doubtful at best. Nevertheless, it is to be hoped that this study will provide something useful on which others will build or, if necessary, dismantle for reuse in the construction of something of more lasting value.

The Virginia colony was established in 1607 and by that date delftware had been in production in England for nearly forty years, its manufacture having begun in Norwich about 1567 and at Aldgate, in London, three years later. Although no controlled archaeological studies of either of these factory sites have yet been undertaken, there is some artifactual evidence, and the Norwich Museum and the Museum of London have been kind enough to allow me to summarize this previously unpublished information (Appendix II). The handful of Norwich and Aldgate fragments helps both to demonstrate the range and quality of delftwares being made by immigrant Netherlandish potters and painters in England before Christian Wilhelm's factory opened, and also to indicate the character of the English wares one may expect to find on Virginia sites dating from the first decade of colonization.

No author of an archaeological study really expects it to be read from cover to cover. Such publications are tools to be used to answer specific questions and, most often, to provide dating evidence for colleagues who "have found a sherd just like your Figure XVII, number 14." Recognizing the manner in which this book will be used, I have elected to permit a degree of repetition. Thus, the introductory sections on the analysis of the illustrated examples discuss collectively the specimens that are later described individually. Consequently, certain details pertinent to both purposes (but possibly to different readers) must be given in both places.

I venture to hope that the book will not only be of use to archaeologists (whose lot in life is to dig up and exult over small chips of once beautiful objects), but also to collectors and curators who may not otherwise have been prompted to look at, or think about, their treasures from the archaeologist's myopic point of view.

Any project that has taken more than a decade to bring to completion inevitably trails in its wake the names of countless kind and helpful people who have commented on this or that, but whose contributions have in the end been churlishly overlooked. To these rightfully indignant friends and colleagues I offer my abject apologies. The names of others are fortunately fresh in my mind for their contributions have been of unforgettable value. Some have now retired from posts held when they assisted me; some have moved on to other positions. Consequently, for the sake of both accuracy and brevity, I propose to omit their affiliations.

It will come as no surprise that my first words of appreciation are due to my longtime friend, Sir David Burnett, Bt., without whose constant help this study could not have been begun, let alone completed. Not only did he provide the archaeological collection but he also assembled most of the original maps and plans from which the new maps have been drawn. Furthermore, his extremely thorough and constructive review of the manuscript not only helped me avoid mistakes but has also led to the acquisition of important additional information. For historical information I am much indebted to Miss Isabel Davies and to Miss Rhoda Edwards. For the provision of parallels, photographs, and opinions I am more than grateful to the following individuals in England: Mr. Robert Allbrook, Mr. D. M. Archer, Mr. John Ashdown, Mr. J. G. Ayers, Mr. K. J. Barton, Mr. Brian J. Bloice, Mr. Alan Carter, Mr. H. J. Case, Dr. F. S. Celoria, Mr. R. J. Charleston, Mr. N. C. Cook, Mr. Graham J. Dawson, Mrs. Philippa Glanville, Dr. D. B. Harden, Mrs. Mary Kaushner, Mr. J. P. M. Latham, Mr. Peter Marsden, Mr. Ralph Merrifield, Mr. William Milligan, Mr. Adrian Oswald, Mr. Cyril Staal, Mr. Hugh Tait, and Mr. James C. Thorn.

For similar assistance in the United States I am equally indebted to Miss Merry Abbitt, Mr. John C. Austin, Mr. John Davis, Dr. Norman F. Barka, Mr. Edward Chappell, Mr. George R. Hamell, Mr. J. Paul Hudson, Dr. William M. Kelso, and Mr. Ross E. Taggart. To Mrs. Judy Hangemanole I offer my admiration and thanks for having brought order and consistency to a sprawling and sometimes incomprehensible manuscript. Needless to add—but appalling to overlook—is my appreciation to my wife, Audrey, whose comments on every fragment (and virtually every sentence) have been of inestimable value.

Most of the excellent pottery drawings are the much appreciated work of Mrs. Paulette Hancock; the maps are by Mr. Daniel Barber; and the color photography is by Colonial Williamsburg staff photographer Miss N. Jane Iseley. For the provision of illustrations of items in their collections, or for permitting me to photograph the objects for myself, I am indebted to the following museums and collectors: to the Museum of London (née Guildhall) for Pls. 3, 6, 41, 43, 44, and 55; to the Museum of London (née London Museum) for Pls. 4, 27, and 37; to the Virginia Historic Landmarks Commission and the Virginia Research Center for Archaeology for Pl. 13; to the Colonial Williamsburg Foundation for Pls. 5, 15, 16, 18 (center), 19, 22 (left), 24, 25, and 28; to the Fitzwilliam Museum, Cambridge, for Pls. 17, 34, and 58; to the Kenneth and Jean Chorley Collection for Pl. 20; to the Victoria and Albert Museum, London, for Pls. 21, 32, 33, 45, and 53; to the Ashmolean Museum, Oxford, for Pls. 23 and 48; to the Nelson Gallery–Atkins Museum, Kansas City, for Pls. 35 and 36; to the National Museum of Wales for Pl. 42; to the Sir David Burnett Collection for Pls. 46 and 52; and to the British Museum for Pl. 56. The items illustrated in Pls. 8, 10, 12, 29, 47, and 54 are in my own collection. The sherd shown in Pl. 39 is in the Colonial Williamsburg archaeological collections and was generously presented by Mrs. Nancy Sweeney; the fragments from Mathews Manor illustrated in Pls. 7 and 14 were deposited in the same collection by Mr. L. B. Weber. Two more sherds illustrated in Pl. 24 were excavated at Carter's Grove plantation and these, also, are in the Colonial Williamsburg archaeological collections. The remaining photographs (9, 11, 18 [left and right], 22 [right], 30, 31, 38A and B, 40, 49, 50, and 51), along with all the items drawn in Figures I–XVIII, are selected from the Burnett Collection of Southwark (now Bermondsey) delftware.

In conclusion, it is imperative to note that although I am indebted to all these individuals and institutions for whatever is correct and useful, they are in no way to blame for errors, omissions, or misinterpretations. For those, I have no one to thank but myself.

January 1, 1976 I. Noël Hume

Introduction

THE beginning of tin-enameled earthenware manufacturing in England in the second half of the sixteenth century was a significant manifestation of Britain's belated renaissance. It also provided a cornerstone for the great English ceramic tradition that was to be built in the eighteenth century and whose faded aura still lingers today. The artifactual evidence discussed in this volume cannot claim to be part of that cornerstone, but it is close enough to the foundation to give considerable support to the subsequent evolution of English delftware. It is important to note, however, that the term *evolution* does not necessarily imply a progressive improvement; indeed, there are both collectors and ceramic historians who contend that, aesthetically, the early seventeenth-century tin-enameled wares were superior to most of the delftware manufactured in the following century and a half.

The collection described and illustrated on these pages was recovered from an area south of the River Thames and east of the present Tower Bridge in what was, in the seventeenth century, the parish of St. Olave, a part of the Borough of Southwark incorporated into the Borough of Bermondsey in 1832. The land whereon the pottery was found is all the property of Hay's Wharf Limited, and the fragments were recovered as a result of building operations carried out by that company between 1954 and 1961 (Pl. 1). Little or no archaeological control was exercised, the bulk of the material being unearthed by construction crews and passed to the present chairman of the Proprietors of Hay's Wharf, Sir David Burnett, Bt., who alone was responsible for salvaging what is certainly one of the more important "documents" in the early history of the English ceramic industry.

There can be no denying that it is tantalizing and disappointing that the collection was not assembled under careful archaeological control. One weeps at the thought of what must have been lost, and bemoans both the absence of photographs of the pottery in situ and of stratigraphic sections showing the chronological relationships between the artifact-bearing layers. However, with that said, the fact remains that the individual pieces often speak eloquently for themselves. It is true that one cannot attribute them to individual potters; nevertheless, the seventeenth-century fragments all come from a relatively small area, thus laying to rest the well-entrenched popular supposition that all London delftware was manufactured at Lambeth—then a village much farther upriver opposite Westminster and close to the modern County Hall. Extant documentary evidence strongly supports the archaeological evidence (or vice versa, depending on one's point of view), the records suggesting that delftware manufacturing may have begun in Southwark by 1612 and showing that the first known factory at Lambeth was not established until about 1676.

As every student of ceramics is aware, the field is strewn with misnomers, with overlapping terminology, and with undocumented traditions—not the least of them being the popular belief that delftware was first manufactured at Delft in Holland. In truth, however, Delft has no valid claim to that distinction. The ware had been in mass production at Antwerp from about 1510 and was being made in England at Norwich as early as 1567. The Dutch city of Delft was, in fact, best known in the early seventeenth century as a brewing center. Delft did not establish its potting industry until about 1640, although its painters did develop the more delicate and sophisticated designs that distinguished the later products from the medieval and renaissance styles of the earlier Netherlandish maiolica. Nevertheless, the technique of manufacture remained similar to that employed by Italian and Spanish maiolica manufacturers of the fifteenth and sixteenth centuries and by French makers of faïence in the seventeenth century. In short, delftware, maiolica, and faïence all refer to a similar body and glaze combination described, by those who dislike all three terms, as tin-enameled earthenwares. Even this description leaves something to be desired, for the potters did not coat their ware with tin, but merely included a sufficient quantity of tin oxide in their essentially lead glaze to make it white and opaque. Furthermore, the majority of English delftware dishes of the first seventy years of the seventeenth century generally were coated on their backs with a semi-transparent and yellowish lead glaze containing little or no tin. There is, however, considerable variation in both the color and degree of transparency of the back glazes, suggesting that they may have been made up from the remains of batches of tin glaze indiscriminately topped up with lead glaze mix.

All this, of course, is extraordinarily confusing and irritating to the layman who finds comfort in neat, all-embracing, one-word descriptive terms. In the sixteenth and seventeenth centuries, the ware was most commonly described as "galley-ware" and later as "painted earthenware." The former's derivation is obscure, but it is thought to relate to the fifteenth-century importation of Italian and Hispano-Moresque maiolicas that reached England aboard galleys. However, for the purpose of this study and in the interest of brevity, the wares manufactured in Southwark in the first half of the seventeenth century will be called delftware—with the lowercase "d" that must always be used to describe any ware having a comparable body and glaze combination but not known to have been made at Delft.

The Historical Background

SEVERAL authorities have claimed that a delftware potter set up a business in or near Sandwich in Kent in 1582 and that he produced a series of bulbous mugs rather similar in shape to Rhenish stoneware examples of the second half of the sixteenth century, but of yellow earthenware coated with a tin glaze colored with zaffre blue or manganese purple. One such jug was encountered in the collection of West Malling church in Kent, and, in consequence, the entire class became known as "Malling ware" (Pl. 5). This is, of course, another misleading appellation suggesting that the jugs were made at Malling—a conclusion for which there is not a shred of evidence. Support for their having been made at Sandwich is actually no stronger; indeed, the existence of a Malling jug having a silver mount bearing the London date letter for 1549–1550 makes it most unlikely that the first of these jugs was made at Sandwich in 1582.

It so happens that the Malling church mug possesses a silver mount with the date letter for 1581–1582, corresponding with the advent of the Sandwich potter. Because these jugs or mugs allegedly represent the beginning of delftware manufacturing in England, it is important to place them in their proper perspective. As already noted, the earliest recorded example has a mount dated 1549–1550, and according to Mankowitz other examples run as late as 1618.[1] How, then, did the Malling jugs come to be associated with Sandwich?

W. B. Honey seems to have been the originator of this belief when he wrote in 1933: "For the sixteenth century besides there is Solon's statement that a Netherlands potter was at Sandwich in 1582, and Chaffers' reference to another at Maidstone in the same year; neither writer gives any authority, and one was perhaps copying from the other. If there actually were maiolica potters in Kent at this time . . ."[2]

This by no means categorical statement by Honey nevertheless occurred in his chapter on the origins of English delftware, and repetition has tended to give greater substance to the maiolica potter of Sandwich. However, going back to Solon, one finds that the unidentified potter is not discussed in the chapter on delftware, but in the section dealing with "Slip-decorated ware." The passage reads as follows: "Howbeit, at the date we speak of, we find this fabrication established in many counties. In Kent it was carried on at Sandwich, where a Dutch potter is known to have settled in 1582; and also at Wrotham, where very elaborate ware was made, including posset pots, dishes, candlesticks, and many different sorts of fanciful jugs and bottles."[3] Clearly Solon was not suggesting that the Sandwich potter made delftware, but that he was a producer of slipware. This might have been the end of the Sandwich legend were it not for the evidence of the town itself. Adjacent to the market were two lanes named Butchery Street and Potters Street, both suggesting that they were named for trades practiced there. Of course Potters Street could refer to potters' shops rather than to actual kiln sites, and being situated in the heart of the town there might be some logic in drawing that conclusion. Besides, there is no evidence that these potters made delftware. Much more interesting, however, is a wider and longer road to the rear of the town named Delp Street.[4] If that name was a corruption of Delph Street,

1. Mankowitz and Haggar (1957), p. 140.
2. Honey (1952), p. 34.
3. Solon (1886), p. 54.
4. John Andrews, Andrew Dury, and William Herbert, *A Topographical Map of the County of Kent* (1769, reprint ed., Lympne Castle, Kent: Harry Margary, 1968).

then it is possible that it dates from the mid-seventeenth century, being named for the galleyware potters who had worked or were still working there.

More convincing is the documentary evidence derived from *The Returns of Aliens Dwelling in the City and Suburbs of London, 1523–1625,* which names several Low Countries potters then living in Aldgate who had come there from Sandwich. Among them were John Fott and William Tande, both of whom had lived in Sandwich prior to 1567.[5] Aldgate would shortly be (if it was not already) associated with the manufacture of delftware, and therefore one is tempted to assume that Fott and Tande were already skilled in that art. But in the absence of further information it must remain just that—a temptation, nothing more.

The Sandwich–Malling connection is by no means accepted by all ceramic historians. Anthony Ray, for example, has contended that "these jugs were probably made by Flemish potters working in London in the reign of Edward VI. During the reign of Queen Mary they were banished, but allowed back under Elizabeth."[6] However, he does not cite his source for this information nor does he produce artifactual evidence to demonstrate that vessels of the Malling type were manufactured in London. At any rate, until wasters are unearthed or an unequivocal documentary reference is located, it can be argued that the jugs were not made in England at all, but were imported from a factory in the Low Countries and later enriched with English mounts. Numerous examples of Rhenish stoneware mugs of the same period have been treated in that way, and no one has asserted that those, too, were made in England. The fact that the known examples of Malling ware span a period of more than sixty years makes it likely that they came from a manufactory that possessed an uninterrupted stylistic tradition, rather than being the products of an on-again, off-again enterprise as suggested by Ray. Were there a great deal of variation among the extant pieces, with some of them copying English rather than Rhenish shapes, there might be reason to take them more seriously. But in the absence of anything identifiably English about these jugs (other than their occasional London mounts) it may be wiser to dismiss them as imports. The fact that three of the examples were discovered in Kent might at first glance suggest that they were the products of direct trade with Flanders, but as they must first have been taken to London to be mounted, their Kent association would appear to be meaningless.

Slightly more tangible are our glimpses of two potters, Jaspar Andries and Jacob Janson, who moved to England from Antwerp in 1567–1568 and set up in business, first at Norwich and then in London (See Appendix II). Although their names are recorded, they nevertheless remain rather shadowy figures and most of what is known about them is derived from Stow's *Survey of London:*

> About the year 1567, Jaspar Andries and Jacob Janson, Potters, came away from Antwerp, to avoid the Persecution there, and settled themselves in Norwich; where they followed their Trade, making Gally Paving Tiles, and Vessels for Apothecaries and others, very artificially. Anno 1570 they moved to London . . . and desired by petition, from Queen Elizabeth, that they might have Liberty to follow their Trade in that City without Interruption; and presented her with a Chest of their Handy-work.[7]

Stow went on to relate that they had claimed in their petition to be the first to bring and exercise "the said Science in this Realm," and that Henry VIII had thought so well of the products made by Andries's father that he had offered him "good Wages and House-room, to come and exercise the same here." This offer had apparently come to naught. The 1570 petition ended by requesting permission to establish a manufactory "in or without the Liberties of London, by the Waterside," and a patent to be the sole manufacturers in England of the aforesaid galleyware.

The petition itself does not survive and there is no record that the Andries–Janson patent was granted. Nevertheless, Janson did move to London, changing his name to Johnson, and setting up a business in Aldgate where he remained until his death in 1597. The range of his products is not known, although it is reasonable to suppose that he produced the types listed in Stow's quotation

5. Archer (1973), p. 7.

6. Ray (1968), p. 33.

7. John Stow, *A Survey of the Cities of London and Westminster and the Borough of Southwark,* II, 6th ed. (London, 1755 [orig. publ. 1598]), p. 327.

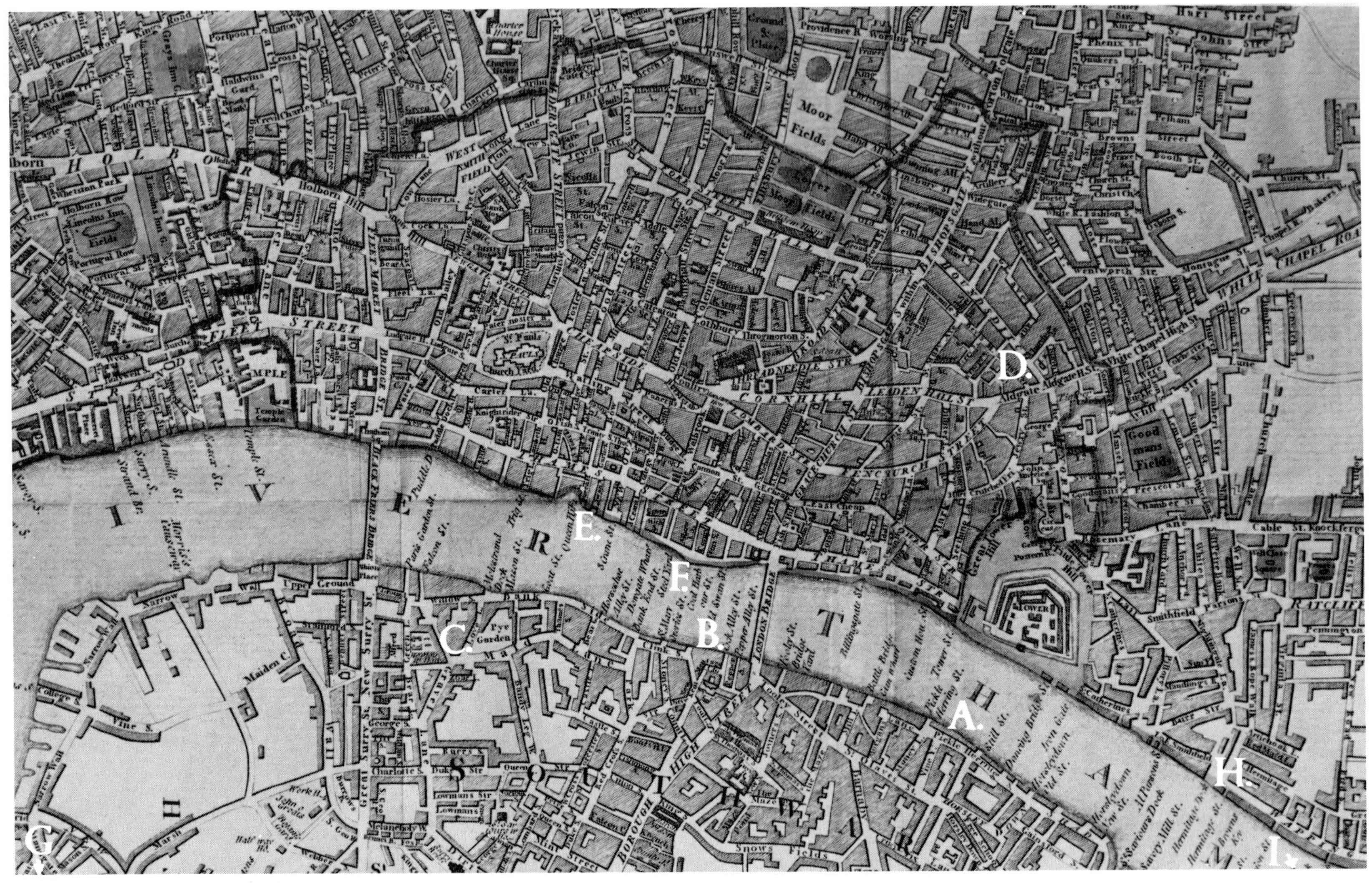

Plate 1.
A map of the city of London and Southwark showing the principal sources of delftware waste products: A, the Pickleherring complex; B, Montague Close; C, Gravel Lane; D, Duke's Place, Aldgate; E, Queenhithe (redeposited material?); F, The Steelyard; and G, Lambeth. Also marked, at H and I, are documentarily identified locations at Hermitage Dock and Rotherhithe.

from the original petition. F. H. Garner, in discussing Jacob Johnson's Aldgate factory, stated that "a large number of dishes, drug-jars, 'vessels for apothecaries,' vases and jugs of the period 1570 to 1600 have been dug up in the City of London. . . .They are decorated in blue, orange, green, yellow, and purple, in many cases rather duller in colour than the similar ware found in Flanders, and whilst some of these may have been imported, there is reason to regard others as probably English."[8] This last contention is now proved to be true, but most of the evidence comes from the Southwark kiln sites and not yet from Aldgate, while irrefutable archaeological evidence found in both England and America shows that the wares Garner attributed to ca. 1570–1600 were common as late as the 1640s.

Johnson had joined, brought over, or otherwise been associated with a number of Flemish craftsmen who worked at the potter's trade in the vicinity of Aldgate, and it is reasonable to deduce that they continued there after his death. The Aldgate enterprise has been linked (for reasons that are unclear) with the establishment in the third quarter of the seventeenth century of a factory near Hermitage Dock east of the Tower of London and St. Katherine's, and west of Wapping, an area that became a major potting center in the following century. Unfortunately, no careful archaeological attention has been devoted to the Aldgate potter and his alleged Hermitage successors, and there is only the slender evidence discussed in Appendix II to suggest what shapes and designs were produced at Aldgate, and none to identify the Hermitage Street wares. It is equally debatable whether Flemish potters from Aldgate were the first to move across the Thames to the somewhat less congested parish of St. Olave in Southwark, or whether the industry was begun there by newly arrived immigrants.

The first name to be associated with the St. Olave venture is that of Christian Wilhelm, who, as Miss Isabel Davies has discovered, came to England from the Rhenish Palatinate in 1604 and rented from Sir William Gardiner "pte of a howse of myne in Southwark called Pickellherringe" and there set up in business as a maker of "Smalte or blew starche."[9] Smalt, incidentally, was used, among other things, to obtain the blue for decorating delftware. A year later, a monopoly for smalt manufacturing was given to another petitioner, and Wilhelm was driven out of the business. In 1617 he was recorded as being a maker of vinegar and in the following year a distiller of aqua vitae. However, in the latter instance he was styled as being an "aquivtay styller" second and a "galley pott maker" first. By 1628, when Wilhelm petitioned for a sole patent to manufacture galleyware, he claimed to have been in that business for sixteen years—which would have put his commencement date around 1612.

In response to his petition, Wilhelm received a royal patent in 1628 granting him "full free and absolute lycense priviledge power libertie and authoritie . . . during the terme of foureteen yeares" to manufacture "earthen gally potte and dishes called by the name of gallyware and all kinde or sorte of bottells of all Colos basons and ewers salte dishes of all sorte drinkinge potte pavinge tyles Apothecaries and Comfittmakers potte of all sorte and all kinde of earthen worke as he the said Christian Wilhelme hath heretofore invented and made."[10] The patent stated that he had been making galleyware in England "for these Twentie yeares past," a claim greater than was his own, and referred to Wilhelm as the inventor of galleyware manufacturing in England. This, of course, was not the case, but it was common practice for patent applicants to make such claims in the hope that no one would challenge them.

Christian Wilhelm died in 1630 leaving the bulk of his estate to his daughter Mary and her husband, Thomas Townsend, who were his executors.[11] As the 1628 patent was granted to Wilhelm and "his executos administratos deputies and assignes," it is reasonable to conclude that theoretically, if not in practice, the monopoly remained in effect until its expiration in 1642. Thomas Townsend's name occurs from time to time in the Southwark court records wherein he was styled a potter or potmaker. In 1638 he was ordered to clean out the sewer and drain "on the west and south sides of his Potthouse and grounde neare Pickleherringe . . ."[12] Two years

8. Garner (1948), p. 4.

9. Davies (1969), 12, quoting S.P. 14/72, No. 84, Public Record Office.

10. S.P. 39/25, No. 42, P.R.O.

11. *Virginia Magazine of History and Biography,* XIV (July 1906), 88.

12. Davies (1969), 21; Edwards (1974), 112.

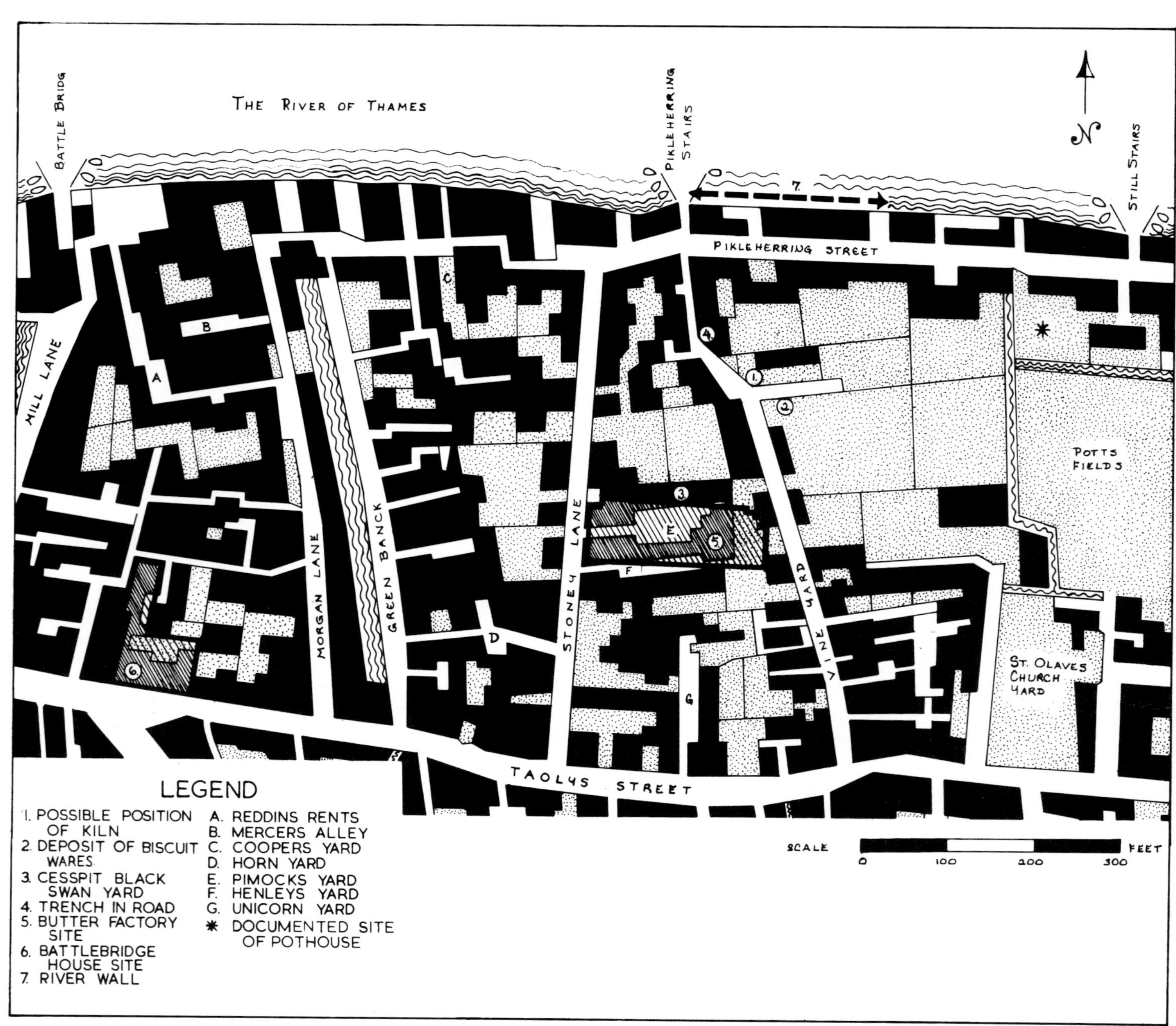

Plate 2A.
A map of the relevant section of St. Olave's Parish redrawn from Robert Morden and Philip Lea's A Prospect of London and Westminster *(1682), superimposing, in diagonal hatching, the areas embraced by the archaeological sites. The original map is derived from the 1720 John Strype edition of John Stow's* Survey of the Cities of London and Westminster. *It should be noted that by the time the 1755 edition was printed, the map had been amended. "Potts Fields" had been deleted and "Gardens" had been substituted.*

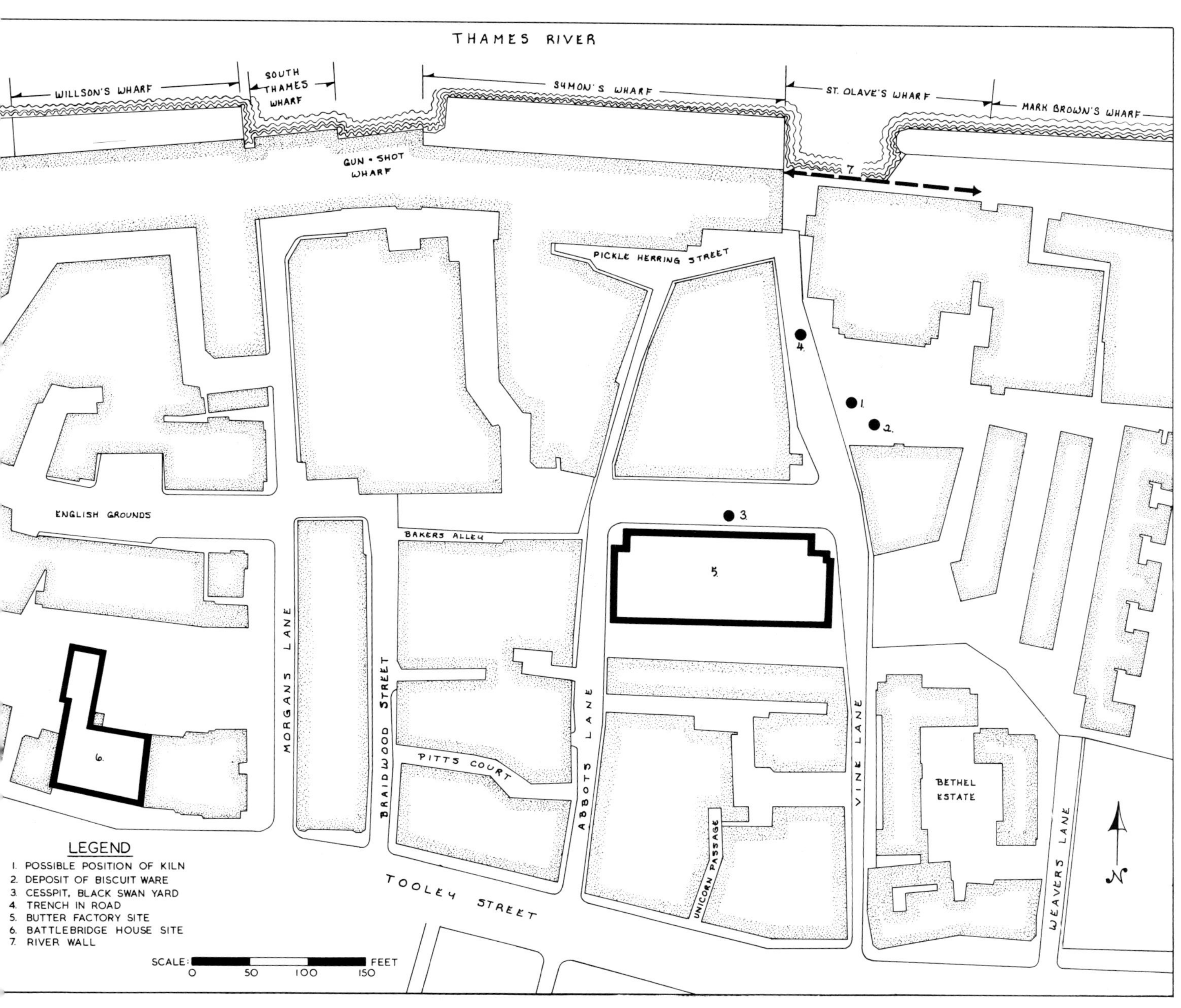

Plate 2B.
A plan showing the modern street configuration in the parish of St. Olave, Bermondsey, and the locations of sites whence came the illustrated delftware fragments.

later Townsend's new landlords, Peter Lister and Thomas Booth, were fined for failing to clean the drains "against theire old Potthouse and theire newe buildinge att Pickleherring in the parish of St. Olave," and in 1642 merchant George Thorogood was instructed to rivet three rods of the sewer bank "against his old Pothouse at Pickleherring in the parish of St. Olave betweene his new house of office, and the next bridge lyeing over the said Sewer."[13]

As Miss Davies has pointed out, the last extant reference to Thomas Townsend as a potter occurs in 1641 in the St. Olave baptismal register. Although the register from 1628 to 1639 does not survive, the record of baptisms is intact from the latter date to 1665 and contains the names of no fewer than twenty-eight potters. It is reasonable to conclude that many of them worked at the Pickleherring factory. Indeed, until the expiration of the patent, theoretically no delftware potter could have worked in London or anywhere else in England or Wales without permission of Wilhelm's heirs.

Although Christian Wilhelm has received more attention than most other early Southwark pothouse entrepreneurs, he was by no means the first to establish residence on the south bank of the Thames. By 1567 another Low Countries emigrant potter, Simon Vandolen, was living in the adjacent Thamesside parish of St. Saviour. There is, alas, no knowing where he worked, where he lived, or, indeed, whether he continued in the potter's trade. In 1613 a London merchant named Edmund Bradshawe entered into partnership with another merchant, Hugh Cressey, and together they obtained a twenty-one-year patent from James I for the manufacture of "all manner of earthen vessell[es] after the manner of Fiansa being a worke not heretofore put in use w[i]thin this kingdome, and hath brought workemen into this kingdome for the p[er]forming thereof." The patent went on to identify the products: "all pavinge tiles of all sises[,] dishes of all sises [,] pott of all sises. . ."[14]

The reference to "Fiansa" is clearly to tin-enameled earthenware (Pl. 3, center), but equally clearly Bradshawe and Cressey were far from being the first to bring the art into Britain. However, they did set up their business in Southwark at Montague Close, hard by St. Saviour's church, where a factory continued to operate for nearly a century and a half. Although the Montague Close enterprise, along with its managerial and floor staff, was closely related to that of the Pickleherring Quay factory throughout its checkered life, it would be more confusing than relevant to recount every twist and turn of Montague Close history. We need note only that archaeological excavations on the kiln sites under the direction of Mr. Graham Dawson of the Cuming Museum, Southwark, have yielded large quantities of sherds indistinguishable from most of the pieces in the Burnett Collection. Furthermore, it may or may not be significant that the Bradshawe-Cressey partnership being short-lived, Cressey secured new backers in March 1613/14, one of them being Sir Thomas Smith, who was both governor of the East India Company and treasurer of the Virginia Company. It is possible, therefore, that the Montague Close factory was exporting delftware to Virginia before Wilhelm entered the picture.

Among the men associated with both the Montague Close and Pickleherring Quay factories is William Bellamy, whose name first appeared in the St. Saviour's parish register in 1631 and who died in 1645. In February 1634/35 "one Pothouse or workhouse built all in brick" was described as being in Montague Close, as were two small tenements occupied by Bellamy and Thomas Irons, both of whom were potters.[15] Since Bellamy lived in the same street as the Montague Close factory, it is reasonable to suppose that he worked there rather than in the neighboring parish of St. Olave. Thomas Irons, incidentally, would later become a partner with Edward Ball and John Townsend in the management of the Montague Close factory. Furthermore, it may be no mere coincidence that John Townsend was involved with that enterprise while Thomas Townsend was operating the Pickleherring Quay factory as the successor to Wilhelm. It is important to recall, as Isabel Davies points out, that the son-in-law of William

13. Davies (1969), 21–22; Edwards (1974), 112.

14. Dawson and Edwards (1973), 57, quoting S.P. 39/3, No. 41, P.R.O.; Patent Roll, C. 66/1982, P.R.O.

15. Dawson and Edwards (1973), 59–60, quoting P. 92/SAV/1326, Greater London Council Record Office.

Bellamy was one Richard Newnham, also a potter, and it is believed that he subsequently went into business with Bellamy's widow, Martha, taking over the management at Pickleherring Quay from Thomas Townsend. Although Martha Bellamy died in 1655, Newnham was still in business as a potter in 1676, for in that year he was one of a group of London potters petitioning Parliament to enforce the embargoes on the importation of foreign "painted earthenwares."

Miss Davies has concluded, however, that in the following year the Pickleherring factory was in the hands of William Fry and Edward Osbaldston. Neither man was originally a practicing potter, Fry being a vintner and Osbaldston a freeman of the Painter Stainers' Company. In 1682 an otherwise unrelated deed of mortgage between Phillip Atkins of the Middle Temple and Alice Stratford of the parish of St. Clemence Danes referred to the "Millhouse and pothouse

Plate 3.
Examples of early Netherlandish and Faenza-style maiolica illustrating the decorative techniques from which English delftware developed. All three were recovered from a rubbish pit filled about 1510 at Gateway House in the City of London. The IHS vase at the left is painted only in blue (height: 5 1/2 inches); the comparable vase at the right is the same size but is decorated in polychrome. Both are of Netherlandish manufacture. The central medallion of the Faenza-style jug is also in polychrome. Height: 10 inches. Museum of London: 23046, 23045, and 23044.

with the Appurtenances and the Yard and Garden plott behinde the same Lyinge on the west-side of the said Pott house now in the tenure of the said Widdow ffry."[16] Although Fry was obviously dead, Osbaldston continued his interest in the delftware trade, his name appearing in 1686 in yet another petition calling for the enforcement of the embargo against the importation of foreign delftware.

Assuming that the factory originally established by Wilhelm remained the principal manufactory in St. Olave's parish, it is logical to assume that any potter domiciled in the parish whose name appears in the records as a spokesman for the London potters was master of the Pickleherring enterprise. On this basis, Miss Davies has pointed out that in 1693 the names of John Robins and Moses Johnson were thus associated, and that Robins figured again in the following year. In that petition Johnson's name was missing, although he is known to have moved westward to the Bear Garden in 1695 and there set up in business as a stoneware potter. In this connection, it may be noted that still further west, on the site of the present Bankside power station, large quantities of both delftware and brown stoneware wasters have been found in use as fill.[17] It is likely that this material came from Johnson's venture and that he not only made stoneware but continued to produce delftware.

According to notes assembled by the late F. H. Garner, Robins or one of his relatives went into business with someone named Grove, who moved the factory from the Pickleherring site to a location in nearby Stoney Lane in 1723[18] where the Grove family continued in business through much of the eighteenth century(Pl. 2A).The name of Richard Grove, "Potter, Tooly-street, Southwark," was listed in London's *The Directory* in 1736 and 1738, while that of Joseph Grove was shown in 1767 as residing in Horsleydowne Lane, Southwark. No trade was cited, but Joseph was previously listed under potters in 1763 as living in Horsley Lane and being a maker of "white" earthenwares.[19] If Garner's information is correct, it would mean that the Groves moved their factory to the west of the Pickleherring site and resided considerably to the east of it. In between, however, and to the north of St. Olave's churchyard, there was a large open space shown on the 1720 edition of Morden and Lea's map as being named Potts Fields (Pl. 2A). This undoubtedly related to a piece of land that figured in a deed of 1679, wherein Daniel Duthais leased a parcel to Humphrey Smith, the land being "part of the Ground now or formerly called Potts Field situate lying and being on the North side of Horsey Downe."[20]

Sir David Burnett has pointed out that as recently as the 1950s, old employees whose families had worked for the Proprietors of Hay's Wharf for several generations referred to this easterly sector of the property as "the farm." It is interesting to note that the 1572 map of London and Southwark by Braun and Hogenberg (see Pl. 57) depicts cattle grazing in that area.[21] To the west is shown an open ditch or sewer, and to the north, and abutting the sewer on the east, a cluster of buildings amid a stand of trees identified as "beere house." These buildings are impaled to the south to enclose a sizable open area, leaving common land to the south and east. A cluster of what appears to be the same group of buildings (five or perhaps seven of them) was shown on Antony van den Wyngaerde's view of London of ca. 1550.[22] More convincing, however, is evidence provided by Radolphus Aggus's view, dated 1563, which shows both the sewer and the cluster of tree-shrouded buildings immediately east of it.[23] Here again the buildings are impaled to the south, fencing them off from what appears to be adjacent common land.

Previously cited evidence has shown that the pothouse operated by Christian Wilhelm's step-

16. Davies (1969), 26, quoting Surrey Deed No. 4886, Minet Library, Lambeth.

17. Oswald (1950), 183–185.

18. Davies (1969), 28.

19. *London Directory,* 1763, prefixed by the following: "Manufactures of Blue and White, and Plain White, Earthen Wares. Brown Stone Potters make only Jars, Jugs, etc. and do not undertake any part of the White branch." Only two potters were then listed under the "Blue and White" heading, John Dunbibin in Coffin's Yard, St. Margaret's Hill, and Joseph Grove in Horsley Lane.

20. Davies (1969), 26, quoting Surrey Deed No. 4882, Minet Library.

21. Facsimile reprint, Topographical Society of London, 1882–1883.

22. Facsimile reprint, Topographical Society of London, 1881–1882.

23. Radolphus Aggus, *London and Westminster in the Reign of Queen Elizabeth, Anno Dom. 1563* (reprint ed., London: J. Wallis, 1789).

son and coheir, Thomas Townsend, was bounded on the west and south by sewers, a relationship appearing in but one location on Morden and Lea's 1682 map, namely close to Still Stairs and north of Potts Fields. We may reasonably deduce that public sewers would have been dug on common land, and thus that the east-west ditch shown by Morden and Lea had been dug at the edge of the common land bordering the fenced "beere house" complex. Hay's Wharf historian Aytoun Ellis has noted that at some time in the second half of the sixteenth century, a Flemish brewer named Peter Van Düren was a resident in the Pickleherring neighborhood and was charged with employing sixteen aliens in his brewery. In the indictment, according to Ellis, van Düren was "given the alternative name of 'Pyckleheryng.' "[24] Peculiar though this may be, it serves to establish van Düren's brewery as being located in the vicinity of Pickle Herring Street. In her invaluable documentary study of sixteenth- and seventeenth-century London potters, Rhoda Edwards has shown that Townsend operated his pothouse next door to the premises of a brewer, Richard Hartford, adding that "it seems that the Pickleherring pothouse was always next door to a brewery."[25] She goes on, however, to equate it with a brewhouse shown between Stoney Lane and Vine Lane on Rocque's map of 1746 (Pls. 2A and 2B, site 5), a location never flanked to the west and south by ditches or sewers and lacking the river frontage shown on the 1572 map by Braun and Hogenberg.

It can be claimed with reasonable conviction that Christian Wilhelm and Thomas Townsend operated a pothouse near Still Stairs at the location asterisked on Pl. 2A. Indeed, it is conceivable that Still Stairs got their name from Wilhelm's aqua vitae distillery.

Even as late as 1755, there remained a considerable amount of lot-divided but undeveloped land in the area east of Vine Yard where most of the Burnett Collection was retrieved and where, in 1961, Sir David Burnett reported that he saw the remains of brick kilns or ovens exposed by the London Electricity Board's trenching. In 1965 Dr. Francis Celoria, then field officer for the London Museum, conducted an excavation in an open area to the west of the previous discovery and recovered additional quantities of pottery fragments. Neither Vine Yard nor Weaver's Lane to the east, which abuts against St. Olave's churchyard, figures in the early documentary sources.[26] There the references were always to "Pickle Herring." On Rocque's map of 1746, this was shown to be the street running parallel to the Thames from Stoney Lane to the dock at Old Stairs, then called Pickle Herring. It is not so identified in Morden and Lea's map illustrating the 1755 edition of Stow's *Survey*, but this was probably an oversight, as the street is marked "Pickle Herring S." in a map of London drawn in 1791 and published in the *Universal British Directory* of 1793 (Pl. 1).

If, as is suggested, Potts Fields was bounded on the west by the sewer referred to in deeds identifying Wilhelm's and Townsend's old potworks, it is strange that Sir David Burnett should have found the remains of kilns so far to the west of that sewer. Furthermore, the relatively intact condition of many of the ceramic items in the collection makes it unlikely that the material was carted from elsewhere as fill. Indeed, the stack of plates that fused together in the kiln (Pl. 30) is so friable that it could hardly have survived if it had been treated at all roughly. On that evidence, we may conclude that the plates were found close to where they were made—although the find spot was in the middle of Vine Yard. It should be noted, too, that the Celoria excavations of 1965 were also located west of the supposed Potts Fields west sewer line, and that there, too, much of the material seemed to have been discarded from a source very close at hand. The most convenient (although undocumented) explanation for these apparent contradictions may be that in the second quarter of the seventeenth century there was more than one pothouse in the vicinity of Pickle Herring Street.

That possibility makes it highly dangerous to attempt to tie much of the Burnett Collection to any specific potter. Nevertheless, the material remains of extraordinary importance in its demonstration of the range of shapes and decorative patterns produced in the parish of St. Olave in the seventeenth and, to a much lesser extent, the

24. Ellis (1952), p. 32. The widespread corruption of foreign names at this time raises the possibility that there might be a family connection between Peter van Düren and potter Simon Vandolen, who had moved from Norwich into the parish of St. Saviour's Southwark in 1571.

25. Edwards (1974), 11.

26. Jean Rocque, ***A Plan of the Cities of London and Westminster, and Borough of Southwark*** (London, 1746), gives the name as Wheelers Lane instead of Weavers Lane.

eighteenth century. This importance is heightened by the fact that potters who learned or practiced their trade in the Pickleherring and Montague Close factories went on to establish or influence potteries elsewhere, first at the Bear Garden, and then perhaps farther westward still to Lambeth, whose industry would later be credited with most of Southwark's achievements.

Less is known about the first years of delftware manufacturing in Lambeth than about the origins of the Southwark industry. Nevertheless, there is no evidence that potters were at work in Lambeth before the middle of the seventeenth century, and in the absence of data to the contrary, the industry that would become so important in the following century is assumed to have begun when another Dutchman, John Ariens van Hamme, settled in Vauxhall in 1676. It is reasonable to contend, therefore, that until that time (and probably for several years thereafter) Southwark was the principal source of London delftware. Consequently, the draft of "an act for encouraging the manufacturers of England" that came before the House of Lords in January 1673/74 may be said to reflect the Southwark potters' opinion of themselves and their products.[27] Asked to give reasons why the importation of foreign wares should be prohibited, they replied that the materials were all of English origin: clay, lead, kelp, and tin. "The Dutch could not make this ware without English earth," the London potters declared.[28] They later submitted further claims stating—rather surprisingly—that "the manufacture has only been brought to its present perfection in England seven or eight years, and that only at much expense."[29] They went on to make even more remarkable statements, claiming that "the Dutch learned the trade from the English," and adding that "the principal workman to this day in Holland, if living, is an Englishman. After the Dutch had attained the way of making fine white and the art of turning hollow ware, by the vast encouragement they had of vending their earthenwares in England, and through the negligence and carelessness of those that then managed this manufacture, they got the profitable part of the trade wholly from us." In connection with the same bill, the potters had earlier asserted that "they did not pretend to make Cologne ware, tiles, and China ware. What they claimed to make," stated the report on the bill, "was white and painted ware, *i.e.*, Gallaway ware. They sent great quantities of ware," the report continued, "to Scotland, Ireland, Barbadoes, and the King's plantations."[30]

The reference to "Gallaway ware" is obviously to galleyware, but the statement that the London potters did not pretend to make tiles is curious and will be considered in more detail later. Important here is the emphasis on exports to America in the third quarter of the seventeenth century, a period in ceramic history about which all too little is yet known.

The Archaeological Evidence

As indicated in the preface, the Burnett Collection is virtually without archaeological context, having been recovered from building site and utility laying operations. Pls. 2A and 2B show the seven locations from which the fragments were recovered, the majority coming from the vicinity of Vine Lane in the area wherein Sir David Burnett stated that he had seen the remains of kiln structures. With one or two minor exceptions, that part of the collection made available for study in Williamsburg was confined to tin-enameled earthenwares. Not all of it, however, is of local manufacture, for the assemblage also includes several Hispano-Moresque pieces, among them a jug that can be attributed to Faenza (Fig. XII, no. 11) and to a date close to 1500. Omitted from the collection are considerable quantities of Siegburg stonewares, most of which were found in the river wall sector (Pl. 2A, no. 7), along with numerous fragments of Flemish-style lead-glazed earthenwares. It will be evident, therefore, that not only is the material without archaeological stratification, but it has also been relieved of several earlier cuckoos.

There can be no denying that one would have preferred to have recovered the material under proper archaeological controls. In that way it might have been possible to draw revolutionary conclusions as to date that would fly in the face of those arrived at through the conventional and certainly more time-consuming pursuit of in-

27. ***Ninth Report of the Royal Commission on Historical Manuscripts,*** Pt. II, Appendix (London: H. M. Stationery Office, 1884), No. 130, p. 32.

28. Ibid., p. 33.

29. Ibid., p. 35.

30. Ibid., p. 34.

scribed and dated specimens in museum and private collections, and from the quest for parallels recovered from stratified deposits in other people's excavations. Although, in this case, the conventional course was the only one open, it is not without merit, and one may hope that the resulting conclusions will usefully stand the test of both time and archaeological criticism. Undeniably, however, reliance on known dated parallels has its limitations, for dates are most often encountered on decorative items. Therefore those that were purely utilitarian enjoy no such support, a fate that has befallen all the plain white wares that seem to have appeared in the 1640s and were in extensive production through the rest of the century.

A manuscript in the Manchester Public Library entitled "For the Taxing of Earthenware for Mr. Bateman, April 4th 1696," divided his stock under the headings "Fine Painted Ware," "Fine Painted Tyles and White Tyles," "White Ware," "Purple and Blew Ware," and "Fulham Ware." The white ware category listed the following items: large and small chamber pots, spitting pots, large basins, large cracknalls and dishes, candlesticks, sillibub pots and caudle pots, drinking pots, plates, saucers, large flower-pots, butter basins with covers, marmalade pots, and close stool pans, plus, of course, the white tiles that were identified as "Large. Fine white Tyles, Ditto. Small. The Best," and "Ditto. ordinary white."[31] It is interesting to note that the lists made no reference to white porringers although they appear under the painted ware heading; the same is true of "Large store potts for Apothecaries, Apothecaires Potts, Pill-Potts," and "gallipots" of six different sizes. Had the list been issued in 1646 rather than 1696, the references to

31. Wills (1967), 443.

Plate 4.
Netherlandish maiolica vase decorated in blue, illustrating the ceramic origins of the ring handles that occur on 17th-century London delftware. This example, with its IHS monogram, was almost certainly imported prior to the dissolution of the monasteries in 1534. Height: 5 5/8 inches. Museum of London: A.378.

Plate 5.
Malling-type maiolica jug, white tin glazed on the inside and decorated with stippled manganese and cobalt. The rim is reinforced and is embellished with an unmarked silver mount. Netherlandish or English, probably last quarter of 16th century. Height: 6 1/2 inches. Colonial Williamsburg Collection: 1955-316.

decorated galley pots would have made more sense. As for the absence of white porringers and pharmaceutical wares, there is ample archaeological evidence to indicate that these predominated at least by the 1670s. Thus, on the one hand, this important document is valuable in that it identifies a wide range of white wares in production at the close of the seventeenth century, but is made questionable on the other by omitting items that we know existed.

Although it now seems clear from archaeological sources that white wares were in fairly general use by the 1640s (and that polychrome-decorated pharmaceutical pots continued later), there is little or no museum evidence to identify the shapes of many of the white items in the Bateman listing. Through archaeology we know, however, that common utilitarian objects such as chamber pots, wash basins, and pharmaceutical pots continued to be made throughout the eighteenth century. Lacking what I call the "keep me" factor (that is, inscriptions that enlighten or decoration that charms), these plain wares were thrown out as soon as they became damaged or outmoded. Even if, by oversight, they should surmount the hurdle of obsolescence and survive in an attic or cellar until such time as they could rightfully claim to be hailed as antiques, they would only be recognized as such if the finder happened to be knowledgeable about ceramic shapes. The posset or caudle pot of about 1645 illustrated in Pl. 8 is a classic example. Unearthed from a cesspit or river bed, its white glaze turned black to conceal its delftware origin, the pot passed into the hands of a dealer who priced it at one shilling. In 1975 it turned up on the shelf of one of London's more exclusive ceramic dealers where it was thought to be stoneware of unknown date. Subsequent chemical cleaning removed the staining to reveal a now apparently unique example of what must once have been a relatively common item.

The shape of the posset pot and its distinctive ring handles revealed the approximate date of the piece, but all too often excavated fragments of plain white delftware have nothing but rim or foot forms to provide loosely datable guidelines, and then one must rely almost exclusively on parallels from closely dated excavations. Unfortunately, these are as yet in short supply. Furthermore, inventory data, so informative in the eighteenth century, tends to be so vague about ceramic identifications in the seventeenth century as to be virtually useless. Here, for example, is an extract from the 1667 inventory of the estate of Mrs. Jane Hartey, of Northampton County, Virginia:

In the little porch loft
3 matted chaires
3 earthen butter dishes
4 earthen plates
3 earthen cupps
2 earthen salts
1 earthen saser [saucer]
3 earthen chamber potts
2 Joynt stooles[32]

These ceramic items are almost certainly of delftware, for it is unlikely that the salts would have been of coarse, lead-glazed earthenware. The compilers of the inventory were presumably using the term "earthenware" to distinguish between pottery and pewter, or perhaps between relatively common wares and porcelain. It remains anybody's guess as to whether the "3 earthen cupps" were decorated or plain white, and only the archaeological excavation of Mrs. Hartey's Virginia homesite can hope to provide the answer.

There are many—American historians among them—who will ask whether it really matters whether Mrs. Hartey's earthenwares were plain or colored. Is such knowledge merely useless antiquarianism, a detail of value to no one but the pedant? The popularity of the refurnished buildings of Colonial Williamsburg is perhaps justification enough, but there is another more pertinent consideration: the need for historians and anthropologists to address themselves to the lives and aspirations of the individuals who make up the statistical group, the family, the voters, the army, and so forth. As long as the researcher is prompted to look at the people of the past as numbers, he will never get to know whether Jane Hartey's earthenwares were white or decorated, and without doing so he cannot imagine what it was like to sit at her table—and if he cannot do that he can hardly expect to fully understand her pleasures or her problems.

Dating Attributions

IT has been established with reasonable confidence that Christian Wilhelm was the first

32. Warren M. Billings, ed., *The Old Dominion in the Seventeenth Century: A Documentary History of Virginia, 1606–1689* (Chapel Hill, N. C.: University of North Carolina Press, 1975), p. 316, quoting Northampton County Deed and Will Book, 1666–1668, fols. 13–14.

Plate 6.
Plain white London mugs discarded about 1670, found in a refuse filled ditch or open sewer during the construction of Southwark's Bankside power station in 1949. The central cylindrical mug is paralleled by a lidded example in the Fitzwilliam Museum's Glaisher Collection (1423) dated 1660. Heights: 4 5/16 inches, 6 3/6 inches, and (surviving) 4 1/16 inches. Museum of London. No accession numbers.

potter to set up a delftware kiln in the parish of St. Olave, and that he did not do so before 1612 at the earliest, and probably not until several years later. Thus, items such as tiles and ointment pots possessing no characteristics that preclude them from dating from the first quarter of the seventeenth century have here been given an opening date bracket of 1612. In most instances the shapes and their dated parallels point to considerably later commencement dates, and when such evidence exists it has been employed.

There is strong support for the contention that many of the wasters and biscuit fragments come from vessels whose shapes preclude their having been made before the end of the Wilhelm monopoly; this evidence is documented in the footnotes. Although most of the dating conclusions are derived from surviving dated pieces, the terminal brackets are in most cases the writer's opinion based only on experience of finding (or not finding) certain shapes and designs in archaeologically datable contexts. Undeniably, opinion is a poor substitute for documented fact, and when none is cited the reader is advised to use the dates with appropriate caution.

Source Attributions

ALL the seventeenth-century biscuit and waster fragments are unequivocally the products of Pickleherring kilns—although it is debatable whether the "kiln" remains observed by Sir David Burnett and the wares from locations in their immediate vicinity are directly related to the "pott house" indicated in the documentary sources as being bounded on the north by Pickle Herring, on the west by a sewer, and on the south by another sewer and the open space known as Potts Fields. To be both accurate and conservative, therefore, one might argue that the wares should be identified only as products of kilns in St. Olave's Parish. One can certainly do no better for the eighteenth-century wasters from the Battle Bridge House site.

Perhaps when the neighboring Montague Close kiln wasters have been thoroughly analyzed and published it will be possible to detect characteristics that distinguish between those and wares of comparable dates from the Pickleherring group. Preliminary comparisons, however, did not hold out much hope that the differences would be distinctive or even that any existed. It must be remembered, too, that delftware manufacturing in the London area was not confined just to Southwark. Jacob Janson's (Johnson's) Aldgate factory is thought to have continued in business until about 1625. Another was operating at Rotherhithe in 1651 that may have started as early as 1638, and by 1660 there was yet another, the Hermitage pothouse at Wapping—and then there was Lambeth. Dates for the beginning of delftware manufacturing there range from 1676 (van Hamme at Vauxhall) to such cautious claims as not "before the middle of the seventeenth century."[33] All that can be said, therefore, is that pieces attributable to London before the mid-seventeenth century are either Southwark or Aldgate products. Once one reaches the third quarter of the century problems proliferate, for not only do we then have to consider Rotherhithe and Lambeth, but also the important Bristol industry, which by about 1645 was off and potting. Established outside Bristol at Brislington, the delftware business was founded by potters (or relatives of potters) from Southwark such as the Bissickes and Bennets. It is certain, therefore, that at the outset Brislington wares were indistinguishable from those made in London.

Ever since W. J. Pountney published his *Old Bristol Potteries* in 1920, collectors have confidently identified seventeenth-century Bristol products on the evidence of Pountney's analysis of fragments found in excavations on the kiln and dump sites. Those that could not be paralleled among the Bristol sherds were equally confidently attributed to Lambeth. This thoroughly specious reasoning was based on the fact that Southwark kiln sites had not then been explored or their products recognized. Conclusions were based on the known, ignoring the possibility that the unknown products of other kilns would have anything pertinent to add. For this reason it is extremely important to keep an open mind now about the eventual contributions to be made by excavations at Aldgate, and Rotherhithe—if, indeed, anything helpful survives.

I have deliberately left until last the biggest problem of all, namely that of distinguishing the difference between early London products and not so early Netherlandish wares.[34] By the eighteenth century the differences are fairly well defined, but in the first half of the seventeenth century, when Netherlandish potters and painters were the backbone of the London industry, and when English clay was used by their confreres in the Netherlands,[35] telling one product from the other is a tricky and often worthless task. Seemingly symbolizing the impossibility of the problem are the arms of the Haarlem ceramic painters that were granted in 1635 and that depict a Wan Li style "bird-on-rock" plate of the type that predominates in the stack of fused plates in the Burnett Collection and which consequently serve to typify the character of the London painters' work in the same period.[36]

33. Garner and Archer (1972), p. 48.

34. While cataloguing the British Museum's English delftware collection, R. L. Hobson (1903), p. 126, attempted to provide guidelines for distinguishing between the English and Netherlandish wares. In discussing glazes and painting techniques he used such subjective terms as thinner, harder, better, and superior, none of which provided a means of identifying a single specimen as having been made east or west of the North Sea. When, however, Hobson discussed body comparisons, he gave us something to get our teeth into, in short, an acid test. "The Dutch [body] is softer and more friable," wrote Hobson, "and contains enough carbonate of lime to make it effervesce under the application of nitric acid; this is not the case with the harder English body." This method has been widely touted in the years since Hobson proposed it, but the test, alas, is worthless. To arrive at that conclusion I took three biscuit sherds from the Pickleherring group (Burnett Collection), three more biscuit pieces from Aldgate, and three glazed fragments excavated at Limburg in Holland. The results were as follows:

	Eff.	No Eff.
Pickleherring	2	1
Aldgate	3	0
Limburg	1	2

Biscuit sherds were chosen to represent the two London factory sites to eliminate any possibility that intrusive Dutch pieces were inadvertently being tested. Realizing, however, that the second firing might have some effect on the English specimens, three glazed wasters from the Burnett Collection were also tested and all effervesced. There being no glazed wasters in the material presently available from Aldgate, a comparable test could not be run for that factory, but even if there were, and no matter how they reacted, Hobson's nitric acid test would gain no more credence.

35. Ibid., p. 2. In 1694 merchant Edmund Warner was shipping East Anglian potters' clay from Aldeburgh to London, to Holland, and even to America. See Edwards (1974), 19, and Jewitt (1878), I, pp. 134–135.

36. De Jonge (1947), p. 74, Fig. 45.

Plate 7.

Fragments of plain white delftware from ca. 1645–1675 contexts at the Mathews Manór site near Denbigh, Virginia. No. 1, pharmaceutical pot base of rare form; no. 2, base from bottle mug or small posset pot of unusual form; no. 3, pharmaceutical pot base; nos. 4 and 5, chamber pot handle and base fragments; no. 6, small mug with handle terminal akin to that of Pl. 6, left; nos. 7 and 8, rim sherds from bowls (?); no. 9, porringer rim and handle sherd; no. 10, plate rim; nos. 11 and 12, fluted bowl fragments similar to Fig. XIII, no. 5; and no. 13, rim sherd from vessel of uncertain form.

The best that can be claimed, therefore, is that evidence from Pickleherring sites and from Montague Close excavations have demonstrated that many designs (particularly among the flooring tiles) hitherto considered to be Netherlandish can equally well be English. It can also be said with some assurance that examples found in Virginia are more likely to be of London than Dutch manufacture due to the influence in the colony of Sir Thomas Smith, Sir John Harvey, and Christian Wilhelm.

Plate 8.
Posset pot with ring handles and expanded lip illustrating one of the more sophisticated forms manufactured in plain white London delftware, about 1635–1645. The foot form is best paralleled by the fragment of a smaller vessel illustrated in Pl. 7, no. 2, and the handles by the 1632 example shown in Pl. 35. Height: 4 3/4 inches. Author's collection: 69.

The Tiles

STOW'S statement that Andries and Janson settled at Norwich in 1567 and there "followed their Trade, making Gally Paving Tiles,"[1] leaves little doubt that tiles were among the first items manufactured by delftware potters in England. Furthermore, it suggests that the tiles were intended to be laid on the floor, because no English dictionary interprets the word "pave" or "paving" as meaning anything other than laying or being part of floors or roads.[2] When Edmund Bradshawe and Hugh Cressey obtained their patent in 1613, the licensed products included "all pavinge tiles of all sises."[3] Similarly, in 1628, when Christian Wilhelm was granted his fourteen-year monopoly, "paving tyles" were listed among the galleywares that it included. No examples of these thick Flemish-style tiles are known to survive in situ in England and there is therefore no evidence (other than the word "paving") to indicate how they were used. Nevertheless, Arthur Lane has stated that "about the middle of the 16th century, maiolica pavements began to go out of fashion in the Netherlands, but the tiles found a new use as wall decoration."[4] It is reasonable to suppose, therefore, that if not by 1567, at least by 1628, tilemakers in England would have ceased to refer to their products as "pavinge tyles" if they were only being used for walls, stoves, or fireplaces. In writing of the early Dutch tiles, Dingeman Korf has declared that "only occasionally were they used as floor-tiles because they were too susceptible to wear and tear."[5] This is a very reasonable contention if one accepts the majority of the Southwark examples as typical of the expected quality. Indeed, the barely vitrified yellow on some examples can be scraped off with a razor blade and would have lasted no time at all if used in a floor. On the other hand, some of the tiles are hard fired and have strong and well-bonded glazes.

The problem with the Burnett Collection tiles (and with any from the Southwark kiln sites) is to know which of them would have been sold and used if they had not been broken. Some, of course (Pl. 9), are irrefutable wasters that were underfired, have glazes that ran to the destruction of the design, or have pieces of kiln furniture adhering to them. To complicate matters, some of these clearly unsaleable products were used, presumably in the vicinity of the kilns, because their edges, including fractures, still have mortar attached. (See Fig. I, no. 4.)

Little or nothing is known about the appearance of the tiles manufactured by Andries and Janson. However, examples having a boar in the center and the arms of the Bacon and Whaplode families in the corners (now in the

1. Rackham and Read (1924), p. 39. John Stow, *A Survey of the Cities of London and Westminster and the Borough of Southwark* II, p. 327.

2. *New World of Words* (London, 1671).

3. Dawson and Edwards (1973), 57, quoting Patent Roll, C. 66/1982, P.R.O.

4. Lane (1960), p. 53.

5. Korf (1964), p. 20.

Plate 9. *See color plate facing p. 20. Examples of flooring tile wasters from Pickleherring sites. Nos. 1 and 2 display glazing flaws exposing the body beneath; No. 3 has run in firing; No. 4 retains a fragment of a clay spacer that had stuck to it in firing; and No. 5 is a biscuit sherd bearing traces of cobalt design indicating that it had been decorated but never fired for the second time. For additional details, see Fig. I, no. 1, and Fig. II, nos. 1, 3, 4, and 10.*

Victoria and Albert Museum) are said to have come from Gorhambury, near St. Albans, a house built by Sir Nicholas Bacon between 1563 and 1568, and have been thought to be from the Norwich or Aldgate factory.[6] Nevertheless, Lane described the tiles as "probably Flemish."[7] The problem, of course, is to distinguish between English and Flemish (or early Netherlandish) products when the craftsmen were members of the same families. Jaspar Andries, for example, was almost certainly a relative of the Italian Guido Andries who established the Nether-

6. Archer (1973), p. 13. pl. 1. This example is in the collection of the Birmingham City Museum and Art Gallery (63.41), but another is owned by the Victoria and Albert Museum (4603-1863). See Garner and Archer (1972), pl. 3B.

7. Lane (1960), p. ix, pl. 31A.

Plate 10.
A "square" of four blue-decorated flooring tiles of the same type as Pl. 9, no. 2, showing how the design motif is quartered. London or Netherlands. Author's collection: 73.

See page 19.

See page 26.

See page 32.

landish industry at Antwerp in or before 1510 and whose son Joris carried it northward to Middleburg in 1564. The persecution of Protestants leading to the revolt against Spain and the subsequent capture of Antwerp in 1585 is thought to have been responsible for the movement of craftsmen northward, and may well have prompted some of them to cross to England—explaining, perhaps, the alleged arrival of the Sandwich potter in 1582.

Nothing is known about Jacob (Janson) Johnson's tilemaking in Aldgate, although there has been a tendency to look on examples of Flemish and supposedly late sixteenth-century type as being his. The many wasters and "seconds" from Southwark now reveal that even if similar designs were produced at Aldgate they are as yet indistinguishable from those made by Christian Wilhelm in his St. Olave factory or from those made at Montague Close in the neighboring parish.

Dating for individual tiles in the Burnett Collection must still rest largely on the published opinions of previous writers who generally restricted their classifications of designs to the late sixteenth century or to the first half of the seventeenth. The earlier types were generally considered to be those with geometric motifs (for example, Fig. II, nos. 6 and 9) while the floral and medallion varieties followed later. However, the presence of wasters of both types in the collection suggests that supposedly sixteenth-century forms continued to be made at least until 1612 and probably later still. Equally disturbing is the presence of a hexagonal tile (Fig. II, no. 8), a type attributed by Lane to Antwerp and to a date around 1525.[8] This tile is slightly thicker than the rest, but the body and palette are comparable, and there is no evidence that it was ever used. It is therefore difficult to divorce it from the rest without some substantial evidence for doing so.

The majority of the designs are closely paralleled by examples in Belgian and Dutch museums, although a few (for example, Fig. II, nos. 1, 2, 6, and 7) exhibit characteristics that are sufficiently different to be possible Anglicizations.

Large numbers of biscuit tile fragments were unearthed by the workmen digging the various holes that yielded the Burnett material, but because the pieces were apparently undecorated, no attempt was made to salvage them. The only biscuit piece in the collection, a corner sherd (Pl. 9, no. 5, and Fig. II, no. 10), is decorated on the clay with part of an unidentified design, leaving one wondering what other significant information was reinterred along with the broken, unglazed tiles. The fact that the decoration appears directly on the clay body has caused some surprise, for the design was normally painted over the already applied but unfired white ground that subsequently vitrified in the second firing. It is likely, however, that in this case the zaffre blue soaked through the glazing composition (tin and lead oxides, sand, soda, and salt) and stained the porous body below. Then, since the tile was never refired, the powdery white surface came off, leaving only the staining behind. Another tile fragment with a bird painted on the biscuit was found among early eighteenth-century delftware kiln refuse farther west near Gravel Lane in 1949, suggesting that such relationships were more common than one might suppose. For years the Gravel Lane bird was dismissed as the doodling of an apprentice painter, but as the skill lay as much in executing the design on the soft glaze base as in drawing the pattern in the first place, this explanation seems suspect.

The designs are believed to have been pounced onto the unfired glaze using stencils and charcoal. As most of the early tiles (Figs. I and II) have small holes in two usually diagonally opposite corners, it has been conjectured that those holes were made to secure the stencils. In reality they resulted from the placement of the forms used in cutting out the green clay after it had been rolled into sheets. The tile-shaped boards had nails driven through them at diagonal corners to prevent any slipping as the workmen cut alongside their edges. These holes are present in most of the thick, Flemish-style examples in the collection, but are absent from later examples of Dutch and English decorative tiles.

Although few of the early examples are complete, measurements seem to range from 5 1/4 x 5 1/4 inches to 5 1/2 x 5 7/16 inches, the commonest being 5 5/16 x 5 5/16 inches and 5/8 inch in thickness, although the full thickness range runs from 1/2 inch to 3/4 inch. In general, the allegedly early specimens are the largest and thickest.

Evidently the tiles were fired for the second time while standing on edge, as the decoration

---

8. Ibid., p. ix, pls. 31C and D. The Burnett Collection example measures 8 inches in length as does Lane's "C," but the decoration is paralleled by his 7-inch example "D."

Plate 11.
Wall and fireplace tiles in the Burnett Collection dating from the late 17th and early 18th centuries. With one exception, none exhibits features to indicate that they are wasters or were made near the Battle Bridge House site where they were found. Nos. 1–7 are decorated with biblical scenes and were known in the 18th century as "scripture" tiles; no. 8 belongs to an even more popular class then called "landskip" or landscape. Nos. 1, 4, and 5 exhibit unusual variations of the standard "ox-head" corner motifs, which were converted into clown-like human faces. It seems likely that these are of English manufacture. Nos. 6, 8, and 10 are decorated in the corners with a "bug" or "spider's-head" device, and although no. 8 could be English, no. 10 is unquestionably Dutch, as is the seascape fragment, no. 9. The latter has been broken at the corner and was not originally intended to be octagonal. The only possible kiln-related item is sherd no. 7, which is inexplicable, coated on the back with what appears to be unfired tin glaze. Nos. 1–5 are painted in manganese, the rest in blue.

could not otherwise have run as vigorously as it did on some of the more obvious wasters (Pl. 9, nos. 2 and 3). Three examples of the geometric form (Pl. 9, no. 4, and Fig. II, no. 6) retain pieces or traces of rolls of biscuit-fired clay that must have served as spacers. However, it may or may not be significant that none of the other designs is found in association with these deficiencies.

The Burnett Collection also includes many fragments of late seventeenth- and eighteenth-century fireplace tiles, but there are no biscuit fragments and no wasters—although one sherd appears to have been coated on its back with unfired tin glaze (Pl. 11, no. 7). It is necessary, nevertheless, to dismiss most if not all of this material as being mere architectural debris not associated with manufacture. The making of "Dutch" tiles in London seems to have begun at Vauxhall at the factory of John Ariens van Hamme, who obtained a patent in 1676 to exercise his "art of makeinge tiles and porcelane and other earthen wares, after the way practised in Holland."[9] However, it would appear from the dispute between potters and potsellers in 1673–1674 regarding the proposed ban on imported wares that very few tiles were being made and the retailers could not be supplied. A "Mr. Sadler (retailer of tiles)" charged that he could obtain no tiles from the London potters "though he had waited long for them." Another deponent, "Mr. Green," also testified that he "had ordered tiles of the Potters, but never could have any of them." To this the spokesman for the potters replied that "the tiles they ordered were to be supplied in the declining time of the year, and they required much drying. They could in a short time make tiles enough." Later in the same deposition it was stated that the potters "did not pretend to make Cologne ware, tiles, and China ware."[10] From this rather confusing evidence it may be deduced that in 1673–1674 the English potters were having difficulty preparing and firing the refined-clay fireplace and wall tiles that had replaced the thick and coarse paving tiles they had successfully produced and marketed earlier in the century. Be that as it may, if the waste found near Gravel Lane in 1949 came from Moses Johnson's factory at the Bear Garden,[11] it would seem that by the close of the seventeenth century fireplace tile manufacturing was well launched there.

Although there is no proof that the later tiles in the Burnett Collection were made in Southwark—and some, such as a fragment decorated with a ship flying the Dutch flag (Pl. 11, no. 9), clearly were imported—they do include a group of biblical tiles painted in manganese whose "ox-head" corner ornaments are unlike those found on Dutch tiles (Pl. 11, nos. 1, 4, and 5). These devices have been converted into faces with human eyes and represent a conscious departure from the long Dutch evolutionary series that began with a fleur-de-lis and ended with something resembling a horned ox. It is possible, therefore, that these "clown's face" corners are late seventeenth- or early eighteenth-century products of a London factory. However, it is not to be supposed that all English "scripture" or roundel tiles exhibited this idiosyncrasy. Furthermore, the presence of late seventeenth- and early eighteenth-century tile biscuit fragments at Gravel Lane[12] reveals the fallacy of attributing all post–van Hamme London tiles to Vauxhall or Lambeth.[13]

Pharmaceutical Pots and Jars

THE firms of both Andries and Janson, and Christian Wilhelm, indicated that the manufacture of "Vessels for Apothecaries" represented a significant part of their endeavor, although it is true that Wilhelm placed them fairly well down

9. Mountford and Celoria (1968), 12–13, no. 18.

10. *Ninth Report of the Royal Commission on Historical Manuscripts,* Pt. II, Appendix, No. 130, p. 34.

11. It is conceivable that Moses Johnson was a descendant of Jacob (Janson) Johnson, founder of the Aldgate factory. Note the fact that both men possessed biblical Christian names.

12. Oswald (1950), 183.

13. Many similar biscuit fragments have been found by the author on the Thames south foreshore east of Blackfriars Bridge as well as on the north foreshore immediately east of Queenhithe and opposite the Bear Garden factory.

on his list.[1] There is no doubt, however, that ointment pots and drug jars were an important part of the St. Olave potters' output and that the shapes and decorative motifs place a great many of the excavated waste products in the period of the Wilhelm monopoly.

The terms *ointment pot* and *drug jar* need defining, for although they are commonly used among ceramic historians, collectors, and archaeologists, they do not parallel the range of terms employed by apothecaries in the seventeenth century. Although for convenience in this report small pharmaceutical pots taller than they are broad and up to 3 1/2 inches in height are called ointment pots, while those of larger size are described as drug jars, in the seventeenth century the former identified but one variety of the smaller pots, while the latter term was not used at all. It is worth noting, too, that large apothecaries' vessels in delftware are divided into two classes, dry and wet, the dry being either large versions of the cylindrical "ointment" pots or olla-shaped vessels inscribed for use on the pharmacy shelf. The wet jars, on the other hand, are generally pedestal footed and possess both a cylindrical spout and a strap handle. It is likely that contemporaries referred to these as jugs rather than jars.

The 1666 inventory of an English apothecary's shop listed the following varieties among its ceramic stock: "Severall syr[up] potts and juggs . . . fifteen quarte[,] four pint and seaven juggs . . . conserve and electuary potts . . . twenty oyntmnt potts . . . oyle potts and 16 juggs no 13 . . . pill potts 24 . . . 2 window potts."[2] This last follows an entry for "34 ordinary boxes" and "six window boxes," suggesting that these were not for flowers but for display in the pharmacy windows. More relevant, however, is the distinction between ointment pots, pill pots, oil pots, and conserve and electuary pots. Electuary pots held sugar confections, but unfortunately none can presently be identified; nor can we be sure of the difference between ointment pots and pill pots. One can only hope that eventually a seventeenth-century delftware potter's catalogue will turn up in England or the Netherlands to illustrate and name the various shapes, and, if we are really lucky, to identify the purposes for which they were intended. Meanwhile it is safer to retain the old, if imprecise, terminology.

The Burnett Collection contains a remarkable array of both pots and jars in biscuit, in glazed but unfired, and in glazed forms, most of the examples belonging to the first half of the seventeenth century. However, a few much later specimens are included, and although there is no evidence of their local manufacture (lacking parallels among the unfinished specimens), they are illustrated to demonstrate the development of shapes. Very few of the small and early ointment pots, be they either in plain white or polychrome, have been illustrated in books on English delftware, and they are poorly represented in museums, save in collections from excavations or building-site salvage. Consequently, published evolutionary studies of delftware pharmaceuticalia have largely been confined to the more costly and more collectible drug jars. It so happens that in the first half of the seventeenth century the same profiles were common to the smallest pots and the largest jars (Pls. 12 and 13). This became less true in the second half of the century, and not true at all in the eighteenth century.

Because the makers of galleyware came originally from Italy, it is hardly surprising that they brought Italianate shapes and designs with them to Northern Europe. Thus the slender and often distinctively waisted albarelli so common in Italy in the fifteenth century began to be made at Antwerp at the beginning of the sixteenth century and in England during the reign of Elizabeth.[3] None of the fragments in the Burnett Collection is of the waisted shape, but the equally Italian slender cylinder pinched inward above the base and below the lip is represented by both miniscule ointment pots and tall drug jars (for example, Fig. III, nos. 1 and 12). The principal characteristic of these early vessels was that, ideally, bases, mouths, and walls were intended to be of the same diameter. As the quality of throwers varied, however, so did the pots, and the collection contains a number of examples whose

1. "Makinge of earthen gally potte and dishes called by the name of gallyware And all kinde or sorte of bottells of all Colo[r]s basons and ewers salte dishes of all sorte drinkinge potte pavinge tyles Apothecaries and Comfittmakers potte of all sorte and all kinde of earthen worke as he the said Christian Wilhelme hath heretofore invented and made." S.P. 39/25, No. 42, P.R.O.

2. Crellin (1970), 194, citing MS 74265, Wellcome Institute of the History of Medicine.

3. Garner and Archer (1972), Fig. 2B.

Plate 12.
Polychrome-decorated pharmaceutical pots typical of Southwark products of the first half of the 17th century. The pot at the left is painted in blue, orange, and purple (height: 3 3/8 inches), and the one on the right in blue and orange. (height: 2 7/8 inches). The latter's foot is raised to create a V-shaped profile, an unusual feature paralleled by examples shown in Fig. V, no.3, and Fig. XVII, no.2. Author's collection: 70 and 71.

walls slope inward toward the top. These were almost certainly anomalies, but contemporary with the straight cylinders.[4]

In the second half of the seventeenth century, ointment pot proportions changed; those that were taller than they were wide disappeared and were replaced by others with the same wall profile but that were as broad as they were tall (Fig. IV, no. 6). Then, at the end of the century, the uniform wall line was abandoned in favor of cup-shaped pots whose lower walls curved inward, often to much smaller feet (Fig. IV, nos. 16–19). At the same time, instead of pinching the wall inward below the mouth to enable paper or textile covers to be tied down with string, the lips were everted. In the second quarter of the eighteenth century, the reduction in the size of the foot became more pronounced (Fig. IV, no. 22) and in some cases became a solid pedestal. This last feature became increasingly common as the century progressed, particularly for shallow pots used for cosmetics and eye ointments.

The larger drug jars for dry preparations (as opposed to those for wet) retained their uniform lip, body, and foot profiles through most of the seventeenth century, but by the end of it these jars, too, were abandoning the sharply indented shoulder in favor of a weaker curve and a small everted lip. In the eighteenth century the shoulder was often omitted and the lip turned outward beyond the girth of the vessel. The constriction above the base continued through the first half of the century and was slowly replaced by no foot at all, the wall dropping straight to the base.

Practically all English delftware drug jars were decorated; those of the Wilhelm period were often painted in blue, green, orange tan, purple, and occasionally yellow, the basic design most often in blue (Pl. 13 and Fig. V, nos. 4–6). By the mid-seventeenth century, the ornament had become more slapdash and the colors were reduced to blue and purple. The elimination of green, orange, and yellow considerably reduced the work involved and, in the case of the overglaze yellow, may have avoided a third firing. The elaborate early patterns gave way to bands of crosses around the girth (Fig. V, no. 7), which in turn surrendered to a less angular chain version of the same idea that was even easier and quicker to execute (Fig. XVII, no. 2). Eventually, in the second half of the eighteenth century, even the chain was omitted and the decoration was reduced to straight blue bands.[5]

The use of polychrome decoration on ointment pots does not seem to have continued after about 1640, probably because the increasing

4. Fig. III, nos. 2 and 3; Fig. IV, nos. 2, 3, and 5; Fig. V, no. 2.

5. Crellin (1969), 16, Fig. 8.

Plate 13. *See color plate facing p. 21.*
Examples of decorated pharmaceutical galleyware. The ointment pots at the left are from the Burnett Collection (Fig. V, nos. 1 and 2). The jar (right) was found in Virginia on the Kingsmill Tenement site in a context of the mid-17th century. Height: 3 3/4 inches. Virginia Research Center for Archaeology: KM. 393A.

demand for them made decoration unnecessary as a marketing factor and because white pots could be produced much more rapidly. Exceptions are provided by two examples in the collection that are of a relatively late shape and that are decorated with vertical blue stripes or wavy lines (Fig. IV, nos. 19 and 20). These are marked on the bases with numbers "1" and "4" respectively, in the same blue color and with strokes of the same size.[6] The ground color used for ointment pots was generally a pinkish white in the seventeenth century with an increasing tendency toward a pale bluish tint as the eighteenth century progressed, a distinction that is also exhibited among such utilitarian wares as chamber pots and wash basins. That is not to say, however, that some of the decorated pots and jars of earlier dates did not exhibit similarly blue-tinted ground colors, but this was generally inherited from the blue used in the decoration.

Relatively few sites of the first half of the seventeenth century have as yet been excavated in America, and consequently it is impossible to determine how widespread was the importing of Southwark ointment pots and drug jars. Two sherds were recovered from Fort Raleigh on the "Lost Colony" site on Roanoke Island, North Carolina, but as there is no evidence of occupation there in the first half of the seventeenth century, it is reasonable to conclude that the fragments were deposited by the Elizabethan settlers.[7] Therefore, unless those pots were made at an Aldgate factory, one must conclude that they are Netherlandish. Many more early pieces of both ointment pots and drug jars have been found at Jamestown, and it is a reasonable assumption that a great many of them were products of Christian Wilhelm's kilns. This probability is increased by the fact that Governor Harvey occupied the statehouse at Jamestown and, as previously noted, Wilhelm was in business with Harvey to such an extent that he described himself in his will as "great adventurer into Virginia."[8] Unfortunately, little of the early delftware pharmaceuticalia from Jamestown is recorded as having come from closely datable archaeological contexts.[9] On the other hand, a

6. There is evidence that by the late 17th century (and probably from the start) drug jars and ointment pots were made in a recognized size progression. Wills (1967), 443. Although the measurements of the sizes are not documented, their numbers and related values in 1696 were as follows: "Large Gallipots 8 Potts" 1/2 d. each; "4 do." 6d. each; "2 do." 2 1/2 d. each; "1 do." 1 1/4 d. each; "1/2 do." 3/4 d. each; and "Small Gallipots, sorted" 1/4 d. each.

7. Harrington (1962), pp. 22–23, Fig. 21. The history of the site points to a deposition date between 1585 and 1590.

8. *Virginia Magazine of History and Biography,* XIV (July 1906), 88.

9. Cotter (1958), pl. 82, p. 184.

Plate 14.

Decorated pharmaceutical pots and jars and manganese-stippled delftwares from the Mathews Manor site near Denbigh, Virginia, and from contexts attributable to the period ca. 1640–1670. The drug pots and jars, nos. 1–4 and 9–11, are decorated only in blue; but in addition to blue, nos. 5–8 and 12 are painted yellow and green, purple, green, purple, and yellow and orange respectively. With one exception, the remaining items are all manganese-stippled and represent the following forms: no. 13, mug rim; no. 14, mug base; no. 15, bowl rim; no. 16, bowl or dish base; nos. 17 and 18, handle and terminal fragments. No. 19 is also a handle fragment, but is white on the inside of the loop and blue on the outside splashed with white in the style of Nevers faïence, a technique usually attributed to the last quarter of the 17th century. This example has a post-1650 association, but is unlikely to date as late as the style would suggest.

considerable range of sherds in plain white, blue decorated, and polychrome have been recovered from stratified contexts at Mathews Manor on the James River below Jamestown toward Newport News (Pls. 7 and 14). This property belonged to Samuel Mathews I, one of the wealthiest of the early settlers.[10] Examples of sherds from this site are illustrated in Pls. 7 and 14, and although most of them were found in contexts of the middle to third quarter of the seventeenth century, it is reasonable to conclude that they were imported during the second quarter of the century, that is, prior to and during the fourteen-year period of the Wilhelm monopoly and, as it happened, during Sir John Harvey's governorship.

The Hollow Wares

THIS rather unsatisfactory heading is here used to embrace a wider range of objects than the term normally implies, and includes such things as candlesticks, salts, tea bowls, and other small bowls. With a few exceptions, the group breaks into two parts: the biscuit wares, most of which belong to the mid and third quarter of the seventeenth century, and the glazed pieces, many of which date from the second half of the seventeenth century and into the eighteenth century.

Some of the more complete biscuit pieces were found in the vicinity of the supposed kiln site in Vine Yard, and from what little information is available, it is believed that they were all extracted from a single, massive stratum of once-fired kiln waste. The fact that some of the most fragile items are the most intact, and that many of those that are fragmentary exhibit new breaks, leads one to suppose that they were, indeed, dumped from a kiln close by rather than having been brought as fill from somewhere else. Had they been repeatedly handled and tipped from one dump to another, the cups and mugs would almost certainly have been more damaged than they are. If, however, the pieces were recovered from a single stratum, one may reasonably conclude that it was deposited over a relatively short space of time, and using normal archaeological reasoning, the most recent items should provide a terminus post quem for the deposition of the rest. There may be significance, therefore, in the fact that some of these key dating items are much later than the period of the Christian Wilhelm monopoly.

The principal items from the Vine Yard site are all illustrated in Fig. VI and include a cup (no. 1), a large mug or bottle base (no. 4), a bulbous jug or mug base (no. 11), the two more or less complete salts (nos. 14 and 15), the candlestick (no. 16), and one of the small "Flower-potts" (no. 18).[1] Dated parallels for the cup shape occur from 1657 to 1682 (Pls. 15, 19, and 20). Delftware wine bottles are known with dates ranging from 1642 to 1671; the broad-rimmed salt is roughly paralleled by an example dated 1675,[2] and is of a class generally attributed to the mid-to-later seventeenth century (Pl. 16), as are larger parallels for the flowerpot shape (Pl. 17). Little close dating information for the candlestick is available. The only dated example yet encountered is marked 1648,[3] but although of the same general class, it differs sufficiently from the biscuit specimen to be of doubtful value as evidence.

A remarkably large number of the extant (and published) English delftware cups, mugs, and bottles of the seventeenth century are painted with dates, but it must be remembered that the survival of these intact pieces may have depended on the fact that they *are* dated. Without those dates to identify them as "old and interesting," they would probably have been broken and discarded along with 99.9 percent of all the other London and Bristol delftwares of the period. If this is a reasonable hypothesis, it may also be argued that the survival of certain dated shapes in the second half of the century fails to prove that *undated* examples of those same forms were not made in the first half of it and simply have not survived. Another possibly significant factor in-

10. Noël Hume (1966b), 832–836. Completion of the full report has been deferred pending publication of the related Burnett Collection material.

1. Wills (1967), 443.
2. Tilley (1969b), 80–81.
3. Tilley (1967b), 270, Fig. 11. The stick is decorated with the arms of the Fishmongers' Company and is in the Victoria and Albert Museum.

Plate 15.
Cup shapes and sizes of the second half of the 17th century. Left: *decorated with portraits of William and Mary in blue, orange, and yellow and initialed W. M. R., thus post-1689.* Center: *decorated in purple stipple and with a blue lettered panel inscribed BE NOT DRVNKE. About 1650–1680.* Right: *decorated with a horned male figure in blue, orange, and yellow, and inscribed IFM COOK COE 1682 OI WAS BORN TO WARE THE HORN. Heights: 3 13/16 inches, 2 3/4 inches, and 3 3/4 inches respectively. Colonial Williamsburg Collection: 1956-530, 1959-50, and 1956-529.*

volves size differences, for it might be argued that because the extant shape parallels are generally much larger than are the Burnett biscuit examples, they need not be of the same date. Pl. 15 shows three well-known specimens in the collection of Colonial Williamsburg, that on the left bearing portraits of William and Mary (thus no earlier than 1688), and the example on the right, the celebrated "cuckold" cup, dated 1682. The center example inscribed "BE NOT DRVNKE" is undated but exhibits a comparable profile to its 1688 companion. The size of this smaller cup is similar to examples in the Burnett Collection. However, its characteristic slope inward above the girth to the rim exhibited in Pl. 18 right, and Fig. VII, no. 1, is paralleled by an example bearing a portrait of Charles II and dated 1663.[4] The majority of the biscuit cups in the collection (e.g. Pl. 18 left, and Fig. VI, nos. 1–3) are more flaring at the rim in the manner of the 1682 specimen and of another Charles II cup dated 1668.[5]

Based on the evidence of surviving dated pieces, it would seem that the bulbous, almost thistle-shaped biscuit mug (Fig. VI, no. 7) is the earliest form in the Burnett Collection. The closest parallel is provided by a manganese-stippled mug with a blue-bordered white reserve in which is inscribed THOMAS * HUNT * OF * EDEN 1635.[6] Although slightly more spherical in the body than the biscuit example, this dated specimen displays a very similar cordon below the mouth, a feature absent from later examples. The Burnett Collection mug is not as tall in proportion as the well-known Elizabeth Brocklehurst mug of 1628,[7] or the Mary Hooper mug of 1629 (Pl. 36), but is less squat than the Bakers'

4. Garner (1948), Pl. 24B.

5. Garner and Archer (1972), Pl. 30B, not to be confused with the 1663 example (Pl. 24B) used in Garner's original edition (1948).

6. Illustrated in Christie's sale catalogue for February 3, 1975 (lot 187); height 4 inches.

7. Garner and Archer (1972), Pl. 6.

Plate 16.
Plain white salt smaller than examples from the Pickleherring and Montague Close sites but belonging to the same general class. Height: 3 1/8 inches. Second half of the 17th century. Colonial Williamsburg Collection: 56-425.

Company arms mug of 1645 in the Colonial Williamsburg Collection (Pl. 19). As the latter does not display the cordon of the Thomas Hunt (1635) mug, it may be possible to detect an evolutionary trend, one that takes another major, if deteriorating, step in a second Bakers' Company mug dated 1657 (Pl. 20).[8] By this time the shape has broadened to a point at which the term cup or caudle cup seems more appropriate than mug. Another 1657 specimen in the Victoria and Albert Museum is related to the second Bakers' arms specimen in that it bears a comparable inscription (NO MONEY : NO CONNY 1657) painted by what may well be the same hand (Pl. 21).

8. Tilley (1968a), 126–127, Figs. 6–8. The cup is now in the collection of Mrs. Jean Chorley, who illustrated it in *Antiques*, LXXXVII (February 1965), 182, Fig. 2. It had previously commanded a high price at Sotheby's and so was illustrated in *Country Life*, CXXXV (January 2, 1964), 12. Note that Tilley's rendering of the inscription is incorrect.

Plate 17.
Chinoiserie-decorated flower vase or pot, painted in blue and purple, and dated 1683. The vessel has three spouts and as many scroll-ended lugs, the latter shorter versions of the cover supports found on salts of the same period. For smaller examples in biscuit, see Fig. VI, nos. 17 and 18. Height: 6 1/4 inches. Fitzwilliam Museum, Glaisher Collection: 1643.

With the exception of Fig. VI, no. 7, the identifiable mugs and cups in the Burnett Collection belong to types not documented prior to 1657, although there are several bases that *might* be from mugs akin to the Brocklehurst and Hooper examples. Unfortunately, the Burnett Collection includes no inscribed mugs or cups, but it does contain several specimens decorated with stippled manganese (and one in stippled cobalt), a technique that goes back to the so-called Malling jugs (Pl. 5) and persisted into the latter years of the seventeenth century. American archaeological evidence indicates that manganese-stipple decoration was more common than the relatively small number of surviving examples in museum collections might suggest. The Mathews Manor site yielded a mug fragment from a mid-seventeenth-century context (Pl. 14, no. 13), related in shape to the Burnett Collection biscuit mug (Fig. VI, no. 7) and to a complete example found in Oxford, England, during 1937 excavations for the new Bodleian Library (Pl. 23). The same Oxford illustration shows another manganese-decorated drinking vessel excavated in Radcliffe Square, a small straight-sided mug that probably dates from the third quarter of the seventeenth century. Fragments of a larger mug, probably of pint capacity, have been found in a 1625–1650 context on a housesite on the Kingsmill tract in Virginia,[9] while another of about half that size has been found in excavations in Bristol, England, in a deposit of 1652–1656.[10]

So far without known parallel are fragments of a shallow bowl or dish from Mathews Manor in Virginia (Pl. 14, nos. 15 and 16) that date from the mid-seventeenth century. Another James River site of the 1640s, now known as Carter's Grove, has yielded the manganese-decorated base of an unparalleled hexagonal salt (Pl. 24). None of the Burnett Collection fragments can claim to be wasters, and only one is illustrated, the base and lower wall of a large bottle or jug, manganese-mottled on the outside and plain white within (Fig. XVII, no. 5), the surviving shape paralleled by an example in the Burnap Collection dated 1673.[11] Not illustrated are several mug handle fragments and the side of a cup of a form com-

9. Virginia Historic Landmarks Commission, "Kingsmill Tenement," base KM382A, rim KM399A, base diameter 3 13/16 inches.

10. Barton (1964), 200–201, no. 6.

11. Taggart (1967), p. 47, no. 98.

Plate 18.
Three typical cups of the second half of the 17th century. Those at the left and right are from the Pickleherring site; the left is in biscuit and the right is white tin glazed. For details, see Fig. VI, no. 3, and Fig. VII, no. 1. The center specimen is akin to the biscuit cup to its left and is described under Pl. 15.

Plate 19.
Cup or mug with contemporary silver mount, decorated with the arms of the Worshipful Company of Bakers in blue, yellow, and white, and inscribed IOHN LARTHMAN & ROSE 1645. Height: 4 5/8 inches. Colonial Williamsburg Collection: 1961-32.

Plate 20.
Transitional mug/cup form dated 1657. Decorated in blue and yellow with the arms of the Bakers' Company with the triple initial cipher AMR and the inscription DRINKE : VP YOVR : DRINKE : AND : SEE MY : CONNY. True to its promise, a slightly surprised blue rabbit is painted on the interior base. Height: 3 1/4 inches. Kenneth and Jean Chorley Collection. No number.

parable to the 1682 specimen shown in Pl. 15. It is possible, however, that the bases shown in Fig. VI, nos. 8, 9, and 10, could have been intended to become jugs or bottles decorated in manganese. Thus, for example, a manganese-stippled bottle in Colonial Williamsburg's collection (Pl. 25) is a close shape parallel for one of these fragments (Fig. VI, no. 9). A similarly decorated base fragment comparable to the Burnett Collection's biscuit cups (Fig. VI, nos. 1–3) was recovered from the cesspit in Black Swan Yard (Pl. 2A, no. 3) and points to a deposition date in the third quarter of the seventeenth century. Further evidence of a relatively late date for the survival of these manganese-decorated cups was provided in Virginia by the recovery of a base and lower wall fragment from a context of ca. 1690–1700 at Clay Bank in Gloucester County. The item was published as being part of a mug or jug and was attributed to the first half of the seventeenth century.[12] In the light of the present study, however, there is ample reason to accept this object as having been manufactured at a date much closer to that of its abandonment.

The Burnett Collection's cylindrical mugs or cans in biscuit (Fig. VI, nos. 5 and 6) would seem,

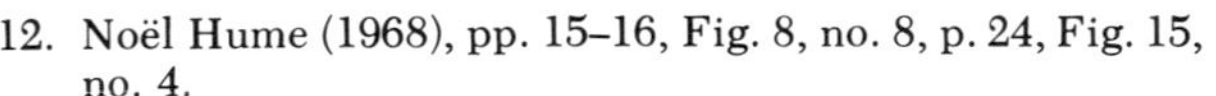

12. Noël Hume (1968), pp. 15–16, Fig. 8, no. 8, p. 24, Fig. 15, no. 4.

Plate 21.
Cup of the same date as that shown in Pl. 20 and inscribed with a rather similar thought in pale blue: NO : MONEY : NO : CONNY 1657. Although the treatment of the letter "C" suggests that both cups were decorated by the same painter, the shapes are very different. Height: 3 inches. The rim form is paralleled by a sherd from Mathews Manor (Pl. 7, no. 7) and the general shape by a smaller specimen from the Pickleherring site (Fig. VII, no. 1). The handle is reconstructed. Victoria and Albert Museum: C.446-1940.

Plate 22. *See color plate facing p. 21.*
At the left is a cylindrical mug or can decorated in blue and yellow with a crowned portrait of Charles II in blue, yellow, and purple, and dated 1660. Height: 3 1/2 inches. Colonial Williamsburg Collection: 1956-531. To the right is a matching mug in biscuit from the Pickleherring site. Height: 3 1/2 inches. For additional details, see Fig. VI, no. 5.

both on archaeological and historical grounds, to date from the third quarter of the seventeenth century, as is demonstrated by the close size and shape parallel decorated with a portrait of Charles II in the Colonial Williamsburg Collection (Pl. 22). A basal fragment from a plain white example of similar diameter but with a more developed foot was found in a mid-seventeenth-century context on the Mathews Manor site (Pl. 7, no. 6). Similar, although larger, white delftware mugs were recovered in 1949 from a ditch or open sewer found during excavations for the Bankside power station in Southwark and are now in the Museum of London (Pl. 6), and other artifacts found with them pointed to a deposition date in the third quarter of the seventeenth century. All in all, there is surprisingly strong evidence for dating the majority of the Burnett Collection's hollow wares to the period ca. 1645–1680, and very little to push them back into the era of the Wilhelm monopoly.

The thickness of so-called tin glazing is such that it tends to conceal the caliber of the potting, a consideration made very evident by the biscuit specimens in the Burnett Collection. The quality of the potting exhibited by the mazer-style bowl (Fig. VI, no. 13), by the cylindrical salt (Fig. VI, no. 15), and by the flowerpots (Fig. VI, nos. 17 and 18), is extremely high.[13] Indeed, both the pedestal-based salt (Fig. VI, no. 14)[14] and the candlestick (Fig. VI, no. 16), although less delicately constructed, exhibit a remarkable command of the medium. It may or may not be significant that the biscuit candlestick's construction differs from that of the glazed specimen (Fig. VII, no. 3). The shaft of the latter is fashioned from a single cylinder, whereas that of the biscuit example is made in two sections joined above the drip tray. Unfortunately, there is as yet no information to indicate a difference of date between these types.[15]

13. The British Museum possesses two more London flower vases, one white glazed and 5 1/2 inches in height, and the other in the biscuit state and much larger, standing 7 1/2 inches tall. Both are of the same, otherwise unparalleled, type, having straight tubular spouts instead of the usual flaring variety, and with interspersed handles which, rather than rolling outward in the normal manner, are twisted laterally into volutes that resemble rams' horns. The smaller vase has two spouts, and the larger three. Their mouths are relatively straight but cordoned below, and the bodies above their pedestal feet are clumsily bulbous and ornamented with another cordon. Both vases were acquired with the rest of Charles Roach Smith's collection of London antiquities in 1856. See Hobson (1903), p. 129, items E 3 and E 4. They were listed in Roach Smith's own catalogues of his London antiquities in 1854, but their find spot was not identified. Because the larger of the vessels is in the biscuit state, there can be no doubting that they were both made in London and probably were found together, but whether they date earlier than the conventional vase forms represented in the Burnett Collection one cannot say—although it is tempting to suggest that they do.

14. The British Museum's English delftware collection includes a biscuit fragment of an even more elaborate salt, described by Hobson ([1903], p. 140, item E 100a) as follows: "Salt-cellar in shape of a star of six points; three scroll feet, imperfect; unglazed." My own examination of this remarkable fragment has led me to conclude that it is far from complete and that the "feet" were supports raising the shallow dish above another decorative element. A footnote in the British Museum's catalogue states that the sherd was given by C. H. Read, F.S.A., in 1903, and that it was "Found in Tooley Street, Bermondsey, London, with a three-pointed kiln rest and some small tin-glazed ointment pots. There was evidently a pottery on or near the spot," Hobson concluded. Dish diameter: 3 1/2 inches.

15. A miniature candlestick or small taperstick 3 3/8 inches in height, in the delftware biscuit state, was found in Bishopsgate Street in 1854 and is now in the British Museum. See Hobson (1903), p. 138, item E 84. The stick's small size may account for the fact that it bears no close stylistic relationship to any London specimens yet known, but its discovery on a site much closer to the Aldgate factory than to any other recorded London delftware pothouses raises the possibility that it may be of very early date. See Appendix II.

Plate 23.
Two manganese-decorated mugs from excavations in Oxford. The cylindrical example at the left was found in Radcliffe Square and is wider in proportion to its height than are the Pickleherring specimens. Height: 3 3/8 inches. The bulbous mug belongs to the same class as a fragment from Mathews Manor (Pl. 14, no. 13), and to the same shape as a smaller biscuit example from Pickleherring illustrated in Fig. VI, no. 7. Height: 4 15/16 inches. Both Oxford mugs can be attributed to dates within the brackets ca. 1640–1670. Ashmolean Museum: 1915.60 and 1937.512.

The mazer cup (if that is what it is) is discussed in detail under its descriptive heading, but it is worth recalling that the recent discovery of the plain white posset pot (Pl. 8) demonstrates that the relatively sophisticated ring handles were not embellishments confined to decorated vessels as had hitherto been supposed (Pl. 35). One may note, however, that the handles of both vessels are externally grooved, creating an exterior concavity akin to the treatment afforded the handles of several silver vessels, whereas the mazer's surviving handle is oval in section.

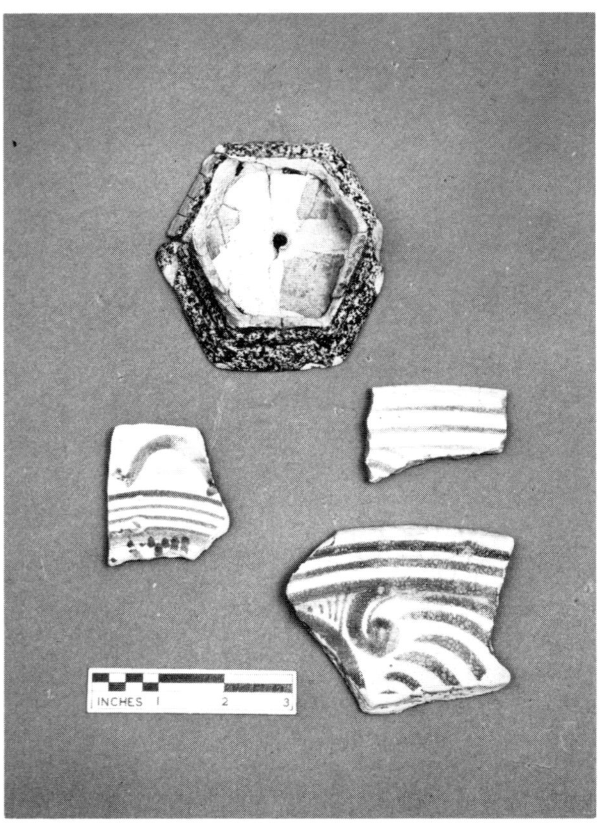

Plate 24. See color plate facing p. 36.
London delftware from Carter's Grove plantation in James City County, Virginia. Nos. 1 and 4 are, respectively, the base from a manganese decorated hexagonal salt, and a rim sherd from an elaborately painted charger; both are from a deposit of the 1640s. Nos. 2 and 3 are dish or charger fragments from an unstratified context, but serve to illustrate the range of colors common on English delftware used in rural Virginia in the second quarter of the 17th century. The salt is partially coated with white tin glaze on both the underside and inside of the base, and the body is pink and extremely friable. Base widths: 3 5/8 inches. Colonial Williamsburg Archaeological Collections, C.G. E.R.989A (1 and 4), C.G. E.R.601 and 1059 (2 and 3).

The realization that so sophisticated an object as the posset pot could be marketed in plain white suggests that many biscuit fragments from London kiln sites may have been intended to be similarly glazed. The occasional recovery of fragmentary white salts, bottles, vases, candlesticks, mugs, and cups is evidence that in addition to the more mundane white wares discussed earlier (p. 14), the more complicated shapes in white were well represented in their day. As further evidence one may point to a small standing cup (perhaps an "oil pot" or lamp) reportedly found in a Seneca grave of ca. 1650–1670 in New York state and now in the Rochester Museum (Pl. 26). Although white chamber pots, ointment pots, and basins are no strangers to the excavators of archaeological sites of the late seventeenth and eighteenth centuries, they are rarely to be seen in the cabinets of collectors or the galleries of art museums. Consequently, therefore, the absence of decoration and the rarity of some of the hollow ware forms in museum collections makes dating extremely difficult. Thus, for example, the white tea bowl(?) illustrated in Fig. VII, no. 2, cannot be dated any more closely than to the last quarter of the seventeenth century or the first quarter of the eighteenth—and that only on the basis of educated guesswork. One is equally at sea in attempting to date the small, handled vase or bottle shown in Fig. XII, no. 12. Nevertheless, they exist and cannot be ignored. One can but hope that as the archaeological study of seventeenth- and eighteenth-century sites continues in Britain and America, firm dating information will eventually be forthcoming.

White chamber pots are well represented in the Burnett Collection, but the majority almost certainly come from domestic deposits and date from the first half of the eighteenth century when great quantities of refuse were dumped on Tooley Street sites. There is, however, an important exception: Fig. XVIII, no. 1, illustrates a biscuit specimen whose broad base and relatively straight walls point to a date in the period ca. 1655–1680, a metallic form predating the ubiquitous bulbous pots of the following century (Fig. XVIII, nos. 2–9). Of these, it may be noted that the strength of the ridge or cordon at the shoulder is an indication of relatively early date. By the mid-eighteenth century the ridge had disappeared. Although this seems to be a clearly defined evolutionary trend, the Burnett Collection includes one such fragment (Fig. XVIII, no.

Plate 25.
Manganese-stippled bottle, white on the inside. The shape is akin to Pickleherring biscuit fragments (Fig. VI, nos. 8 and 10), and is paralleled in white by an example dated 1649 ([Hodgkin], 1891, p. 75), both weakly contoured at the mouth. Height: 6 1/4 inches. Colonial Williamsburg Collection: 1958-300.

9) that lacks the cordon but possesses other characteristics (pink hue and thickness of glaze coupled with broad crazing) that point to a date no later than the beginning of the eighteenth century.

Porringers whose decoration is reminiscent of ointment pot palettes and designs can generally be attributed to the second and early third quarter of the seventeenth century (Fig. XIV, nos. 1 and 2); less easily dated are the plain white varieties of the remainder of the seventeenth century, although the character of their handles has something to offer. Alas, there is but a single biscuit porringer handle in the collection (Fig. XIV, no. 5), one that appears to represent a transitional step between the early "frilled" form (Fig. XIV, no. 1), and the more restrained lobing of the eighteenth century (Fig. XIV, no. 3).

The later material in the Burnett Collection is largely unsupported by biscuit specimens and therefore there is less information to associate shapes with the St. Olave or Tooley Street kilns. There are, however, a few irrefutable and presumed wasters, notably those shown in Fig. XVI, nos. 5 and 6, a tea bowl and basin, both of which are assumed on stylistic evidence to date in the period ca. 1720–1740. The only biscuit specimens are two bowl fragments (Fig. XVIII, nos. 10 and 12) and a candlestick socket (Fig. XVI, no. 11), all three of which appear to be eighteenth-century shapes. Unfortunately, none of them comes from properly identifiable archaeological contexts.

Plate 26.
Small pedestal-footed cup, white glazed; from a Seneca grave on the Marsh site, northern New York state, attributed to ca. 1650–1670. Height: 3 5/8 inches. Rochester Museum and Science Center: 71.69.153. The specimen is illustrated to further demonstrate the variety of 17th-century forms manufactured in plain white. No parallels for this shape seem to be recorded. Although the vessel resembles a lamp, no documentary evidence of their existence *in delftware is forthcoming, and it may be more reasonable to relate it to the "oyle potts" listed in a 1666 English apothecary's inventory. Crellin (1970), 194.*

The Chargers, Dishes, Plates, and Saucers

BEFORE discussing the objects, it is necessary to define one's terminology. A word should first be said about the term "charger," which collectors and dealers commonly apply to the larger delftware plates and dishes of the seventeenth century. The word was promoted in 1919 by Edward A. Downman when he published his important early book *Blue Dash Chargers* subtitled *And Other Early English Tin Enamel Circular Dishes.* He began by saying that "there has been collected in England a considerable number of chargers, or circular dishes, of coarse earthenware, varying in diameter from 8 1/2 to 16 1/2 inches." It is evident, therefore, that to Downman size did not distinguish a charger from a dish. However, if the term is to be usefully retained, it must surely refer to a "master" dish, one from which others of lesser size were served or charged. This, then, brings us to the problem of correctly distinguishing between a dish and a plate. Downman did not make any such distinction, but it may be suggested that a plate is best defined as a shallow and broad based vessel having a wide shelf-like rim or marly. A dish, on the other hand, can be deeper and has only a narrow rim.

Size inevitably plays a part, limiting, for example, the use of the word "plate." It is hard to imagine a specimen more than a foot in diameter being described as anything but a platter—or, perhaps, a dish. A plate can reasonably be used to define examples measuring up to 10 1/2 inches in diameter; any size above that is a platter. This terminology does not apply to dishes, for an oversize dish is not a platter. Here, therefore, is an opportunity to retain Downman's "charger," using it to describe delftware dishes of more than a foot in diameter. There may be flaws in this reasoning, but for better or worse, these are the criteria for the nomenclature used in this monograph. With that said, however, it must be admitted that such distinctions are absent from the contemporary letters patent, which referred only to dishes.

There is as yet insufficient evidence to point to any surviving tin-enameled plate or dish of the sixteenth century and to claim for it an English origin. Nevertheless, there is evidence that the Aldgate factory included plates in its inventory (see Appendix II), among them, perhaps, the well-known specimen now in the collection of the Museum of London dated 1600 (Pl. 27). We know that in 1613 Edmund Bradshawe's twenty-one-year patent put "dishes of all sises" high on its list.[1] By the end of the year "potts dishes tiles posts for gardens and other vessells" were in production.[2] When Christian Wilhelm sought a similar monopoly in 1628, he claimed that he had been in the galleyware (delftware) business for twenty years, and cited "earthen gally potte[s] and dishes" at the head of a list that included "bottells of all Colo[r]s basons and ewers salte[s] dishes of all sorte[s] drinking potte[s] paving tyles Apothecaries and Comfittmakers potte[s] of all sorte[s]."[3] There is no knowing why Wilhelm

Plate 27.
Plate decorated in Italianate style in blue, yellow, green, brown, and purple. With its inscription in English and date of 1600 (or perhaps 1602), this is considered to be the earliest inscribed example of English delftware. Diameter: 10 1/4 inches. Presumably an Aldgate product (see Appendix II, pp. 117–118). Museum of London: C.84.

1. Dawson and Edwards (1973), 57, quoting S.P. 39/3, No. 41, P.R.O.; Patent Roll, C. 66/1982, P.R.O.
2. Dawson and Edwards (1973), 58.
3. Davies (1969), 29.

See page 34.

See page 42.

listed galley pots and dishes twice, but the fact that he placed them at the top of the list suggests that they were considered staples of the trade. The evidence of the Burnett Collection can support such a view, for biscuit examples of pharmaceutical pots and dishes predominate. It would be useless, however, to base a quantitative chart or histogram on that fact, since the fragments retained were limited to those that were large or provided sections through the objects. Such an exercise was attempted by Mr. Graham Dawson for one of the Montague Close deposits, but as he gave no dates, and as the sampling was relatively small (representing fewer than eight examples of any biscuit vessel save "drug jars" of which there were fourteen), a slightly smaller ratio of plates to chamber pots is surprising but not disconcerting.[4]

4. Dawson (1971), 250–251, no. 11.

It seems clear from the overwhelming preponderance of biscuit fragments over recognizable glazed wasters that most of the losses occurred during the first firing, or at least prior to glazing. A few sherds of drug pots and other hollow wares have been found with unfired glaze adhering to them, indicating that they were discarded after decorating but before entering the glost oven. It must also be noted that very few of the biscuit wares exhibit flaws (for example, firing cracks, blisters, chips) to indicate that they were rejected after spoiling in the kiln. Indeed, the only indisputable firing wasters are those that were damaged in the second burning (Pl. 9, nos. 2–4, Pls. 30 and 31, Fig. V, no. 3, Fig. VIII, nos. 1–3, and Fig. XVI, no. 5).

Before considering the range of dish designs included in the Burnett Collection, a further word should be said about its principal documentary artifact, a stack of fourteen (surviving) plates and a dish fused together with their trivets between them (Pls. 30 and 31). The discovery was made by laborers laying electrical lines who were less than "archaeological" in the care with which they shoveled the fragments out of the trench. The stack has not been fully reassembled, there being many breaks both new and old and too few sherds

Plate 28.
Platter decorated in polychrome with Adam and Eve motif; the rim unthickened, the edge rouletted or notched, and the marly pressed up from beneath to create a row of small bosses. The central motif is painted in blue, orange, yellow, and green; the back is unevenly lead glazed. The footring for this massive platter is pierced by two, rather than by the usual single, suspension holes. The design is derived from an undated engraving by Crispin van de Passe of Zealand (1568–1637). This platter is attributable to about 1635 on the evidence of a close parallel bearing that date in the Victoria and Albert Museum. Mactaggart (1959), p. 58, pl. 1. Diameter: 19 1/2 inches. Colonial Williamsburg Collection: 1959-52.

Plate 29.
Charger decorated in polychrome with Adam and Eve motif, the rim everted, slightly down-turned, and decorated with blue dashes. The central design is painted in blue, orange, yellow, and green, with the figures drawn in purple. The back is yellow lead glazed, and the footring is pierced by a single suspension hole. Diameter: 14 1/8 inches. Author's collection: 72.

Plate 30.
Stack of plates and dishes fused in firing; side view showing trivets in situ. *From the Pickleherring site. For details, see Fig. VIII and related text.*

to match them. Nevertheless, several important pieces of information were garnered.

The kiln had overheated to a disastrous degree, causing the plates and the intervening trivets to melt. No traces of a sagger were attached, and it was evident that the plate rims had not been supported by the triangular-sectioned sagger pins that one associates with delftware and other quality pottery manufacturing in the late seventeenth and eighteenth centuries. The presence of one dish with polychrome pomegranate decoration (Fig. VIII, no. 3) among thirteen plates painted in oriental designs in blue indicated that both polychrome and monochrome wares were fired in a single trivet-spaced pile. Two chinoiserie designs could be identified (Fig. VIII, nos. 1 and 2) but were stacked in no identifiable order. Using Fig. VIII's numbers for identification, the contents of the two fused lumps present the following equations. There being a single polychrome dish in each unit (no. 3), that type is used as an anchor in seeking a relationship between the two fused blocks.

Unit A (Rims)	1 1 1 2 1 2 1 2 1 ? 1 3 1 1 . .
Unit B (Bases)	. . . . 1 1 2 2 3 1 1 1 1

On the basis of the foregoing evidence, it seems likely either that the two fused units do not come from the same stack or that the pile comprised twenty or more items. If the rims do not belong to the stacked bases, it is likely that the utility trench cut through the debris of a disastrous firing from an entire kiln and that much more evidence was either discarded unnoticed or still lies buried beneath Vine Lane. Sir David Burnett's notes state that the fragments came from a point "very close to the site of [the] Pickle Herring kiln," that is, close to the location wherein he had seen traces of what he believed to be brick-built kiln structures.

The principal plate design (Fig. VIII, no. 1), represented by at least nine examples in the fused pile, is a relatively direct copy from contemporary Chinese porcelain (Pl. 32). The central motif was common in the Wan Li period (1573–1619) of the late Ming Dynasty and is generally known as the bird-on-rock. The central elements are a bird standing at the left on a bulbous rock, and a fronded plant to the right, the top of which bends over the bird. Above the rock to the left there is generally a lozenge-shaped flower with widely spaced radiating petals. This flower often seems to be floating, but is intended to be attached to a stem that in turn is anchored to one of several leaves protruding from the rock. As Pl. 32 shows,

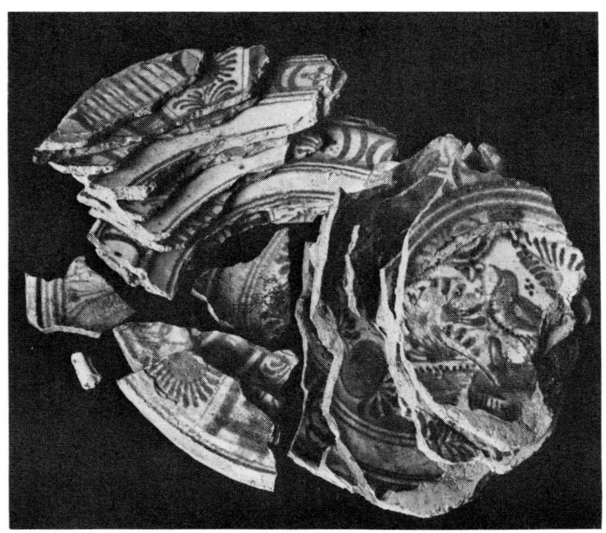

Plate 31.
The plates and dishes illustrated in Pl. 30 showing blue-painted bird-on-rock and other motifs borrowed from Wan Li period porcelain.

Plate 32.
Chinese porcelain dish decorated with bird-on-rock motif in blue. Late Ming. Diameter: 8 inches. Victoria and Albert Museum: C.539-1922.

Plate 33.
Platter decorated in blue with bird-on-rock and well-executed Wan Li style border; the back yellow lead glazed. About 1630–1645. Diameter: 19 1/2 inches. Victoria and Albert Museum: C.59-1961.

Plate 34.
Plate decorated in blue with floral pattern containing elements commonly encountered in the bird-on-rock design. The rim is notched at the edge and the marly is pressed up from beneath to create a series of blue-painted bosses. Dated 1636. (See also Pl. 28.) Diameter: 10 7/8 inches. Fitzwilliam Museum, Glaisher Collection: 1298. For a related example with a crudely executed bird-on-rock central design, see Archer (1973), p. 60, no. 12.

the Chinese drawing could be very sloppy and it was small wonder that the Southwark potters were uncertain in their copying.

The illustrated porcelain dish has been chosen because it is a relatively simple version of the bird-on-rock motif and most closely parallels the designs of the excavated delftware plates. There were many larger Chinese porcelain dishes of this type, which naturally contained additional design elements; those too were copied by Southwark painters decorating larger delftware pieces such as the 19 1/2-inch platter in the collection of the Victoria and Albert Museum (Pl. 33). This specimen has in its "sky" a curious striped "cloud" that is present on the much smaller Burnett Collection plates in the form of a snail-like scroll. That scroll, in a rather more hesitant hand, also appears on a plate dated 1636 in the Glaisher Collection at the Fitzwilliam Museum (Pl. 34). Although the rest of the Glaisher plate's design bears no resemblance to the standard bird-on-rock, it is clear that the latter design outlived Christian Wilhelm at the Pickleherring factory. A rather similar scroll feature is present on the previously discussed globular jar in the Burnap Collection at the Nelson–Atkins Gallery, Kansas City, which is dated 1632 (Pl. 35). Other features, notably the curving fernlike plant and the long-petalled flowers, are closely akin to the Burnett Collection examples. The same may also be said of another fine specimen in the Burnap Collection, inscribed MRS. MARY HOOPER 1629 (Pl. 36), and of a mug in the Museum of London dated 1630 (Pl. 37).

Plate 36.
Mug decorated in blue with simplified bird-on-rock motif, inscribed MRS. MARY HOOPER 1629. Height: 4 7/8 inches. Nelson Gallery–Atkins Museum, Burnap Collection: B 185 A.

Plate 35.
Double-handled jar or large cup, painted in blue with the bird-on-rock motif, and dated 1632 under the left handle. Lightly painted vertical and horizontal lines may have served as guides for a painter not working with a previously pounced subject. Note that the flower at the left is closely related to that to the right of the platter in Pl. 33. The jar's handles are externally concave and belong to the same class as those on the posset pot illustrated in Pl. 8. Both pot and jar may originally have possessed lids. Height: 5 1/16 inches. Nelson Gallery–Atkins Museum, Burnap Collection: B185 A2. For the painting of the other side, see Taggart (1967), p. 44, no. 75.

Based on the foregoing evidence, therefore, the bird-on-rock motif might appear to date in the period ca. 1628–1636 or to the period immediately before and after Wilhelm's death. This is not a valid conclusion, however, as another fragment from the Burnett Collection reveals. This, the only dated specimen in the entire collection, comes from a small dish marked on the underside within the footring E Ç S over the date 1651 (Pl. 38A and B). The decoration, although somewhat more sophisticated than the treatment of the ca. 1630 bird-on-rock designs, nevertheless retains the essential elements, including the gratuitous plunging bug that is a major feature of the Glaisher Collection's 1636 plate (Pl. 34).

Returning to the Burnett Collection's bird-on-rock motif, it will be noticed that below and to the left of the standing bird a curious molelike crea-

Plate 37.
Tankard or can painted in blue with bird-on-rock motif divided into two zones containing matching elements and divided by a panel inscribed THE : GIFT : IS : SMALL : GOODWILL : IS : ALL : Below the rim is a band of similar lettering reading JAMES AND ELIZABETH GREENE ANNO 1630. Height: 6 1/8 inches. Museum of London: A.6807.

A.

B.

Plate 38A–B.
Upper and underside views of a dish or bowl base fragment decorated in blue with an elaborate version of the bird-on-rock design. Dated on the back 1651 with the owners' initials ECS. Foot diameter: 2 3/16 inches. Probably from the Pickleherring site. For details, see Fig. XII and related text.

ture sits atop the rock. This, presumably, is a poor rendering of another bird whose body is intended to be largely concealed by the stone and is much better rendered in the examples shown in Pls. 33, 35, 37, and 38A. Mention should also be made of the lozenge-shaped flowers that appear on these delftware pieces in differing styles. The petals are sometimes shown as blue dots on stalks, as blue dots above two lines representing the petal edges, or (as in the case of the Museum of London's 1630 mug) with the petal outlines complete and the dots spaced between them. On the Burnett Collection plates, two flowers rise like the rays of the morning sun, there being no petals below the horizon. This feature is to be seen intermittently throughout the date range of the delftware bird-on-rock design from the 1629 Hooper mug to the Burnett Collection's 1651 dish fragment (Pl. 38A and B). The same feature is present on an extremely important fragment (actually three fragments) found at Lee Hall, Virginia, which shows one such flower resting on a blue line and part of another below it (Pl. 39 and Fig. VIIIA). A comparison between this fragment and the central motif from the Burnett Collection plates (Pl. 40) shows that, with the exception of the blue line and the solid cloud substituting for the snail-like scroll, the designs are strikingly similar, and there is every reason to assume that they are from the same factory.

Before leaving the flower elements, one must turn to the second and much more elusive design represented among the fused plates (Fig. VIII, no.

2), which almost certainly also belonged to the bird-on-rock school, but for which no intact parallel can yet be found. The principal remaining feature is a pomegranatelike ball (replacing the usual fern) from which project dot-and-stalk petaled flowers, a combination that appears to the upper left of the central design of the Victoria and Albert Museum's platter (Pl. 33) and the Museum of London's 1630 mug (Pl. 37). Something akin to it also occurs on an abominably painted little seven-inch plate in the collection of the Museum of London (Pl. 41) that was found in the city in a ca. 1625–1650 context. Here, however, the "pomegranate" is surrounded by extremely small petals which, of course, make the object look much more like a flower. It is worth noting, however, that regardless of its atrocious painting, the rock has a hole in it, a common Chinese feature in the eighteenth century that is absent from all the other specimens discussed above. One might deduce, therefore, that the plate was copied from a different Chinese source, one that also included a mountainlike element above the bird instead of the clouds usually seen there.

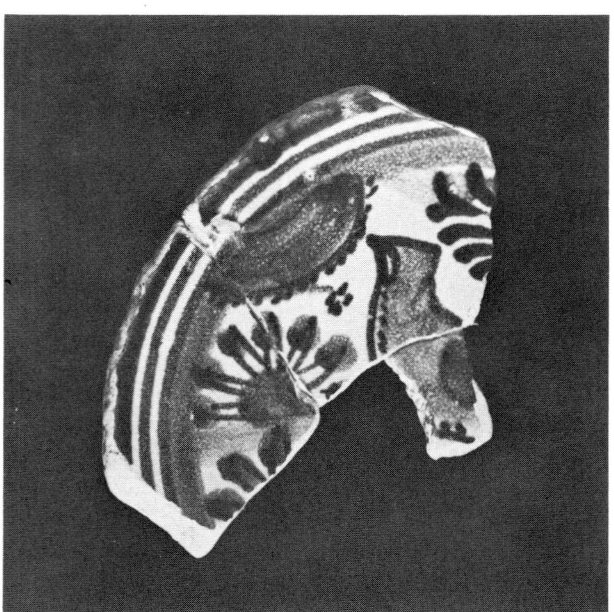

Plate 39.
Base fragments from a dish or bowl decorated with a Wan Li style bird-on-rock motif similar to examples from the Pickleherring site. Found at Lee Hall, Virginia. See Fig. VIIIA. Colonial Williamsburg Archaeological Collection: O.C.6940.

Frequent reference to the Chinese origins of the bird-on-rock design must not obscure the fact that the design on delftware is as characteristically Dutch as it is English. Thus, for example, virtually all the elements discussed above occur on a group of Netherlandish tiles in the Victoria and Albert Museum.[5] However, Dutch dating is no closer than the English.

As previously noted, the third type included among the fused wasters is represented by but one identifiable specimen (Fig. VIII, no. 3), a dish decorated in polychrome colors in a pomegranate motif. Dated examples of this design are rare and there is today less certainty as to the English origin of several important specimens which, until a few years ago, were firmly attributed to London. It may be significant that the waster differs from most recorded pomegranate dishes in that it lacks the thick blue dashes commonly found on the rims. Instead, the edge is undecorated, but is accented by three concentric blue bands akin to those on a possibly comparable dish in the collection of the National Museum of Wales (Pl. 42).

The majority of the seventeenth-century chargers, dishes, and plates in the Burnett Collection are lead glazed on their backs employing a formula differing from that used to create the

5. Lane (1960), p. 60 and pl. 33E.

Plate 40. *See color plate facing page p. 37.*
Detail of blue-painted bird-on-rock motif on fused plate stack from Pickleherring site.

thick white tin glaze of their upper and decorated surfaces. It is frequently claimed that early English delftware potters omitted the tin oxide opacifier from the "back" glaze to conserve that expensive ingredient. This, one is told, distinguishes between English and Netherlandish products, the latter invariably being similarly tin glazed on both sides. This certainly is not valid, for many comparable fragments found on Dutch and German sites are not identically glazed on both faces. It is true, however, that the vast majority of the Burnett Collection's early examples (be they plates, dishes, saucers, or porringers) do exhibit such a difference. A slightly whitened glaze is either so thin that the yellow or pink body shows through, or it is richly yellow and apparently devoid of tin. There is therefore every reason to suppose that the potters were, indeed, trying to save tin, either by omitting it altogether or by thinning the last of a supply of facing glaze. There seems to be no consistency in the use of either expedient, and no close dating conclusion can be drawn from them, although the practice certainly seems, with rare exceptions, to have been confined to specimens dating prior to ca. 1680. That the back glazing was not always of inferior quality is demonstrated by Pl. 38, A and B, where the 1651 dish is clearly identically tin glazed on both sides, and by the "daisy" charger in Pl. 46. The same is true of the later seventeenth century armorial plate fragment shown in Pl. 51, Fig. XII, no. 2. By the last decade of the seventeenth century glazing was generally the same both front and back.

The decline of polychrome decoration and a growing taste for the clean appearance of white glaze is to be seen among dishes and plates just as it is among drug pots and hollow wares. Surviving dated specimens indicate, however, that for plates and dishes this was a trend that developed in the mid-seventeenth century, and therefore it may be convenient (if not convincing) to associ-

Plate 41.
Small plate extremely crudely decorated in blue with bird-on-rock motif; thin tin glaze on the back over a pink to yellow body. Note that the flower at the right is related to that on a plate in the Pickleherring fused stack (Fig. VIII, no. 2), and to the items shown in Pls. 33 and 37. The rock is of special interest, being pierced in the manner common both on Chinese porcelain and on English ceramic copies in the 18th century, but absent from other recorded 17th-century examples of the bird-on-rock design on delftware. The plate is one of a pair from a brick-lined cesspit in Church Alley, adjacent to London's Guildhall; found in a context of 1625–1650. Diameter: 7 inches. Museum of London: E.R.1016, 24368. The dish shown in Pl. 43 is from the same deposit.

Plate 42.
Dish decorated in polychrome with grapes, pomegranates, and leaves, enclosed within three blue circles. Painted also in green, orange, and purple, the dish is believed to closely parallel the only polychrome decorated example amid the fused stack from the Pickleherring site (Fig. VIII, no. 3). Lead glazed on the back. A close parallel rather more tidily painted, but with none of the pomegranates opened, is in the collection of the Boymans–van Beuningen Museum, Rotterdam (A.3209) and is attributed to the mid-17th century. See Archer (1973), p. 18, no. 18. Diameter of illustrated example: 8 1/4 inches. About 1628–1640. National Museum of Wales: 2092.

ate the new style with Puritan purity during England's regretted experiment in revolutionary democracy. The only plain white plate in the collection is of much later date (ca. 1700), but is important as evidence that such things existed (Fig. VII, no. 14). They are not to be seen in museum collections and only one is recorded as having been found in close to half a century of Williamsburg excavations. One might add that the appallingly bad glazing of the Burnett specimen suggests that for some unexplained reason the glazing of white plates could be more difficult than coating porringers or chamber pots. It should be noted, however, that in the second half of the seventeenth century and early eighteenth century the glaze used on all three forms was prone to craze, and in spite of its thickness to flake away from the body. These characteristics are less common on the white wares of the earlier years of the seventeenth century (see Pls. 8, 15, and 22), but they are clearly visible on the mugs illustrated in Pl. 6.

One is on slightly safer ground in attempting to define evolutionary trends in dish and plate designs, at least at the beginning and end of the seventeenth century. At the outset, designs were generally in polychrome and clung to the heraldic traditions of renaissance Europe. The border encircling the famous 1600 plate in the Museum of London (Pl. 27) is typical of this genre,[6] as is the strikingly two-colored diamond pattern used on the dish shown in Pls. 43 and 49, no. 4. The latter design is closely related to the decoration to be seen on early drug jars and ointment pots (Pls. 12 and 13) and employs a similar palette of blue and orange. By the 1620s, these traditional Italianate and Germanic motifs were being challenged by the new taste for porcelain and chinoiserie ornament. Nevertheless, this was slow to oust the old styles, and one finds oak-leaf and pomegranate designs persisting at least into the mid-seventeenth century. Both are present, for example, around the rim of the well-known Charles II yacht plate of 1668, now in the Burnap Collection in Kansas City.[7] The pomegranate design, so common not only on delftware but also on crewel (from which the potters probably borrowed it), seems to have gone out of fashion by the 1670s and to have been overtaken by tulip patterns, which persisted to the end of the century (Pl. 49, no. 5), although the latest dated example known to me is marked 1676 and is in the Glaisher Collection.[8]

Owing much to the elaborate maiolica designs of the fifteenth and sixteenth centuries were those delftware dishes decorated with biblical and historical scenes, most of which date between ca. 1635 and 1665. To the same period belong the best of the well-known "Adam and Eve" chargers (Pls. 28 and 29), although there is one in the Victoria and Albert Museum dated as late as 1741.[9] Royal portraits are relatively common in museum and private collections, and most of these date between 1662 and 1691, although there is at least one recorded charger bearing a standing portrait of George II, thus dating it no earlier than 1727.[10] In using the word "common" in connec-

Plate 43.
Dish decorated in polychrome with central pinwheel motif and exhibiting striped diamond elements in the outer design related to the decoration used on early polychrome painted pharmaceutical pots and jars. Three bands of blue are at the rim (see Pl. 42) and around the central element; other colors comprise orange, yellow, and green; yellow lead glazed on the back. Possibly Netherlandish. Diameter: 8 3/8 inches. From the same ca. 1625–1650 context as the example shown in Pl. 41. Museum of London: E.R.1016, 25319.

6. A comparable design persisted as late as 1642 on a dated mug made for Ann Chapman, now in the Victoria and Albert Museum (C.1107-1853). See also Archer (1973), p. 19.

7. Taggart (1967), p. 46, Fig. 89.

8. Rackham and Read (1924), pl. VI.

9. Victoria and Albert Museum, C.278-1926.

10. Downman (1919), p. 73, illustrated facing p. 74. Item in the Fitzwilliam Museum, Glaisher Collection, No. 1638, attributed to ca. 1740.

Plate 44.
Small dish, blue dashed at the rim, polychrome decorated with central pinwheel motif and with lozenges reminiscent of those on early delftware flooring tiles (Fig. II, no. 8). Note the use of the striped triangle ointment pot element, suggesting a date no later than ca. 1650. An 8 1/4-inch dish exhibiting both the pinwheel and lozenge design elements has been found in a well at Potters Bar, a deposit attributed to about 1650–1660. Ashdown (1970), p. 97, Fig. 1, no. 1. Besides blue, the illustrated dish is painted in orange, yellow, and green, and is yellow lead glazed on its back. Possibly Netherlandish. Diameter: 8 1/16 inches. Found in excavations for the Bank of England subway; no archaeological dating recorded. Museum of London: 6075.

tion with any of these elaborately decorated dishes and chargers, I refer only to their presence in collections. Negative archaeological evidence indicates that these objects were never in common household service, for they are rarely found in the ground. It must be supposed, therefore, that they were intended almost exclusively for decorative use and thus would have been protected from the attrition of fair wear and shatterage. There are no fragments of any such items in the Burnett Collection, nor have any been found in Williamsburg or in other Virginia excavations. Nevertheless, it would be improper to fail to mention them, as they are the focal point of most museums' seventeenth-century delftware collections.

The common designs among the Burnett Collection dishes (and saucers) are geometric and based either on daisy or pinwheel centers. The latter can be dated at least as early as the second quarter of the seventeenth century on the evidence of an excavated specimen in the collection of the Museum of London (Pl. 43) that retains the previously mentioned two-color diamond pattern associated with polychrome drug jars and ointment pots of the first decades of the century. The same central design occurs on another dish excavated in London (Pl. 44), although its rather crude lozenge design suggests that it may date in the period ca. 1645–1670. Variations on the pinwheel—or Catherine wheel—motif are illustrated in Pl. 49, no. 4, in Fig. XII, nos. 4, 5, and 8, and in Fig. XI, no. 2, whose design also includes the hook-ended fronds that are an important element in the dish shown in Pl. 43.

The pinwheel feature usually occurs on plates decorated in polychrome, although the wheel itself is generally only in blue occasionally ringed in yellow. The daisy design, on the other hand, is invariably employed only on chargers, dishes, and bowls decorated in blue, probably because the wall or outer design was taken from Wan Li porcelain and was intended to give the piece a Chinese "blue and white" appearance. Fig. IX illustrates the two key examples in the Burnett Collection, but central fragments shown in Pl. 49, nos. 1–3, more fully define the central pattern. Although fragments of these dishes seem to be relatively common in London excavations, they are not well represented in museum collections other than those derived from archaeological excavation and salvage. The three examples

Plate 45.
Dish painted in blue with solid color at the rim, and with Wan Li style border and "daisy" central element, a combination that is one of the most common among dishes from the Pickleherring sites as well as at Montague Close. Dawson and Edwards, 1973, p. 49, Figs. 5 and 6. Lead glazed on the back. Diameter: 12 7/8 inches. About 1640–1650. Victoria and Albert Museum: C.3859-1901.

shown in Pls. 46–48 illustrate both the consistency and the minor variations to be encountered in this design. The relatively tight daisylike floral centers of Pls. 45 and 46 are almost identical to examples from the Pickleherring sites, but that of Pl. 47 is reduced to six narrow spokes (as opposed to the eight "petals" of the others) and it is tempting to see this much lighter treatment of the design as a later development. That the design was originally fully floral (as opposed to the purely geometric debasement shown in Pl. 47) is demonstrated by a small dish (diameter 7 3/8 inches) found in a dubiously dated context at Dover Castle and assumed to be Dutch.[11]

The same basic daisy and Wan Li border combination also occurs in bowl form as is demonstrated by an example found in Oxford and now in the Ashmolean Museum (Pl. 48), and by another found at Colchester.[12] A bowl having a comparable wall design, but regrettably lacking all of its base, has been found in Virginia at the Kingsmill Tenement site in a context attributed to ca. 1640.[13]

Plate 47. *See color plate facing p. 84.*
Dish similar to, but larger than, those shown in Pls. 44 and 45, but the decoration more thinly painted, the central "daisy" with only six petals instead of the usual eight, and the back yellow lead glazed. Diameter: 13 1/2 inches. About 1650. See n. 1, p. 77. Author's collection: 74.

Plate 46.
Dish comparable to that shown in Pl. 44, but with a groove at the rim and tin glazed on the back. Diameter: 12 1/4 inches. About 1640–1650. Sir David Burnett's private collection. No number.

Both bowls and dish forms in the pinwheel–Wan Li combination tend to be yellow glazed on their backs. It is not, however, an infallible rule, for the charger shown in Pl. 46 is tin glazed on both faces. What does seem to be consistent, however, is the presence of a solidly blue-painted rim rather than the blue dash feature common to so many seventeenth-century dishes and chargers dating after about 1635.

A third geometric pattern well represented among the Burnett Collection fragments is incompletely illustrated by Fig. VII, no. 4. The dishes generally run to charger diameter and the decoration is usually painted in a pale blue. In the absence of evidence to the contrary, the sloppi-

11. Mynard (1969), 34–36, Fig. 10, no. 1. After this book was already on its way to publication, the largest yet recorded charger of the "daisy" type was found in a rubbish pit at Kingsmill plantation in James City County, Virginia. Unfortunately, none of the charger's central motif survives, but the character of the wall and rim leaves no doubt as to its identification. Painted in very pale blue and lead glazed on the back, the Kingsmill charger measures 14 1/8 inches in diameter. K.M.639R. Collection of Virginia Research Center for Archaeology. The pit is thought to have been filled after ca. 1640, but the dearth of associated datable artifacts causes the terminus post quem to be based on this writer's dating of the delftware charger which, in turn, is derived from the accumulated evidence discussed herein.

12. Blake, Hurst, and Grant (1961), 6 and Figs. 33 and 34. The bowl is said to be "typical of early 17th century Netherlands Maiolica" and is so identified perhaps because the authors were unaware of the London parallels.

13. Diameter 7 3/8 inches, KM.382A.154C, collection of Virginia Research Center for Archaeology.

ness of the painting and the lack of uniformity in the designs suggests that these represent the last gasp of the multiple-stroke diamond tradition (Pl. 43) and therefore date from the third quarter of the seventeenth century.

Although not represented among fragments in the Burnett Collection, mention must be made of another rim form that archaeological evidence shows to have been made at the Pickleherring factory in the 1630s (Pl. 28). This is a ring of equidistant protuberances. The edges of such plates are generally notched to create a shallow "dog tooth" pattern. Both biscuit and glazed fragments of such plates were among the kiln waste recovered by Dr. Francis Celoria in his 1965 excavations east of Vine Lane. In addition to the examples illustrated in Pls. 28 and 34, two fine specimens of this type dated 1635 and 1637 are to be seen in the collection of the Victoria and Albert Museum.[14] It does not seem to have been a long-lived style, probably because the marly was time-consuming to shape, easily damaged before firing, and weak at the rim. It should be noted that De Jonge ([1949], p. 58, Pl. 31) illustrates a Netherlandish example that differs from the English specimens in that the rim is gently scalloped rather than notched.

The Burnett Collection includes a considerable range of seventeenth-century plate, dish, platter, and charger designs, and a selection of these is to be seen in the photographs and drawings. Not all can be safely claimed as Pickleherring products; indeed, some clearly are not (Pl. 49, nos. 6 and 7). Of considerable interest, if of questionable origin, is the base of a dish or charger decorated in blue with a ship in full sail (Pl. 50), which from the friable nature of the yellow back glaze can be said with reasonable confidence to be a local product, if not necessarily from the Pickleherring factory. Unfortunately, nothing but the central design survives, but the encircling narrow and broad lines are reminiscent of fragments found in the Netherlands having an outer decoration of painted fluting in the Italian manner.[15] The treatment of the sky behind the sails in the Burnett Collection example is akin to that employed in the cited parallel whose central motif is a running dog of the kind often found on flooring tiles of the late sixteenth and early seventeenth centuries.[16]

Plate 48.
Bowl with "daisy" pattern and Wan Li style border painted in blue, lead glazed on the exterior. London manufacture. Found in Oxford. Rim diameter: 9 5/8 inches. Ashmolean Museum: 1938.1169.

The major public and private collections of seventeenth-century London delftware may lead the casual observer to assume that items made for city livery companies, members of titled families, and "personalized" pieces for private individuals were among the most abundant of any factory's output. Archaeological evidence does not support such a thesis, and the fragments represented in the Burnett Collection are equally negative. It is true that the collection does include one incomplete armorial plate (Pl. 51 and Fig. XII, no. 2), but it must be remembered that this was salvaged for that very reason from among many thousands of other less obviously interesting sherds. The survival of so many named, dated, and armorial items must be explained by their strong "keep me" factors enabling them to eloquently beg for survival.

Before leaving the dishes and plates, one eighteenth-century specimen must be considered, for being an unquestionable waster, it is important evidence of at least one of the designs being manufactured in the parish of St. Olave in the

14. Garner (1948), p. 8 and pl. 14; Garner and Archer (1972), pl. 5; Victoria and Albert Museum, C.278-1919.

15. De Jonge (1947), p. 54, Fig. 28. This example is in the collection of the Rijksmuseum, Amsterdam, and is attributed to ca. 1600.

16. Korf (1964), p. 60, Fig. 77.

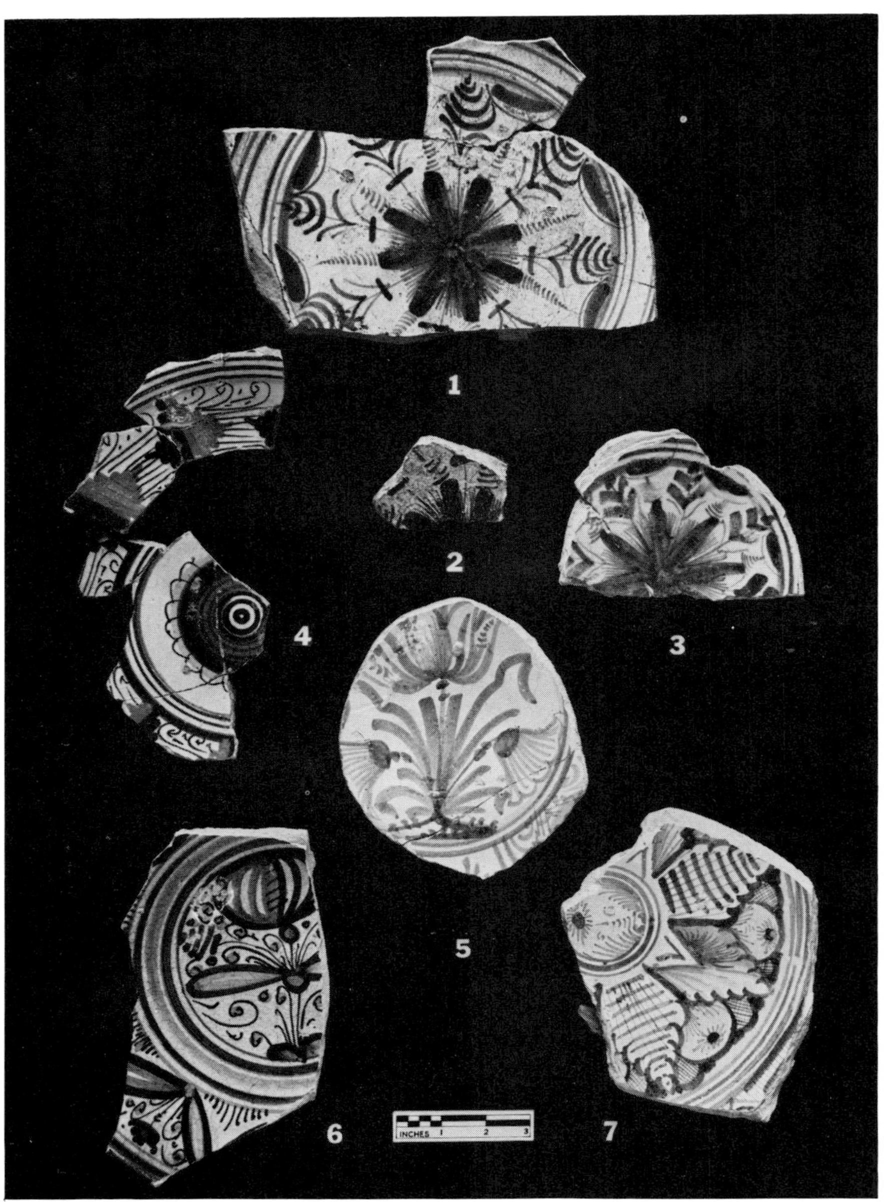

Plate 49. *See color plate facing p. 85. Dish and bowl designs from the Burnett Collection. Nos. 1–3, dish variations on the "daisy" pattern on blue (see Fig. IX). No. 2, a possible waster, about 1640–1650. No. 4, dish with pinwheel center and divided diamond outer decoration in blue, orange, and yellow; thinly tin glazed on the back, blue scrolls on the lower wall, and a large $ painted in blue on the bottom; Netherlandish, about 1620; see De Jonge (1947), p. 63, pl. 37. No. 5, tulip design on dish, with Wan Li type outer design, all in pale blue (see Fig. X, no. 2), about 1650–1665. No. 6, plate with polychrome floral device in Italianate style (see Fig. X. no. 1); probably Netherlandish, about 1600–1640; see De Jonge (1947), p. 45, pl. 16, for a ca. 1565 design parallel. No. 7, bowl with elaborate pomegranate and leaf design in a palette of blue, orange, yellow, and green; probably Netherlands or Italian; about 1600–1640.*

1740s. Lest it be thought that this may be a single anomalous and intrusive item, the reader's attention should again be drawn to other eighteenth-century wasters in the collection (Fig. XVI, nos. 5, 6, and 11), suggesting that all are products of a nearby factory. In the absence of another named potter, it may be deduced that they come from the kilns of Richard Grove who was in business in the Stoney Lane area in the second quarter of the century. It must be noted, however, that both the waster plate and the fused bowls come from the Battle Bridge House site three blocks west of Stoney Lane.

The waster plate is decorated in blue, red, green, and yellow, and was discarded after the blue-tinted glaze had slid away from the wall to reveal the body beneath (Fig. XVII, no. 6). The central basket-of-flowers motif can be found both earlier and later on Rouen faïence, which in turn borrowed it in a simplified form from the vase-on-table design seen on late Ming porcelain. The delftware waster is closely paralleled by two intact examples in the collection of Sir David Burnett (Pl. 52) and the Victoria and Albert Museum (Pl. 53), and in a debased and presumably later form by another specimen in the writer's collection (Pl. 54). However, it is reasonable to suppose that all three are from the same factory, for although there is a great difference in quality between the specimens shown in Pls. 52 and 54, the debased treatment of the flower centers in the second example (Pl. 53) provides a link between them.

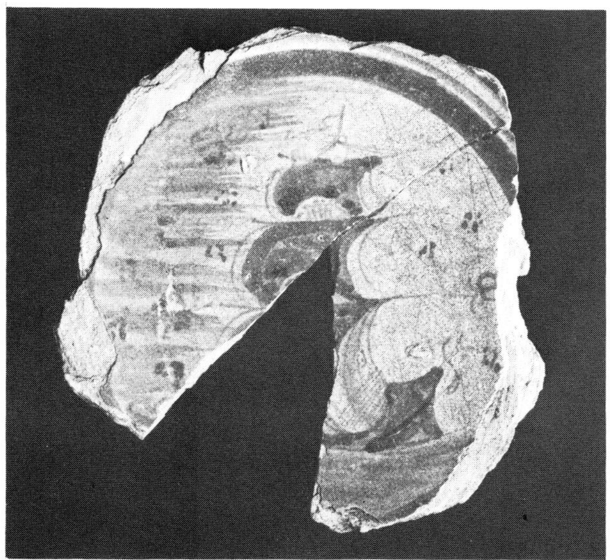

Plate 50.
Base of dish or plate painted in blue with a ship in full sail, lead glazed on the back, probably a Pickleherring product. Foot diameter: 3 7/8 inches. About 1640–1675. *See p. 86.*

Plate 51.
Armorial plate fragment painted in blue. London manufacture. Diameter approximately: 8 3/4 inches. About 1650–1680. (See Fig. XII, no. 2.)

Plate 52.
Platter decorated in blue, red, yellow, and green; the floral design paralleling the waster illustrated in Fig. XVII, no. 6. Diameter: 14 inches. About 1740. Sir David Burnett's private collection. No number.

The saucers have been left to last, not only because they are the smallest, but also because they are the most enigmatic of the "flat" shapes. The term "saucer" is perhaps misleading in that these vessels were not at first used in conjunction with cups or tea bowls but were containers for salt, sauces, spices, and so forth.[17] The majority were about 4 1/4 inches in diameter, and were busily, if crudely, decorated on their upper surfaces. There is considerable variation in depth, ranging from those that are relatively flat (Fig. XII, no. 6) to others that are more akin to small, shallow bowls (Fig. XII, nos. 7 and 9). Some have small footrings in the manner of the conventional saucer (Fig. XIII, no. 6), while others have small, almost pedestal feet (Fig. XIII, no. 7). Like the larger plates, dishes, chargers, and porringers of the mid-seventeenth century, saucers occur with a yellow lead glaze on their backs, but they are most often found tin glazed on both sides. The examples in the Burnett Collection are decorated only in blue, suggesting that they belong to the "post-polychrome" period, that is, after about 1640. It may also be deduced that the broad brush-stroke designs are sufficiently akin to the painting of earlier polychrome pharmaceutical pots, and are so lacking in even the smallest hint of chinoiserie, that a manufacturing date range between the brackets 1640 and 1670 seems reasonable. No doubt firm archaeological dating will eventually be forthcoming, but so far few examples have been found in closely datable contexts. Indeed, the only specimen known to me was found in a ca. 1702–1710 context at Tutter's Neck plantation, Virginia.[18] This seemingly unique saucer is decorated in "reverse Nevers" style (that is, blue splashed on white), a technique which, in its white on blue form, is attributed to ca. 1680–1700 (Fig. XV, no. 2). Ceramic saucers do occur considerably earlier in Virginia, however, figuring in inventories by 1667.[19]

Decoration among the Pickleherring fragments is generally limited to geometric patterns built from lines and swags of graduated lengths, but in one instance something a little more elaborate is attempted, the painted area being divided by a cross reminiscent of the medieval

17. The ***Oxford English Dictionary*** attributes its first saucer reference to 1607, at which date it meant "any small shallow dish or deep plate of circular shape." The same dictionary recalls that in 1742 the word meant "a dish or deep plate in which salt or sauces were placed upon the table." Samuel Johnson's ***Dictionary of the English Language,*** 3rd ed. (1765) gives the primary definition as "a small pan or platter in which sauces are set on the table." His second definition is the first dictionary reference to saucers as an element of tea-drinking equipment: "A piece or platter of China, into which a tea-cup is set." That the term *saucer* was uncommon in the late 17th and early 18th centuries is suggested by the absence of the word from the much used 1737 edition of Bailey's *Etymological Dictionary* (1721).

18. Noël Hume (1966a), 65–66, Fig. 18, no. 8.

19. Billings, ed., ***The Old Dominion in the Seventeenth Century,*** p. 310, inventory of Jane Hartey, 1667, Northampton County Deed and Will Book, fols. 13–14.

Plate 53.
Plate decorated in blue, red, yellow, and green; a close parallel in both design and size for the waster illustrated in Fig. XVII, no. 6. Diameter: 9 inches. About 1740. Victoria and Albert Museum: C.65-1965.

Plate 54.
Plate decorated in blue, red, yellow, and green; a debased version of the design shown in Pls. 52 and 53, and represented by the waster in Fig. XVII, no. 6. Diameter: 9 inches. About 1750. Author's collection: 68.

Plate 55.
Saucer with geometric pattern in pale blue comparable to specimens from the Pickleherring sites; tin glazed on both sides. Diameter: 4 1/2 inches. From an uncertain deposit in Cheapside (Pit T.R.B.). About 1650. See Fig. XIII, no. 6, for shape. Museum of London: 26782.

quartering on the reverse faces of English silver coins (Fig. XIII, no. 1). Citing such a parallel may well be seen as an attempt to read vastly more into these simple designs than they merit, and there is certainly no doubting that the artist sometimes conceived his motif with little in his head but the products of lead- or alcohol-poisoning (Fig. XIII, no. 2). On others, however, the effect was distinctly pleasing in its naiveté. The example illustrated in Pl. 55 is in the collection of the Museum of London and was found in a now unrecorded pit in Cheapside. As already stated, its central spiral or pinwheel element is a well-represented Southwark feature (Fig. XII, nos. 4 and 5, the former a waster), and one that persisted on English delftware at least into the mid-eighteenth century.[20] It should also be noted, however, that in the seventeenth century the same pinwheel or Catherine wheel design occurred on Netherlandish specimens, and so is not by itself diagnostically useful.

Although no more skillfully painted than the rest of the saucers, one example bears a triple-initial cipher, further evidence that their surfaces were not intended to be concealed beneath cups or bowls (Fig. XII, no. 6). Nevertheless, regardless of the occasional personalizing initials, these saucers seem to belong to a uniformly crudely decorated class. One may wonder, therefore, whether they were of sufficiently little consequence to be left to the talents of the most junior apprentice painters.

20. Noël Hume (1970), p. 111, Fig. 31, no. 6.

The Kiln Furniture

KILN equipment included in the Burnett Collection comprises sagger fragments and trivets, all apparently of seventeenth-century date. Recognizing that the collection is limited to large sherds or pieces having obviously interesting designs or shapes, it is reasonable to deduce that the seven trivets were all that were found, but that the sagger fragments are but a few of the many that were unearthed and subsequently reinterred. Consequently, no quantitative analysis has meaning and no valid conclusions can be drawn as to the range of sagger shapes or the relative preponderance of one size over another. These negative factors aside, it is unquestionably significant that none of the saggers exhibits triangular holes in its sides and that no matching sagger pegs were found. As previously noted, such pegs are characteristic of delftware manufacturing in the eighteenth century,[1] although evidence of their occasional earlier use is revealed by scars on the backs of seventeenth-century plates.

The sagger fragments present in the collection range in projected exterior diameter through the following: 4 7/8 inches, 6 1/4 inches, 6 3/4 inches, 6 7/8 inches, and 7 1/16 inches, suggesting that they were intended to represent sizes of 5-, 6-, and 7-inch diameters. Only three examples provided sections from top to bottom, and these measured 3 1/2 inches (Fig. XVIII, no. 14), 4 inches (Fig. XVII, no. 13), and 5 3/8 inches (Fig. XVII, no. 12). It will be noted from the diameter range, therefore, that none of the fragments in the collection represents saggers large enough to contain plates, dishes, or chargers. Consequently, one may be forgiven for asking whether perhaps in the seventeenth century such items were fired in the open kiln. This might better explain the disaster that befell the stack of plates (Pls. 30 and 31) that should, by rights, have been protected within

1. Bloice (1971), 118, Fig. 52, nos. 9 and 10.

their sagger and so unable to slip sideways as these appear to have done.

The triangular trivets served to space and balance the stacked plates or dishes without support at the rims. Assuming that such rim support was unnecessary, one might argue that there was no need for saggers—although it remains true that the plates could be stacked much higher if they were enclosed in saggers that could be piled one upon another. This, however, only becomes a major factor if the kiln chambers were tall rather than long; the shape and character of the Pickleherring kilns have yet to be demonstrated.[2]

With one exception (Fig. XVIII, no. 13), all the sagger fragments in the collection are made from a poorly wedged clay in which no attempt was made to minimize the iron oxide inclusions. The resulting saggers became extremely friable after use and were inclined to flake along the structural flow lines of their roughly mixed bodies. The interiors of the saggers are generally coated with a thin lead glaze that has apparently volatilized from the finished wares in the process of glost firing. It is extremely likely, therefore, that any large group of stacked plates piled within a sagger would have included some that came in contact with the sagger wall. If so, the fluid glaze adhering to the latter could have been expected either to have caused traces of the friable sagger wall to become attached to the plate rims or, alternatively, for small sections of rim glaze to have broken away from the finished products and thus remain fused to the saggers. It is significant, perhaps, that neither condition is present among the Burnett Collection specimens, suggesting that the plates, dishes, and chargers were not fired in saggers. An additional factor supportive of this conclusion is the fact that the previously discussed stack of fused plates had evidently fallen over, and yet not one of them has so much as a trace of sagger adhering to it.

The shallow and tall sagger forms that make up the range of examples represented in the Burnett Collection generally exhibit a central hole in the base (like that of a flowerpot) and an opening in the side from the lip to within approximately half an inch of the floor to allow the free passage of air, and, when necessary, to permit handles to project beyond the interior diameter. Sagger rims are usually thickened, but on smaller examples they sometimes are straight and only slightly beveled (probably wiped when soft) at their exterior and interior edges. There are few published examples of comparable saggers, the most important being those found during 1968 excavations in Lambeth (Norfolk House) on a site for which there is documentary evidence of the presence of a delftware potter no earlier than 1680.[3] Both Pickleherring sagger types are represented, but so, too, are the peg-walled cylinders characteristic of delftware manufacturing in the eighteenth century.[4] The early forms range in size from 6 3/8 x 3 1/2 inches to 10 3/8 x 6 inches, but although the largest might seem almost big enough to hold a ten-inch plate, its interior diameter is actually only about nine inches.

It has been noted that one sagger in the Burnett Collection is of a different body composition from those previously described. The specimen in question is illustrated in Fig. XVIII, no. 13, and is made from the same clay formula as the contemporary delftware products. It does not exhibit the friability common to the others, and was capable, one presumes, of withstanding higher temperatures and longer usage. Adhering to the interior at the junction of base and wall is a small rim fragment of a pharmaceutical ointment pot (comparable to Fig. III, no. 5). The sherd lies on its side imbedded in a thick but localized deposit of tin glaze, making it impossible to determine whether the pot was either glazed or decorated on the outside; on the inside, however, there is no

---

2. The foundations of two delftware kilns found by Mr. Graham Dawson in Montague Close are reportedly rectangular in plan. Ibid., 149; Dawson (1970), 184. However, there seem to be no surviving illustrations or plans of 17th-century delftware kilns either in England or the Netherlands. Consequently, the majority of writers have used Diderot's encyclopedia (ca. 1765) and the well-known tile panel in the Rijksmuseum, Amsterdam, showing a delftware kiln at Bolsward, Friesland, in 1737 (De Jonge [1947], p. 3, Fig. 1), neither of which necessarily relates to kiln styles in the first half of the 17th century.

3. Bloice (1971), 100; contribution on documentary evidence by Rhoda Edwards.

4. Although no fragments of pegged, cylinder saggers are represented in the Burnett Collection, they are present in two groups from the vicinity of Montague Close. One example is in the collection of the Museum of London and was acquired by Guildhall Museum in 1947; another is on loan from Southwark Cathedral to the Cuming Museum (Acc. No. 58/2/25). Dawson and Edwards (1973), pp. 48–49.

Plate 56.
Delftware waster and biscuit specimens in the collection of the British Museum, all found in Tooley Street, Bermondsey, in 1907. At the left is the base of a saucer with its solid trivet adhering, the saucer decorated in blue in a design similar to that shown in Fig. XIII, no. 7. The biscuit ointment pots are akin to Fig. III, nos. 4 and 15; and the biscuit cup is closely paralleled by the example illustrated in Pl. 18, left, and Fig. VI, no. 3. The trivet measures 1 3/8 inches. See p. 68, n. 2. British Museum: 1907, 10-14, 7, 2, 4, and 1.

surviving glaze, and it may be that the pot never progressed beyond the biscuit stage.

It is noteworthy that the largest sagger in this collection had been used as a container for one of the smaller of the factory's products, and that although the sagger exhibited a large handle opening, the wares fired in it did not, in this instance, possess them. It may be concluded, therefore, that then (as later) large saggers were often used to contain several small items. It seems likely, on the other hand, that the smaller and taller saggers generally were used to contain single mugs, jugs, and so forth.

The previously mentioned Lambeth site yielded several significant items not included in the Burnett Collection, notably unglazed yellow ware discs ranging from 8 1/2 inches to 1 foot 2 inches in diameter, each with a central hole. It is conceivable that these were lids for seventeenth-century-type saggers; however, it is much more likely that they represent floors and covers for the peg-walled open cylinder saggers of the eighteenth century. There are no lid fragments among the Burnett Collection's kiln furniture.

Also from the Lambeth site are several pieces of red roofing tile of the type in use in Britain from medieval times onward (and, of course, in America in both the seventeenth and eighteenth centuries). The Burnett Collection includes fragments of two such tiles, one of them containing nodules and specks of the yellow delftware clay. The red clay of the tiles bonds poorly to itself and is almost certainly the same as that present in the saggers and, to a lesser degree, in most of the biscuit wares. Thus the roofing tiles are in composition precisely the reverse of the blend used in the delftware. It is reasonable to assume, therefore, that the two are related, indicating that roofing tiles as well as domestic wares may have been produced in the vicinity of Vine Lane. One of the tile fragments is warped at the crack between two otherwise joining sherds, suggesting either that it is itself a waster or that it had seen service in a kiln where it had broken and warped in the course of refiring.

As noted above, seven trivets are present in the collection, six of them of the same size, having a point spread of 3 1/4 inches, and the seventh slightly larger with a point spread of 3 3/4 inches. These do not parallel the point spread range represented by the collection's finished products, which start at 1 3/4 inches for saucers (Fig. XIII, no. 7) and increase in size to 4 1/2 inches for large dishes (Pl. 49, no. 1). If nothing else, this disparity demonstrates the fallacy of drawing conclusions based on limited archaeological evidence. For the same reason, the 2 1/2- to 3-inch range of trivet sizes from the Norfolk House site in Lambeth is equally inconclusive—although it is worth observing that neither size parallels either the Pickleherring examples or the point spread range of the finished products.

There is evidence in the British Museum to indicate that the trivets used for saucers were not of the standard "crow's foot" type, but were pads of clay cut into equilateral triangles whose corners were pinched or pricked up into small prunts. One such specimen, still attached to the underside of a saucer, was recovered from a site in Tooley Street in 1907 (Pl. 56, left).[5] No examples of this type appear to be represented in any London delftware collection, but its absence may be explained by the small size of the triangles (in this instance 1 3/8 inches) and the chance that they would be dismissed as triangular sherds from biscuit plates or dishes.

Surviving examples prove that delftware chargers continued to be manufactured into the reign of George II, and that scars on the upper surfaces of such pieces show that trivets were still employed in their firing. Supportive evidence comes from the Lime Kiln Lane factory site in Bristol where excavators found a trivet, mold-shaped with the initial PI and the date 1730. It may be significant that this example is much more waisted than are those from seventeenth-century sites in London.[6]

If trivets continued to be used to support large delftware items as late as 1730, it is important to consider how early pegged cylinder saggers may have been used for smaller plates and dishes. A partial answer is provided by an 8 1/2-inch plate in the Colonial Williamsburg Collection decorated in blue with the triple-initial cipher R^{C}M and the date 1670.[7] This plate is clearly, even damagingly, scarred on the underside of its rim with the marks of three narrowed-edged and, presumably, triangular-sectioned pegs.

---

5. See p. 68, n. 2, for additional site details.

6. Lipski (1969), 149 and pl. 153a. Another rather slender example with a 4 3/16-inch spread is in the collection of the British Museum and was found in Thames Street in 1840 by the antiquary Charles Roach Smith (Acc. No. 56, 7-1, 370). Smith's notes stated that the trivet was found in association with Roman Samian ware—which helps not at all. Although there is no evidence that a delftware pothouse existed on the north bank of the river near Thames Street, many 18th-century delftware biscuit sherds have been found along the foreshore in the vicinity of Queenhithe Dock. It has always been supposed, however, that this was waste brought from the south bank pothouses and was used to improve the "hards" along the river frontage. Noël Hume (1956), p. 193.

7. Colonial Williamsburg Collection, 64-445, the shape rather similar to that of the biscuit example shown in Fig. VII, no. 12.

THE FIGURES

Representative Examples from St. Olave's Parish Sites

ALL the delftware fragments in the Burnett Collection were recovered from six locations shown on the two maps (Pls. 2A and 2B). In the interest of brevity the sources of the illustrated items are given at the end of each description as "Site 2," "Site 6," and so forth. The majority of the unglazed (biscuit) items were recovered from locations 2 and 4. Unfortunately, nothing in the collection is derived from recognizable or datable archaeological contexts—with the possible exception of the artifacts from Site 3, a brick-lined cesspit in Black Swan Yard. On the evidence of several clay tobacco pipes, this deposit may date from ca. 1675. However, there are a sufficient number of seemingly anomalous items in the group to make even this association questionable.

The Battle Bridge House material (location 6) was recovered from a building site, and all that can be said of it is that it includes eighteenth-century wasters that are not present amid the collections from sites in and around Vine Lane. In several instances, seemingly significant items are without any firm location, and these, along with others about which there is doubt, are noted as coming from unrecorded sites.

Although graphic scales are present in each of the figures, they are intended only to provide a visual dimension. A key measurement is therefore included when a full height or diameter can be ascertained. These are cited in inches rather than centimeters, the former being retained regardless of the European archaeological transfer to metric measuring on the grounds that it was in inches that the items were measured in the seventeenth and eighteenth centuries, and therefore any documentary evidence (for example, contemporary inventories or shopkeepers' advertisements) would be given in that form.

FIGURE I

1. (and Pl. 9, no. 1). Medallion tile with dromedary motif, the design painted in blue

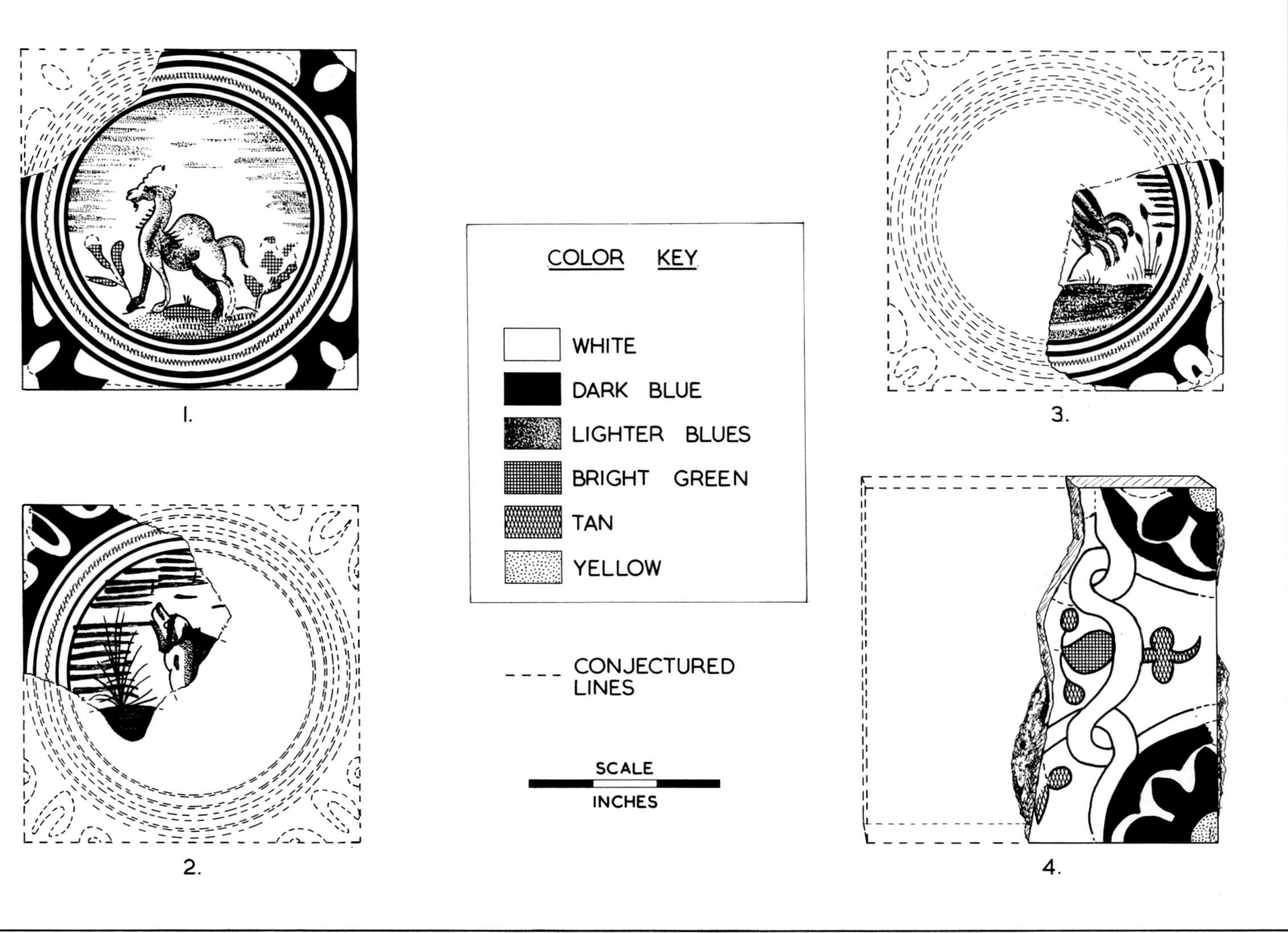

FIGURE I

and enriched with green, yellow, and tan, this last used over green as a ground color and as the third of the five concentric rings. The yellow has been applied over the glaze after the second firing and it is conceivable that yet another firing was intended. The glaze is heavily puddled leaving the pink body exposed here and there. However, there are traces of lime mortar on both back and sides indicating that the tile was not discarded as a waster. There is a manufacture hole in the bottom right corner. The design is fairly well paralleled by an example in the collection of the Museum of London and found at Aldgate.[1] It also belongs to the same general class as another in the Victoria and Albert Museum illustrated by Lane, who

1. Cat. No. A.3908. An alleged waster of this dromedary design was found by Francis Celoria in his 1965 excavations east of Vine Lane, unpublished.

states it to be Dutch.[2] However, the corner ornament differs slightly, and the animal on the Burnett example is less competently executed. Three more tiles of the same class are illustrated by Korf,[3] although, like the Lane specimen, they have blue elements dividing the central lozenge in the corner devices. Unfortunately, this minor difference cannot be used as evidence of English origin as the dividing features are present on other tiles in the collection (see nos. 2 and 3), while another Netherlandish specimen illustrated by Korf lacks the lines.[4] 5 5/16 x 5 5/16 x 5/8 inches. Site 7. First half of 17th century.

2. Medallion tile fragment of type generally similar to no. 1, but with central bear and blue stripe largely dividing the corner lozenge; the design executed in blue but with an orange tan line as the second and widest of the border rings; manufacture hole in top left corner. The body is a hard yellow with many red ochre (iron oxide) inclusions. A close parallel in the Museum of London collection was found in Clements Lane.[5] Thickness: 5/8 inches. Unrecorded site. First half of 17th century.

3. Medallion tile fragment of similar type to no. 2 but with a central rooster (?) motif, the design apparently painted only in blue but with an orange tan third border ring as in no. 1. The body is a soft yellow, poorly wedged, and containing large flecks of red ochre. Thickness: 5/8 inches. Site not recorded. First half of 17th century.

4. Tile with snakelike pattern, Islamic in character; the basic design executed in blue with details in yellow, orange tan, and green; the colors having run somewhat in firing. There is a manufacture hole in the top right corner;[6] the body is yellow. This tile is coated on the back, sides, and fracture with a coarse granular mortar and had been used in its present broken condition. However, the glaze dips at the fracture, suggesting that the break occurred in firing rather than that the tile was deliberately broken by the pavior to fit a small space. 5 5/8 x ? x 5/8 inches. Site not recorded. Examples of this general type have been attributed to the late 16th century.

2. Lane (1960), pl. 33A.

3. Korf (1964), p. 60, nos. 74, 76, and 77. All three are attributed to the beginning of the 17th century.

4. Ibid., no. 73. The treatment of the border rings is more elaborate here.

5. Cat. No. A.27809.

6. When the design fails to make it clear which way up the tile was intended to be laid, descriptions such as "top right corner" refer only to the location of the hole or holes in relation to the drawing.

FIGURE II

1. (and Pl. 9, no. 3). Quadrant tile (that is, one of four required to complete a design) with quarter of "Tudor rose" motif in the lower right area, the decoration painted only in blue. This example is drawn from a specimen whose glaze ran and puddled in firing, the smeared design being reconstructed with the help of other comparable fragments in the collection. The body is yellow and hard fired, and manufacture holes are present in the top left and bottom right corners. Mortar adheres to the edges indicating that in spite of the tile's ruined appearance it was put to some practical use.[1] Although quadrant tiles of this general character were common in the Netherlands, it is tempting to suggest that the multipetalled rose may be an English innovation. It would certainly appear to have been one of the commonest types manufactured in Southwark, and it occurs in the collection in both monochrome and polychrome (see no. 2). A close parallel in the Museum of London collection was found in Fenchurch Street.[2] 5 5/16 x 5 1/4 x 1/2 inches. Site 7. First half of 17th century.

2. Polychrome version of no. 1, the drawing derived from three overlapping fragments, the design executed in blue, yellow, orange

1. The fact that numerous examples of tiles whose decoration has been ruined in firing were actually used suggests that they were employed for paving floors around the factory. It is unlikely that they could have been sold, particularly if their intended purpose was decorative rather than useful. This argument tends to support the contention that these thick tiles were still being made for use as paving.

2. Cat. No. A.22937.

1.
2.
SCALE
INCHES
3.
4.
5.
6.
7.
8.
9.
10.
COLOR KEY
WHITE
YELLOW
DARK BLUE
TAN
LIGHT BLUE
ORANGE
BRIGHT GREEN
BROWN
YELLOW GREEN
---- CONJECTURED LINES

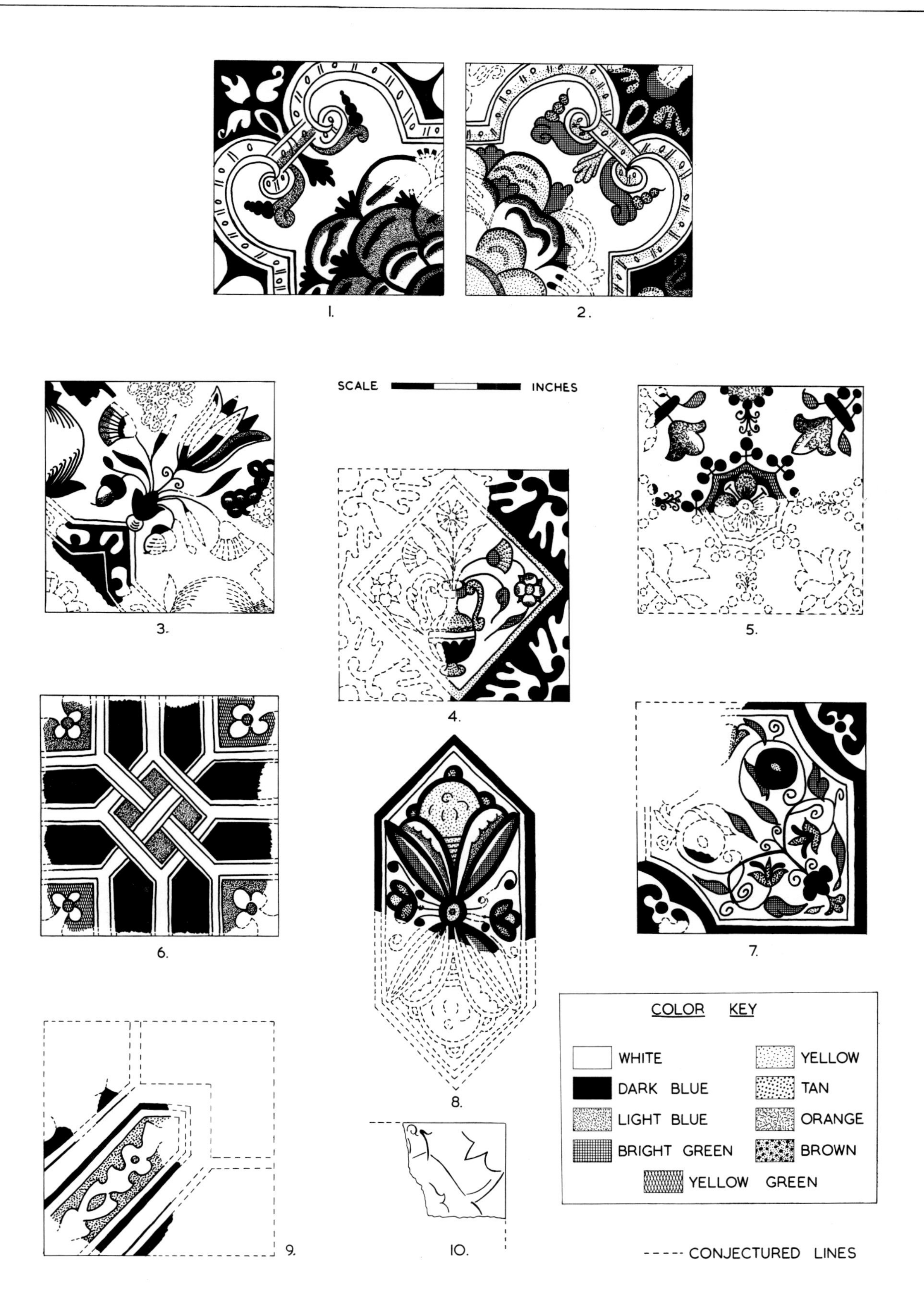

FIGURE II

tan, and green; the body differing in all three pieces: soft yellow with red ochre inclusions, hard yellow, and yellow core with pink exterior—this last merely the result of atmospheric variation in the firing. The third sherd can be classified as a waster insofar that the glaze has run, ruining the design. However, all three pieces retain traces of mortar and so had been used. Manufacture holes are present in the top left and lower right corners. 5 3/8 x ? x 5/8 inches. Site 7.[3] First half of 17th century.

3. (and Pl. 9, no. 2). Quadrant tile with so-called "star and tulip" design, the star created by the juxtaposition of four units (see Pl. 10). The drawn example is derived from two fragments, the larger of them a waster that lost much of its design and glaze in firing. The decoration is executed in blue, the tulip having buds and acorns below it, flanked by bunches of grapes and what are presumably intended to be unripe pomegranates. The class is common in the Netherlands, and numerous variations are illustrated by Korf and attributed to the first half of the 17th century.[4] Both the Southwark fragments are pink bodied, the clay poorly wedged, and contain red ochre and other inclusions. The waster fragment has mortar attached. 5 1/4 x ? x 5/8 inches. Site 7. First half of the 17th century.

4. Quadrate or flower vase tile,[5] the decoration in polychrome, corners and outline in blue, the diamond created in yellow, and the vase and flowers painted in yellow, orange tan, and green. The glaze is unusually matt and the body is hard and pink. 5 3/8 x ? x 5/8 inches. Site not recorded. First half of 17th century.

5. So-called "star" tile of a type tentatively attributed by Korf to Haarlem;[6] the design in polychrome: blue, orange tan, and pale green, this last created by laying yellow over darker green. It should be noted that the two fragments in the collection differ from Korf's parallel in that the corner fleur-de-lis motifs are polychrome and his are in blue. The body is yellow with red ochre inclusions, both pieces rather poorly wedged. A manufacture hole is present in the top right corner. 5 1/4 x ? x 1/2 inches. Note that both specimens are only half an inch in thickness. Site 7. First half of 17th century.

6. Geometric tile decorated in dark blue, with pale blue and yellowish green in alternating corners, and a pale blue ground in the central diamonds. The body is a light yellow with red ochre inclusions; manufacture holes occur in the top right and bottom left corners. No exact parallel for this design has been found, but the general style is dated by Korf to the late 16th century.[7] Although the drawn specimen is not a waster, two irrefutable and identical waster fragments are included in the collection (Pl. 9, no. 4), both having pieces of kiln pads adhering to them. These were found during digging for a new river wall at St. Olave north of Pickleherring Street.[8] 5 1/2 x 5 3/8 x 5/8 inches. Site 7. First half of 17th century.

7. Floral and foliate scroll tile, Islamic in character, the design executed in blue, green, orange tan, and overglaze yellow, the yellow not properly adhering. The drawing is derived from two fragments, one with a hard yellow to pale pink body, the other a much darker pink and the clay containing fine particles of gravel and ochre. A manufacture hole occurs at the bottom right corner. No close parallel has been found. 5 5/16 x ? x 9/16 inches. Note that another example is 5/8

---

3. A similar fragment was found in association with vessel and dish biscuit to the south of the supposed kilns in a cutting across Vine Yard; Site 4.

4. Korf (1964), pp. 68–70, nos. 104–110; see also Lane (1960), pl. 31A, and Hurst and Golson (1955), Fig. 15, no. 18, and p. 68. A comparable fragment was found in the filling of the city ditch and was attributed to the first quarter of the 17th century. It is tempting to seek a connection between this sherd and the Andries and Janson tilemaking operation started at Norwich in 1567.

5. The term "quadrate" is used by Korf to describe those tiles decorated with central devices enclosed within squares or diamonds and should not be confused with "quadrant," whose meaning is explained under Fig. II, no. 1. For parallel, see Korf (1964), pp. 85–86, Fig. 160.

6. Ibid., p. 74, no. 121, and pl. 6, top.

7. Ibid., p. 48, no. 42.

8. A third sherd, although not an identifiable waster, was found to the south end of Vine Yard in Tooley Street.

inches in thickness. Site not recorded. First half of 17th century.

8. Hexagonal tile with stylized floral motif painted in blue, green, tan, and yellow, the body a hard yellow to pink. There is no mortar on any surface and therefore no reason to suppose that this specimen was ever used; at the same time, however, there is no evidence that it was discarded due to manufacturing imperfections. Four tiles of this type are illustrated by Lane, who classified them as "Flemish (Antwerp)" and dates them "about 1525."[9] Nevertheless, similarities between the palette used for this example and that characteristic of the obviously Southwark products previously discussed might be used as evidence in favor of its St. Olave origin. On the other hand, this specimen is the thickest of all the fragments recovered.[10] Width: 3 3/4 inches; thickness: 3/4 inches. Site 5. 16th or early 17th century.

9. Geometric tile of a type requiring four or more to complete the motif;[11] painted in blue and orange tan. Being extremely friable, this example is an undoubted waster and the body contains so much red ochre that it could not bond together. A manufacture hole occurs in the bottom left corner. A fair parallel illustrated by Korf is attributed to the late 16th century.[12] Thickness: 11/16 inches. Site not recorded. First half of 17th century.

10. Biscuit fragment with remains of decoration painted directly on it in black;[13] the clay yellow, poorly wedged, and with many ochre and chalk (?) inclusions. Thickness: 9/16 inches. From trench 10 yards south of supposed kiln site in Vine Yard, Site 4. First half of 17th century.

9. Lane (1960), p. ix, and pl. 31 C, D, E, and F. The pattern is most closely akin to "D," but its 8-inch length is paralleled by "C." See also Biddle, Barfield, and Millard (1961), 186–188, Fig. 21, no. 7. The Netherlandish tiles from this site bear some similarities to those in the Burnett Collection, and although recovered from destruction debris of about 1650, they are stated to have been installed prior to 1552.

10. For the manner of laying these tiles, see Korf (1964), p. 27, Fig. 22.

11. As the design is not so obviously incomplete without four tiles abutting (as are Fig. II, nos. 1 and 2), the term "quadrant" has not been used in this description.

12. Ibid., p. 49, no. 44.

13. For a possible explanation, see p. 21.

FIGURE III

1. Ointment pot of cylindrical albarello type, pink biscuit, a size and shape frequently decorated in polychrome. (See Fig. IV, nos. 2 and 3.) Height: 2 9/16 inches. Site not recorded.[1] About 1612–1645.[2]

2. Ointment pot of cylindrical type, pale pink to yellow biscuit, poorly potted, the foot very uneven and the wall unintentionally ribbed on the exterior. The idiosyncrasies have been omitted from the drawing to better illustrate the type. Height: 2 3/8 inches. Site not recorded. About 1612–1645.

3. Ointment pot, a miniature version of no. 2, the wall sloping inward toward the top, the sandy biscuit yellow on one side and pink on the other. Height: 1 1/2 inches. Site not recorded. About 1612–1645.

4. Ointment pot of Italianate form, extremely crudely potted and probably the work of an apprentice; the biscuit yellow to pale pink. So poorly made is this example that the angle below the lip is obscured at one side. Height: 2 inches. Site not recorded.[3] About 1612–1630.

5. Ointment pot, a broad version of no. 1; hard pink biscuit, well potted. Height: 2 1/8 inches. Site not recorded. About 1612–1645.

1. The biscuit pots, nos. 1–5, 7–9, and 15, are noted only as having been found in Tooley Street.

2. The opening date of 1612 is derived from Christian Wilhelm's implied claims to have been the first delftware potter in Southwark and to have started his manufactory in about 1612.

3. Another biscuit example of this type, but considerably better potted, was found in Tooley Street in 1907 and is now in the British Museum (Pl. 56, center). For additional information on the source of this example see p. 68, n. 2.

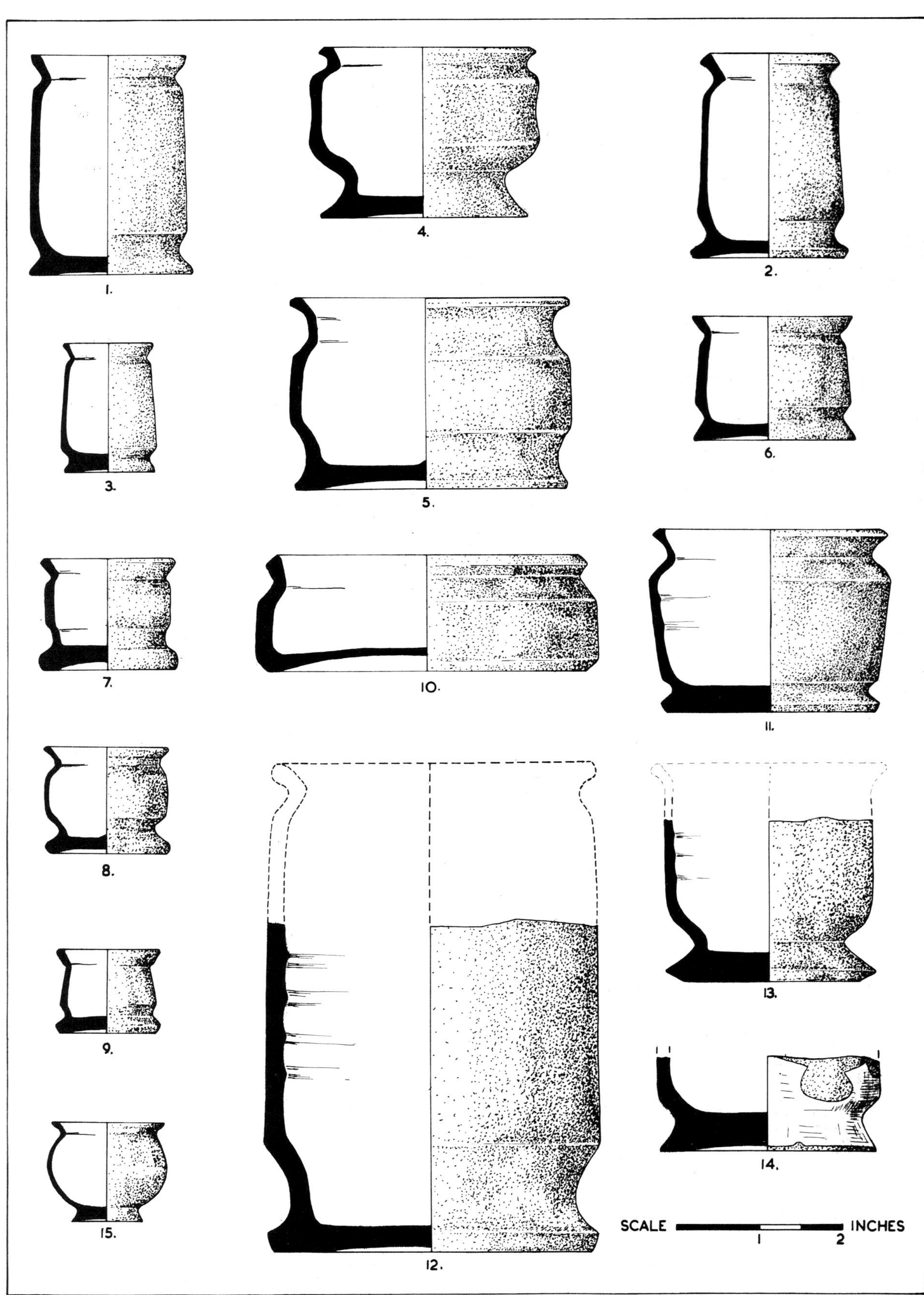

FIGURE III

6. Ointment pot, a squat example of intermediate size, the biscuit pink, hard fired, and well potted. Height: 1 1/2 inches. From a trench 10 yards south of the supposed kiln adjacent to Vine Yard; Site 4. About 1612–1650.

7. Ointment pot of small size; soft yellow biscuit poorly potted, the foot disproportionately heavy. Height: 1 1/4 inches. Site not recorded. About 1612–1645.

8. Ointment pot of small size; yellow biscuit better potted than no. 7. Height: 1 3/16 inches. Site not recorded. About 1612–1645.

9. Ointment pot of miniature size, yellow biscuit relatively well potted. Height: 15/16 inches. Site not recorded. About 1612–1645.

10. Ointment or confection pot of shallow form; pink biscuit, well potted. The shape has not been recorded from closely datable archaeological contexts, and differing as it does from the common 17th-century forms, dating must rely on this example's own archaeological associations. It was found along with many other biscuit fragments of shapes and types common in the first half of the 17th century in a trench dug in Vine Yard 10 yards south of the supposed kiln site; Site 4. Height: 1 3/8 inches. About 1612–1650.

11. Ointment pot; hard pale yellow biscuit, the base thick and the walls leaning badly. The proportions suggest a manufacture date later than that of the preceding examples. Height: 2 1/8 inches. Site 6. About 1660–1700.

12. Pharmaceutical drug jar of albarello form; pink biscuit with small red ochre inclusions. A firing crack had split the bottom and presumably caused the jar's rejection. The shape and size are well paralleled by the glazed example shown in Fig. XVII, no. 3. Base diameter: 3 9/16 inches. Site 4. About 1612–1640.

13. Ointment pot with strangely flaring and cut foot; the biscuit yellow on the outside and pink inside. There is a wide firing crack through the bottom. Base diameter 2 7/16 inches. Site 7. About 1612–1660.[4]

14. Ointment pot base, the glaze a thick drab gray, the body pink to orange.[5] Base diameter: 2 1/2 inches. Site 4. About 1640–1700.

15. Ointment pot, the shape reminiscent of a Roman "poppyhead" beaker; pinkish yellow biscuit, well potted. No glazed parallels for this form have been found.[6] Height: 1 3/16 inches. Site not recorded. Date uncertain.

4. If the pot is of early date, it almost certainly had a V-shaped shoulder and lip relationship akin to that of nos. 1, 2, and others. For similar feet see Pl. 12, right, Fig. V, no. 3, and Fig. XVII, no. 2.

5. Another base fragment of the same size and shape, and with the normal yellow body, is coated with white tin glaze that has bubbled and pooled in firing; an obvious waster.

6. Roman pottery of this shape has been unearthed on building sites in Southwark, and no doubt other examples were found in the 16th and 17th centuries when Southwark was developing. It is conceivable, therefore, that the potter may have been influenced by them. Another comparable biscuit specimen, slightly less classical in style, was found in Tooley Street in 1907 (Pl. 56, center). See n. 3 above.

FIGURE IV

1. Ointment pot of similar style to Fig. III, no. 1, poorly potted, pink bodied, and the thick white glaze matt, pitted, blistered, and crazed; a possible waster. Height: 2 3/8 inches. Site not recorded.[1] About 1612–1645.

2. Ointment pot, the wall sloping inward toward the top in the manner of Fig. III, no. 2. The thick pad foot is an unusual feature that makes the pot very heavy. The white glaze is thin in places and appears pink where the body color shows through. Height: 2 1/2 inches. Site not recorded. About 1612–1645.

---

1. Pots 1–5, 7–12, and 14–18 are noted only as having been found in Tooley Street.

3. Ointment pot generally similar to the above, the glaze greenish gray, and pink where the body color shows through. In those places where the glaze has failed to cover, the body is a pale yellow. Height: 2 7/16 inches. Site not recorded. About 1612–1645.

4. Ointment pot similar to the above, the white glaze somewhat blistered on one side, the body pale yellow. Height: 1 15/16 inches. Site not recorded. About 1612–1645.

5. Ointment pot with even white glaze; the yellow body very thick at the base and generally poorly potted. Height: 1 3/4 inches. Site not recorded. About 1612–1645.

6. Ointment pot with white glaze,[2] retaining the albarello wall profile but in a wide and generally later form, the body a well-fired pale yellow with red ochre inclusions. Height: 1 7/8 inches. Site 3. About 1650–1680.

7. Ointment pot of squat form, the white glaze speckled with black and broken away at one side where it adhered to another object in the kiln, the body pale yellow. Height: 1 9/16 inches. Site not recorded. About 1640–1680.

8. Ointment pot of squat form, the wall sloping inward toward the top in the manner of Fig. III, no. 6. The grayish white glaze was fired close to an object decorated with manganese, and the purple has discolored the glaze. In addition, the glaze had puddled and pulled away from the pink body in the kiln both inside and out, making this an almost certain waster. Height: 1 3/8 inches. Site not recorded. About 1640–1680.

9. Ointment pot of similar shape to no. 8; the glaze a pale gray extending overall (including the base) and the pale pink body unnecessarily heavy. Height: 1 5/16 inches. Site not recorded. About 1640–1680.

10. Ointment pot with the lower wall somewhat bulbous, a transitional form between nos. 9 and 16; the glaze burned, pitted, and turned pink, the body pale yellow. Height: 1 3/8 inches. Site not recorded. About 1660–1700.

11. Ointment pot, a miniature version of Fig. III, no. 5, the glaze very pink and occasionally flecked with zaffre, the body yellow to pale pink. A small hole pierced the bottom in firing and made this example a probable waster. Height: 1 1/8 inches. Site not recorded. About 1630–1670.

12. Ointment pot of miniature size, the wall shape akin to no. 10, but the small size makes this a dangerous dating criterion. The white glaze has been tinted pink and kiln waste adheres to one side; the body pale yellow. Height: 15/16 inches. Site not recorded. 17th century.

13. Ointment pot of unusually shallow form; a thick white glaze over the yellow body. The rim of another vessel adhered to one side in the kiln and was broken off afterward; a possible waster.[3] Base diameter: 2 3/16 inches. Site 4. About 1630–1660.

14. Ointment pot, smaller version of no. 13, pinkish white glaze over a yellow body. Height: 15/16 inches. Site not recorded. About 1630–1660.

15. Ointment pot, smaller version of no. 13, white to pinkish glaze over a very soft yellow body. Most of the glaze has flaked off, but it is not known whether this happened before or after it was discarded. Height: 1 1/8 inches. Site not recorded. About 1630–1660.

16. Ointment pot with wall somewhat bulbous above the foot, the latter thick and flat; white glaze much damaged by burning, although

2. The glaze has been blackened by contact with the organic content of the cesspit in which it was found. For other artifacts from this deposit, see Fig. XV.

3. It is possible that both are of the same shape.

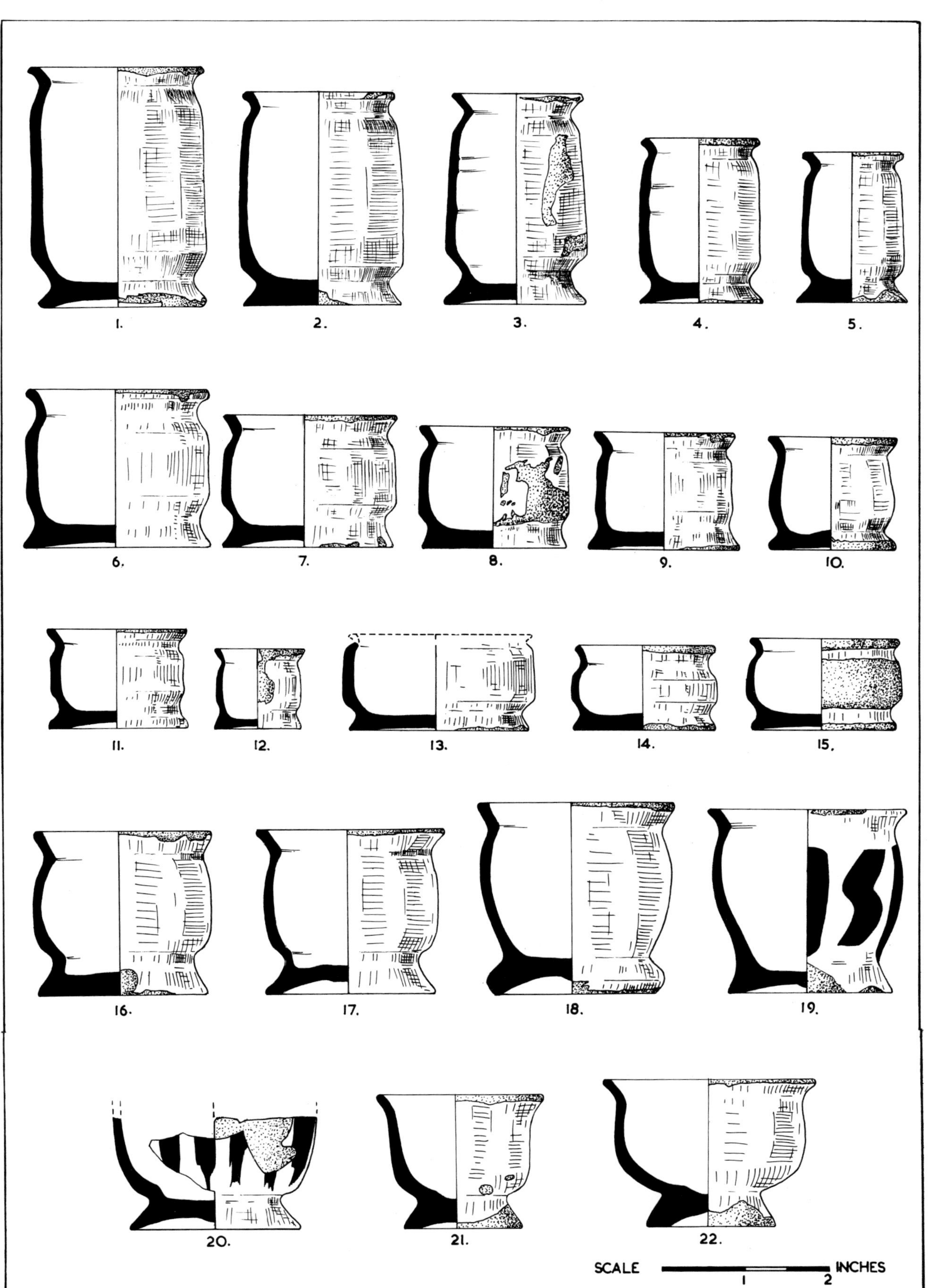

FIGURE IV

not necessarily in the kiln. The body is yellow and exhibits swirled pulling marks on the bottom where the pot was cut from the wheel with a wire.[4] Height: 1 7/8 inches. Site not recorded. About 1670–1710.

17. Ointment pot similar to no. 16, but with rising base; the white glaze poorly fired, matt, and discolored, but probably not a waster. Height: 1 7/8 inches. Site not recorded. About 1670–1720.

18. Ointment pot with typical 18th-century body form, but with an unusually heavy and almost conical foot. The glaze is a thick white over a yellow body. Height: 2 1/4 inches. Site not recorded. About 1680–1710.

19. Ointment pot, the walls somewhat lopsided, exhibiting the wider lip than foot characteristic of the eighteenth century; the body yellow, the glaze white and painted with vertical and wriggled lines in blue. The base is also glazed and marked with a straight line similar to those used to decorate the exterior. (See also no. 20.) Height: 2 1/8 inches. Found in Abbot's Lane "80 yards from kiln." Site 5? Late 17th or early 18th century.

20. Ointment pot similar to no. 19, but all the vertical blue lines straight and an Arabic "4" painted in blue on the white glazed base. The body is a pale yellow. This pot almost certainly came to pieces in the kiln; glaze fell off and fragments of clay adhered to what remained. Base diameter: 2 1/16 inches. Site not recorded. Late 17th or early 18th century.

21. Ointment pot of small size, with pedestal foot and thin white glaze over a yellow body. Height: 1 1/2 inches. Site not recorded. Probably second quarter of 18th century or later.

4. Less pronounced but just as recognizable pulling marks occur on many of the earlier examples in the collection. The scar is characterized by a hooked or "quotation mark" arc to one side of the base close to the edge. It occurs on the following specimens: Fig. III, nos. 1, 3, 6, 12, 13; Fig. IV, nos 1–3, 5, 7, 8, 11, 13–15; and Fig. XVII, no. 2.

22. Ointment pot with pedestal foot, the glaze bluish white and the body pale yellow. Height: 1 3/4 inches. Site 6. About 1730–1770.

FIGURE V

1. (and Pl. 13, left). Ointment pot of shape comparable to Fig. IV, no. 1, but decorated in blue; the glaze matt, seemingly underfired, and adhering poorly;[1] the body pink. Height: 3 1/8 inches. Site 4. About 1612–1640.

2. (and Pl. 13, center). Ointment pot of shape comparable to Fig. IV, no. 2, but decorated in polychrome, the ground glaze a bluish gray and the characteristic chevron design painted in blue and orange tan, the body pale yellow and the base exhibiting the curved pulling mark referred to in n. 4 below. Height: 2 5/8 inches. Site not recorded.[2] About 1612–1640.

3. Ointment pot of form generally similar to nos. 1 and 2, but the walls warped and a large lump of clay adhering to the side, making it an almost certain waster. The ground glaze a bluish gray and the design executed in blue and orange tan, the painting unusually crude and broad orange arcs substituted for the

1. Sir David Burnett's notes indicate some "glaze removed in cleaning."

2. A good collection of this type of polychrome ointment pot was found at the bottom of a brick-walled cesspit on the site of the present Gateway House in Cannon Street, London, and is now in the collection of the Museum of London (E.R. 166B), the deposit attributed to the period about 1590–1610. However, a date up to 30 years later seems more reasonable in the light of subsequently acquired knowledge. Other comparable fragments have been found in Virginia at Mathews Manor, near Newport News, in contexts of the mid-17th century. (See Pl. 14, nos. 8, 9, and 12.)

COLOR KEY
DARK BLUE
LIGHT BLUE
ORANGE
PURPLE
1.
2.
3.
4.
5.
6.
7.
SCALE
INCHES
1
2

FIGURE V

usual angular chevrons. The body is pink with red ochre inclusions. The foot differs from the usual type, the base being trimmed upward at the edges, a technique paralleled by the biscuit fragment shown in Fig. III, no. 13, and also by the much larger drug jar in Fig. XVII, no. 2. Base diameter: 1 1/2 inches. Site not recorded. About 1612–1640.

4. Drug jar base fragment with unusually white ground glaze speckled with black and the decoration in light blue and manganese purple, the latter blistered and largely brown, perhaps caused by using a mix containing too little frit; the body a pale yellow. Approximate base diameter: 4 5/8 inches. Site 5. About 1630–1660.

5. Drug jar, a larger version of no. 1, the glaze badly discolored from burial, but the ground color originally a pinkish white, the decoration in blue; the body pale yellow to pink with red ochre inclusions.[3] Approximate rim diameter: 4 1/2 inches. Site 5. About 1612–1640.

6. Drug jar of type comparable in profile to ointment pot no. 1, although probably somewhat later in date; the glaze badly discolored from burial, but the ground glaze originally a good white; the decoration in blue and purple; the body pale yellow. Base diameter: 3 3/4 inches. Site not recorded. About 1630–1660.

7. Drug jar of large size, the ground glaze white and flecked with black,[4] the decoration in blue and purple, and the body a pale yellow. The base cracked in firing but not necessarily sufficiently for this jar to have been rejected.[5] Base diameter: 6 7/16 inches. Site 5. About 1630–1670.[6]

For other drug pots and jars, see Fig. XV, no. 5, and Fig. XVII, nos. 1–4.

3. For a fair parallel see Garner (1948), pl. 3B center, and p. 4. The author stated of the illustrated specimens that all were "possibly English work and the products of Janson's pottery." See also ***Guildhall Museum Catalogue*** (London, 1908), pl. LXXIII, no. 4, and p. 214, no. 72. This last example was found in Fountain's Court, London, but differs in that it is decorated in blue and orange.

4. It is possible that the black flecks in the glaze exhibited by this example and others from Black Swan Yard resulted from burial in the ground and not from any original imperfection in the glaze. Similar flecks are visible in the posset pot (Pl. 8), which, when purchased, was dark brown to black, almost certainly as the result of burial.

5. A biscuit base of this size and shape was found among the wasters recovered from the London Electricity Board's trenching in Vine Lane (Site 4) near the supposed kiln.

6. Close dating for this type is difficult as the chevron decoration (debased into a chain) continued well into the 18th century, as did this foot form. Little is known about the evolution of these annular-decorated drug jars in the second half of the 17th century, but as they were common in the 18th century, it is unlikely that they ceased to be painted around the time of the Commonwealth as did the cheaper and expendable ointment pots. However, in the absence of evidence to the contrary, a date prior to 1650 for this example seems probable.

FIGURE VI

1. Cup with single handle, thinly potted, buff to pink biscuit, but pale yellow on the outside to a point approximately 9/16 inch above the base. The wall flares above the handle, but its original height is uncertain. Base diameter: 2 1/8 inches. Site 1. About 1650–1685.[1]

2. Cup of similar shape to no. 1, but larger and the biscuit body pale yellow throughout. The base is small and the handle would seem to

1. For a shape parallel bearing the arms of the Carpenters' Company and dated 1666, see Berry (1933). However, a cup of similar shape decorated with the arms of the Watermen's Company is dated 1682. See Bedford (1966), p. 37, top, or Garner (1948), pl. 33A. Between these poles is another similar cup bearing the arms of the Carpenters' Company dated 1676. See Tilley (1968a), 123, Fig. 1. To the same class belongs the "cuckold" cup in the Colonial Williamsburg Collection (Pl. 15, right), which is dated 1682. However, as noted in the introduction to this section, all these dated specimens are considerable larger than the examples in the Burnett Collection.

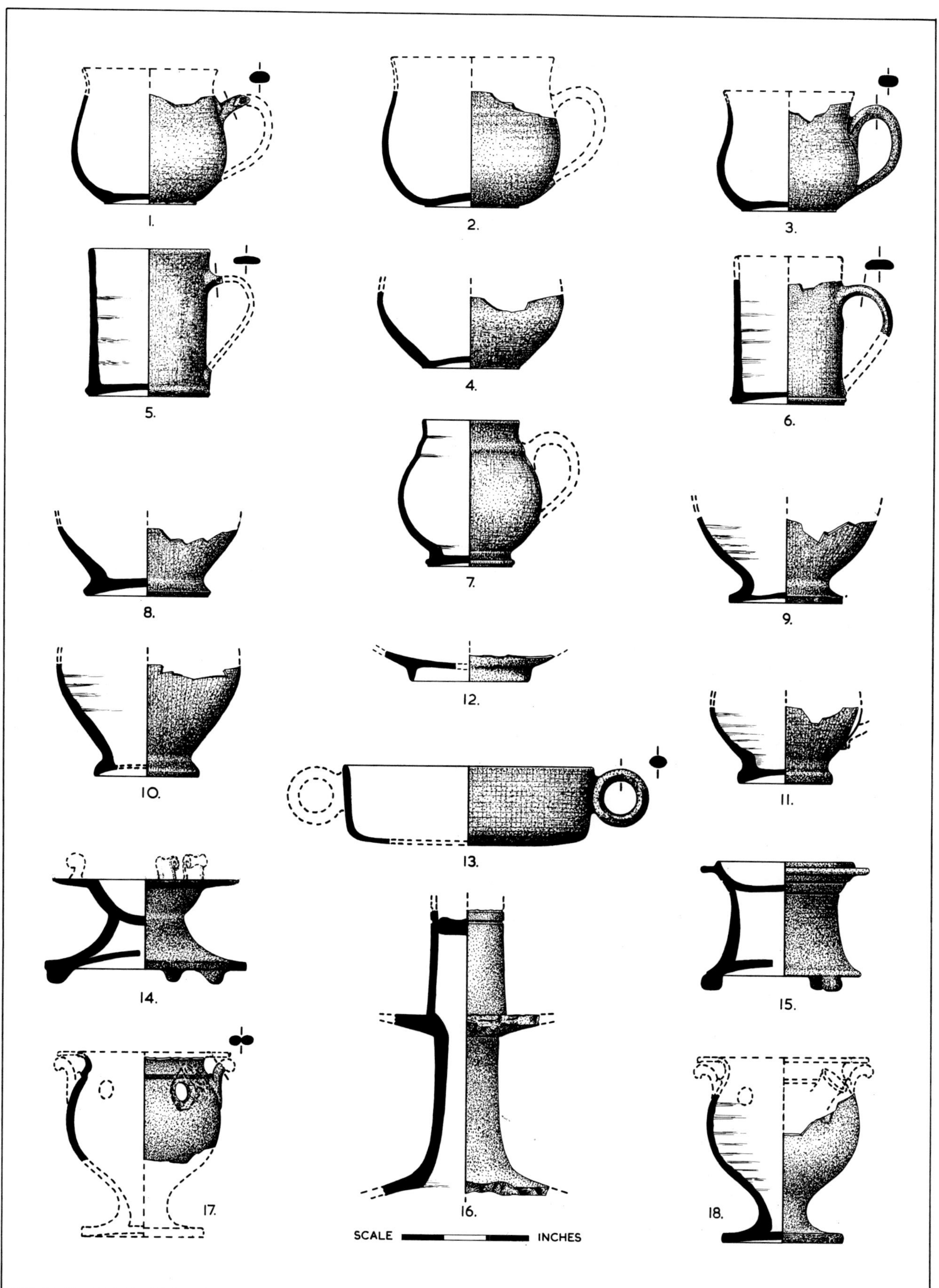

FIGURE VI

have been a relatively light strap. For shape parallel see Pl. 21 dated 1657. Base diameter: 2 1/8 inches. Site 5. About 1650–1685.

3. (and Pl. 18, left). Cup similar to no. 1, pale yellow biscuit but orange in the core. The intact handle, although delicately shaped, is heavily applied and resulted in a thick and poorly anchored pad attached to the upper terminal. For shape parallel see Pl. 15, right, dated 1682. Base diameter: 2 1/8 inches. Site 5. About 1650–1685.[2]

4. Base of large posset cup or bottle, yellow-surfaced biscuit, buff on the inside, rather heavily potted. Base diameter: 2 1/4 inches. Site 1. About 1640–1675.

5. (and Pl. 22, right). Cylindrical can with remains of a light strap handle; pink biscuit with locally yellow surface on the sides leaving the handle section pink, as is a stripe immediately opposite it, perhaps corresponding with the openings in the walls of a sagger. Height: 3 1/2 inches. Site 7. About 1650–1675.[3]

6. Can similar to, but smaller than, no. 5, the biscuit body a bright orange, upper fragment of strap/handle surviving. Base diameter: 2 5/8 inches compared to 2 15/16 inches for no. 5. Site 7. About 1650–1675.[4]

7. Bulbous mug or caudle cup originally with single small strap handle, a decorative cordon below the rim, and the foot well turned.[5] The biscuit ware is a pale yellow but pink where the handle has come away. Abbot's Lane near Tooley Street. Height: 3 9/16 inches. About 1630–1650.[6]

8. Jug or mug foot, the biscuit largely orange pink but yellow on part of the exterior surface. Base diameter: 2 7/8 inches. Site 1. About 1628–1650.[7]

---

2. This cup, with its body somewhat more bulbous than those of nos. 1 and 2, is closely paralleled by an example in the collection of the British Museum (Pl. 56, right). That specimen, also in the biscuit state, was acquired from dealer G. F. Lawrence in 1907 who obtained it, along with several other delftware items, from an unspecified building site in Tooley Street. Sir David Burnett has determined that the only construction work carried out north of the street in 1907 was confined to Nos. 115 to 121, thus placing the archaeological source between Morgan's Lane and Braidwood Street, and some distance from the other known deposits of pothouse waste (see Pl. 2A). British Museum: 1907, 10-14.1.

3. The shape is paralleled by a can in the Colonial Williamsburg Collection, decorated with a portrait of Charles II and dated 1660. See Pl. 22, left. A manganese-stippled mug of similar form was found in a context of 1652–1656 at the St. Nicholas Almhouses site in Bristol. Barton (1964), 200–201, no. 6.

4. A small, undecorated mug of this general style, although with a rolled rather than a strapped handle and a slightly broader foot, was found in a mid-17th-century context at Mathews Manor, near Newport News. (See Pl. 7, no. 6.) The handle terminal style of this Virginia specimen is akin to that of the small example from Bankside (Pl. 6, left) found in a context of the third quarter of the 17th century. If, however, the Mathews Manor mug was expanded at the mouth in the style of the Bankside example, it would differ markedly from the Burnett mugs. On the other hand, the third of the Bankside specimens (Pl. 6, right) has no expanding foot, possesses a flat, strap handle, and, save for a cordon above it, is a much closer parallel for the Burnett examples.

5. A mug of comparable shape with a similar cordon below the rim was sold at Christie's on February 3, 1975, lot 187. The mug is inscribed in blue with a rectangular panel THOMAS ∘ HUNT ∘ OF ∘ EDEN 1635. There is a blue band at foot and lip; the ground between manganese stippled. Height 4 inches, and therefore slightly larger than the illustrated specimen. The girth, too, is slightly higher.

6. Sir David Burnett's notes state that this mug was found "approx. 80 yds from the [Vine Yard] kiln."

7. The beginning date for this fragment is based on the by no means proven assumption that the complete object was similar in character to the Elizabeth Brocklehurst mug. Garner and Archer (1972), pl. 6. Another of rather similar body shape, but with a more flaring foot, is inscribed MRS. MARY HOOPER 1629, and is in the Burnap Collection; see Pl. 36. However, it is possible that the Burnett base comes from a much more bulbous mug in the style of one marked THOMAS BALARD and dated 1644, Tait (1960), 42, Fig. 16, or the even squatter example inscribed IOHN LARTHMAN & ROSE 1645 and bearing the arms of the Bakers' Company of Exeter (Pl. 19). It is significant that the rounded foot disappeared from these bulbous mugs or caudle cups soon after 1660 and was replaced either by a straight and flaring foot or by no foot at all. For a good example of the flaring type on a mug or tankard bearing the Salters' Company arms and dated 1674, see *The Connoisseur,* CXLV (March 1960), xxvii.

9. Lower body and delicate spread foot from a vessel of uncertain form, but one that probably was small necked, as the fold of the interior lower wall over the base rarely, if ever, occurs on wide-mouthed vessels. It is possible, therefore, that this was part of a jug or bottle, although the foot is unusually thin and pedestallike for the latter.[8] The drab yellow biscuit is marked on the outside with traces of what may be brown unfired slip, but if so, no identifiable decoration survives. Base diameter: 2 5/8 inches. Site 5. About 1630–1665.

10. Mug, jug, or bottle foot and lower wall fragment; orange to pink biscuit with traces of unfired white glaze in slip form adhering. The foot shape is paralleled by that of the Elizabeth Brocklehurst mug (1628), by a marriage (?) mug inscribed WILLIAM AND ELIZABETH BURGES, 24th AUGUST 1631 and dated under the handle 1632, and by yet another bearing the names John Potten and Susanna, dated 1633.[9] However, this evidence is insufficient to necessitate so early a date for the Burnett example. Base diameter: 2 7/16 inches. Site 7. About 1625–1640.

11. Small mug or jug foot and wall fragment with the lower handle terminal surviving; pink biscuit with red ochre and chalk (?) inclusions. Numerous cracks may have occurred in firing. The heavy foot shape and the bulbous body curve above it make it evident that this vessel differed in character from no. 10. It is possible, however, that it belongs in the same class as nos. 7 or 8.[10] Base diameter: 2 3/16 inches. Site 1. About 1630–1650.

12. Basal fragment from small bowl with V-shaped footring and the base raised within it; the ware a pale orange pink biscuit thinly potted. There is an incised groove around the exterior wall above the footring. Dating for such a sherd is extremely difficult, but the foot form was used in the last quarter of the 17th century and through much of the 18th. Base diameter: 3 3/8 inches. Site 5.[11] Date uncertain.

13. Mazer bowl (?), very thinly potted yellow to buff biscuit, the surviving handle formed as a separate ring and luted to the wall. Handles of this type occur on a silver-mounted mazer bowl bearing the date letter for 1585–1586, and on a silver cup stamped with the date letter for 1657–1658.[12] Similar handles are present on a globular delftware jar dated 1632 (Pl. 35) and on a white undated posset pot (Pl. 8). However, they also occur on Netherlandish maiolica flower vases of the early 16th century (Pl. 4). Diameter: 4 3/4 inches. Site 5. About 1612–1660.

14. Salt with wide pedestal foot closed at the base save for a small central hole, and standing on three nipple-shaped feet. Each of the feet was applied separately and all have cracked in firing. The bowl with its wide flat rim appears to have been made separately and then luted to the foot. The ware is a thinly potted pale yellow to buff biscuit. Napkin supports have been added to the drawing only because salts of this type generally possessed them. However, no traces of them survived on this example.

---

8. Tait (1960), 40, Fig. 13. The cited example (dated 1634) possesses a rather similar foot, is described as a jug, and is identified by the author as English delftware, in spite of the fact that it is in the Museum fur Kunsthandwerk at Frankfurt-am-Main, Germany.

9. Ibid., 38, pl. 7, 40, pl. 11.

10. See n. 6.

11. Sir David Burnett's notes state that the fragment was recovered from "Excavations for petrol tank, Black Swan Yard, S.W. of kiln at Pickle Herring Wharf."

12. Berry (1933), pl. XXXI, no. 78, pl. LXVI, no. 133. Also illustrated in this catalogue (pl. XXXIII, no. 80) is a shallow but handleless wooden mazer bowl 2 1/4 inches in height and 8 3/4 inches in diameter, and with a silver mount dated 1642. The ring handle form goes much later as is evidenced by a London-made silver college cup dated 1720. See *The Illustrated London News* (March 27, 1971), 37.

Height: 2 3/8 inches. Site 4. About 1650–1700.[13]

15. Salt standing on a cylindrical pedestal in turn raised on three ball feet; the rim narrow and offset over two stepped cordons. The base is closed save for a central hole, and the ware is a well-thrown pink biscuit. Parallels for the shape, glazed in plain white, have been found at the Kingsmill Tenement site in James City County, Virginia, in a context dated post-1640.[14] From a trench in Vine Lane 10 yards south of supposed kiln; Site 4? Height: 3 3/8 inches. About 1640–1680.

16. Candlestick made in at least two sections and joined at the median drip tray, the upper barrel of wider diameter than the lower pedestal. The stick has a rough clay plug thrust into the upper unit to provide a bottom for the holder, at which point the exterior wall is decorated with two grooves. The ware is a well-potted pale yellow biscuit appearing buff in the fractures. Surviving height: 6 5/8 inches. Site 4. About 1640–1700.[15]

17. Upper body fragment from small "flower pott" or posy holder, probably originally with three tubular orifices at the shoulder, equally spaced between three ornamental "handles" made up from pairs of abutting clay rolls, and similar in appearance to the napkin supports found on delftware salts of the same period (see Pl. 16). The biscuit body is orange pink in section but pale yellow on the exterior. Only one example of this small size seems to be recorded as being in museum and private collections,[16] but larger versions of the same shape are known and appear to have been relatively common in the second half of the 17th century, the most important of which is dated 1683 (Pl. 17).[17] Site 5. About 1650–1690.

18. Foot and part of body from "flower pott" or posy holder as above; solid pedestal; a terminal for one of the "handles" is just visible at the uppermost fracture line. A very pale yellow biscuit with unfired white glaze adhering to the inside.[18] Vine Lane immediately west of supposed kiln. Base diameter: 2 7/8 inches. Site 1? About 1650–1690.

---

13. The only dated parallel for this salt type bears the blue painted inscription "A W 1675" and was illustrated by Tilley (1969b), 80–81. Unfortunately, Mr. Tilley did not give the measurements of the dated specimen, nor did he describe the underside of the base. A silver salt of this type dated 1676 is in the collection of the Skinners' Company. See *The Antique Collector,* XXXVI (February–March 1963), 10. For a small, undated delftware specimen in the Colonial Williamsburg Collection see Pl. 16. A fragmentary example has been found in Virginia at the Joseph Pettit site in James City County in a context of ca. 1690. Virginia Research Center for Archaeology: GL. 1A. For an unstratified example from Montague Close see Dawson and Edwards (1973), 53, Fig. 26.

14. Virginia Research Center for Archaeology Collection: KM.393D.

15. The only recorded, dated candlestick of the 17th century is in the Victoria and Albert Museum and bears the arms of the Fishmongers' Company and the date 1648. See Tilley (1967b), 270, Fig. 11. This specimen differs from the Burnett example in that it has knoplike features at the base of the holder and above the foot, paralleling reinforcements found on metal sticks. The foot is scalloped at the edge, again a feature with metallic associations. Another undated stick, with a bulge at the base of the holder and with raised prunts around the circular foot, is illustrated by Garner and Archer (1972), pl. 29A, and dated "about 1650." A much closer parallel complete with double grooves, although slightly smaller, is illustrated by Wills (1969), p. 47, pl. 6, and is attributed to Lambeth in the mid-17th century. An unstratified biscuit example from Montague Close is illustrated in a conjectured drawing by Dawson and Edwards (1973), 53, Fig. 25. See also the glazed example in the Burnett Collection, Fig. VII, no. 3.

16. The specimen is in the collection of the Colonial Williamsburg Foundation (G.1974-681), stands 4 5/8 inches in height, and is decorated in blue in the chinoiserie style characteristic of the 1680s. It differs from the Burnett Collection fragments in that it has only two "spouts" and two handles, and has a separately thrown foot and pedestal.

17. A much more complete example than either of the Burnett Collection specimens (nos. 17 and 18), although minus its foot, is in the British Museum and is stored unnumbered amid other delftware found in the vicinity of Tooley Street. The vase is in the biscuit state, but the interior retains a considerable quantity of unfired tin glaze. Unlike the majority of the surviving finished specimens that possess cockled rims, the British Museum specimen has a broad, flat mouth, and it is this form that has been copied in the conjectural reconstructions of both the illustrated specimens. This British Museum specimen has a surviving height of 5 inches. Yet another biscuit specimen of comparable size has been recovered in the course of the Southwark Archaeological Excavation Committee's unpublished 1968 digging in Lambeth High Street (Object No. S.19, trench 2, layer 6), thus adding support to a post-Wilhelm date for this shape. See also Dawson and Edwards (1973), 49, Fig. 3, for a squatter, biscuit example from Montague Close.

18. Another example of similar size and shape (but the biscuit body harder and a pale orange on the inside and on the bottom of the foot) was found in the same location. Not illustrated.

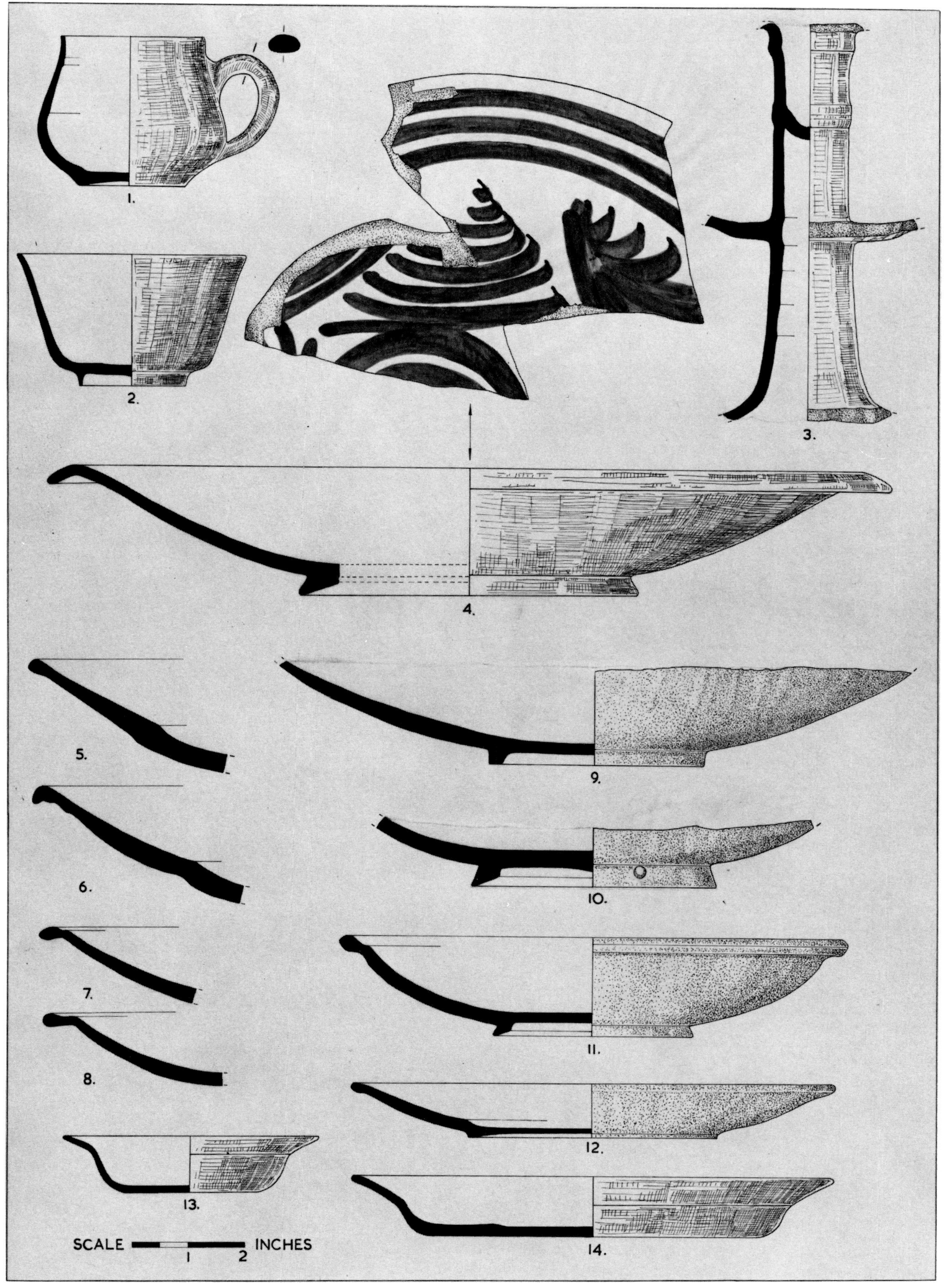

FIGURE VII

FIGURE VII

1. (and Pl. 18, right). Small cup with thick strap handle thickly white glazed over a yellow body. The shape is rather similar to the biscuit example shown in Fig. VI, no. 3, although the latter is less angular above the base and has a more delicate handle.[1] Height: 2 5/8 inches. Site not recorded.[2] About 1650–1670.

2. Small handleless cup or tea bowl with flaring wall and slender footring, white glazed over a buff body. Height: 2 1/4 inches. Site not recorded. About 1670–1710.[3]

3. Candlestick with thick white glaze inside and out over a yellow body. This specimen is of lighter construction than the unglazed example (Fig. VI, no. 16) and it differs significantly in that the elements above and below the drip tray are of comparable diameter, also in that the base of the candle socket is concave-convex. That of the biscuit example is no more than a flat plug. Surviving height: 7 inches. Site not recorded. Second half of 17th century.[4]

4. Charger,[5] the upper surface tin glazed and decorated in pale blue; the back also glazed and with some tin oxide in it, and light greenish where the glaze thickens; the body pale yellow. Approximate diameter: 15 inches. This reconstruction is derived from two fragments having overlapping design elements, but the sherds are not proven to be from the same dish although they are identified as coming from the same location at Battle Bridge House; Site 6. About 1650–1680.

5. Platter rim and bowl fragment, biscuit; pale yellow surfaces over a pink body, the ware thick. The junction of rim and bowl is indicated by a shallow step that might well have been obscured after glazing. Approximate diameter: 14 3/4 inches. From trench 10 yards south of "site of Pickle Herring Kiln"; Site 2. About 1630–1670.

6. Platter rim and bowl fragment, biscuit; similar surface and body to no. 5 above, but with fewer red ochre inclusions. The rim differs in that it is slightly downbent and undercut, and in that the exterior wall is slightly more ridged. The foot is likely to have been of the type suggested by no. 10. Approximate diameter: 15 1/2 inches. Site 2. About 1630–1670.

7. Small dish, rim, and bowl fragment, biscuit; buff to pale yellow surface, pink core with sizable red ochre inclusions. There is a small groove at the interior junction of rim and wall that would almost certainly have been hidden after glazing. (For a rather similar shape see Fig. VIII, no. 4.) Approximate diameter: 8 1/2 inches. Site 2. About 1640–1670.

---

1. For a cup dated 1664 with a closely paralleling handle and of comparable size, see Parkinson (1969), p. 35, no. 63. Another dated 1660, painted in blue with a front view portrait inscribed KING CHARLES THE 2D, also BE : MERY : & WISE, and initialed R E G, was sold at Christie's on February 3, 1975, lot 186. The mug is attributed to Lambeth (for no good reason) and is 3 inches in height, thus slightly larger than the illustrated example.
2. Here, as elsewhere, examples without site designations were noted by Sir David Burnett as coming from sites on the north side of Tooley Street in St. Olave Parish.
3. Fragments of three such cups have been found in unrecorded contexts on the Chiswell site in Williamsburg, pointing to the type's continuing use into the 18th century. 2H2, 2H6, and 2H10.
4. Dating for delftware candlesticks of the 17th century is difficult. However, it seems that the more elaborately shaped specimens, i.e., those with pressed up bosses around their feet and with frilled socket rims (for example, Garner and Archer [1972], pl. 29A) date within the brackets 1645–1665. That conclusion is based on the similarity between the embossed candlesticks and comparably ornamented posset pots (e.g., ibid., pl. 26B) which occur bearing dates between 1651 and 1661. An example of the latter date was illustrated by Hughes (1957), 98, Fig. 2. Not all early candlesticks are embossed, however, as is demonstrated by an example painted in blue with the arms of the Fishmongers' Company and dated 1658. Tilley (1976b), 270, Fig. 11. Here the foot is scalloped in what one might suppose to be a much later metal form. There are, it should be noted, other even simpler delftware candlesticks in plain white (such as those in the Bayou Bend Collection and illustrated in *Antiques,* XCIV [December 1966], 808), some of which may well be of Continental origin. A good paralleling example of what can be supposed to be an English stick is illustrated by Wills (1969), 47, pl. 6. More helpful from a dating point of view is a chinoiserie-decorated (chinaman amid rocks) stick in the Greg Collection (Parkinson [1969], p. 32, pl. 47) that can be attributed to the period 1680–1700.
5. For charger, platter, dish, and plate nomenclature discussion, see p. 36.

8. Dish akin to the above, biscuit; pale yellow surface to a poorly wedged pink body. The wall is more concave-convex than no. 7, and the groove at the rim has developed into a dishing of the rim itself. Approximate diameter: 11 1/2 inches. Site 2. About 1640–1680.

9. Charger base, biscuit; pink body with pale yellow exterior surface (that is, the underside), the footring unusually square cut and with a trace of the pierced hole at the fracture. Base diameter: 3 3/4 inches. Site not recorded. About 1640–1680.

10. Charger or platter base, biscuit; pink body with pale yellow exterior surface, the footring rather similar to that of no. 4. The base center is unintentionally thickened and is scored on the underside with concentric circles of varying width and depth. The footring is crudely pierced with a single hole, the tool having been tapered and rectangular in section—perhaps a nail. Base diameter: 4 3/8 inches. Site 2. About 1640–1680.

11. Dish, biscuit; pale yellow surfaces over a pink body with many red ochre inclusions. The rim is relatively heavy and although exhibiting a profile related to that of no. 7, it differs in that it is more upturned and square cut. The interior ridge is smeared below to create an unintentional cordon that would have been obscured after glazing. Approximate diameter: 9 1/2 inches. Site 2. About 1640–1670.

12. Plate or paten with broad rim and flat slightly rising base, biscuit; pinkish yellow ware throughout, but with considerable staining, apparently as a result of burial. The base is very thin and exhibits an encircling ridge at its junction with the wall giving the appearance of a footring. Approximate diameter: 7 3/4 inches. Site 2. About 1650–1675.

13. Small dish or plate, perhaps from a food warmer; a thick pinkish white glaze over a very thin body, the glaze containing small black flecks. The weakly contoured base is darkened, the glaze matt and badly pitted, apparently in manufacture. Two sagger peg scars are clearly visible on the underside of the slightly upturned rim. Diameter: 4 1/2 inches. Site not recorded. Late 17th or early 18th century?

14. Plate with narrow rim and no footring, the shape attributed by Garner to Lambeth and to the period 1690–1780.[6] The pale yellow body is covered with a white glaze (up to 1 mm. in thickness) that is both pitted and gathered into drops along the rim edge at one side and is heavily crazed overall, the latter feature being common among plain white wares such as chamber pots of the late 17th and early 18th centuries. The potting is poor and the center of the plate is unintentionally dished creating a rippled effect on the upper surface. Diameter: 8 1/4 inches. Site not recorded. About 1680–1720.

FIGURE VIII

1. (and Pls. 30, 31). Plate, waster, tin glazed on the upper surface and decorated in Ming style in blue, the back glaze much damaged by overfiring but exhibiting greenish patches that are absent from the upper surface, suggesting that the back was intended to be a greenish yellow as is the properly fired example no. 4. The footring is square cut and pierced by a tapering but round-sectioned tool to create a single hole. It should be noted that the drawing is derived, not from one plate, but from elements of at least nine specimens found fused together as the result of a kiln accident.

The central bird-on-rock motif is paralleled in a general way by numerous examples of jugs and mugs previously attributed to Southwark and to the factory of Christian Wilhelm. However, comparable designs occur on a group of jugs whose forms are typically European (and so far absent from the shapes found in waster or unfinished states in

---

6. Garner and Archer (1972), p. 81. See also pl. 51, a "Merry Man"-type plate dated 1720, and another in praise of George I, dated 1719, pl. 66D. Two further related specimens dated 1693 were illustrated in *Country Life*, CXXXII (August 9, 1962), 311.

3.
1.
4.
2.
COLOR KEY
DARK BLUE
LIGHT BLUE
GREEN
ORANGE
BROWN
BLUE-GREEN
SCALE
1
2
INCHES

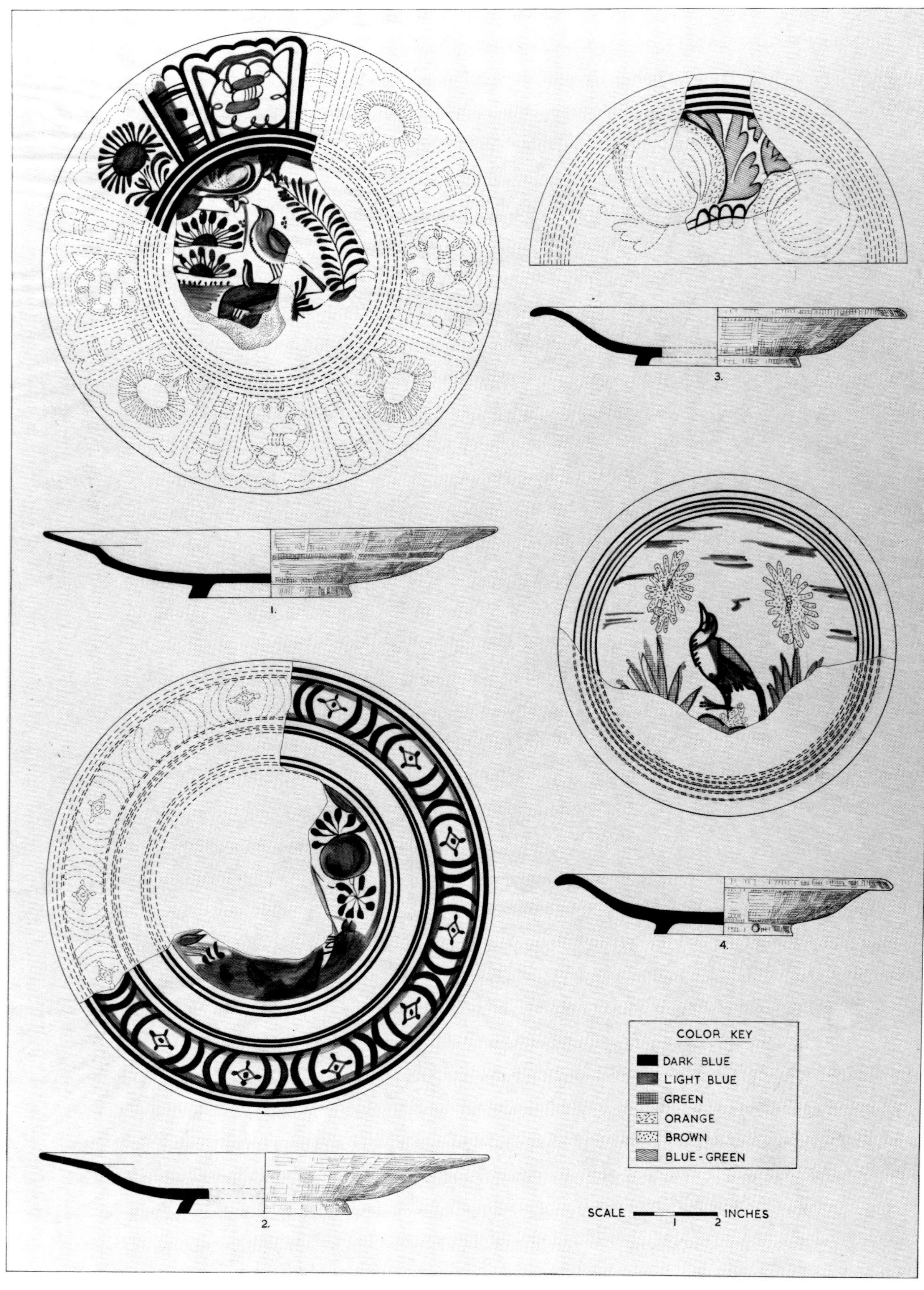

FIGURE VIII

Southwark),[1] and therefore the decoration alone is not enough to identify plates of this type as products of the Wilhelm or any other London kilns.

Very similarly decorated plate fragments have been found in Bremen, Germany, and are attributed to the Netherlands.[2] There is no doubt that this Chinese bird-on-rock design was used by Dutch painters, for as de Jonge shows, the arms of the Haarlem ceramic painters include a rendering of a dish of this type.[3] As yet there is no evidence to prove that the English preceded the Dutch in developing this design—or vice versa.[4] Approximate diameter: 10 1/4 inches. Site 4. About 1628–1640.[5]

2. (and Pls. 30 and 31). Plate, waster fused to nos. 1 and 3, tin glazed on the upper surface and decorated in blue with a central floral motif of uncertain character (see below), and with a geometric pattern at the rim. The back glaze is comparable to that of no. 1, but the footring is lighter. However, not enough of it is visible in the pile to be certain that it was pierced. Three identifiable rims of this type are represented in the largest fused mass (14 plates), but only two bases are recognizable in the block of six.

   Although it is dangerous to draw conclusions as to the style of the decoration based on so little visible evidence, it is a reasonable supposition that it was also of Ming-derived bird-on-rock character. That suggestion is based on the fact that the surviving ball-like "fruit" with a flower above and beneath is closely paralleled by others on a bottle in the British Museum dated 1628[6] and the London Museum's 1630 tankard (see Pl. 37), each of which forms part of a bird-on-rock motif. If this interpretation is valid, it follows that the vertical line with the shaded zone to its left (at the edge of the obscuring kiln trivet) is actually part of the tail of the bird. Approximate diameter: 10 1/2 inches. Site 4. About 1628–1640.[7]

3. (and Pls. 30 and 31). Dish, waster, fused to nos. 1 and 2, tin glazed on the upper surface and decorated with a pomegranate motif in polychrome colors that included blue, orange, and green; the back glazed as nos. 1 and 2. Whether or not the footring was pierced cannot now be determined, but in all probability it was. The angle of the rim is conjectural due to the fact that the only surviving fragment had flattened in the kiln.

   The pomegranate design is well known in a generally Italianate style in the first half of the 17th century, but continues into the third quarter in a rather flat and lifeless form. An excellent example of the early type occurs on a charger dated 1640 illustrated by Garner[8] and in the Burnett Collection by a bowl base of uncertain origin (Pl. 49, no. 7). The later pomegranate type is well represented by an undated specimen in the Burnap Collection, there attributed to Lambeth and to a date around 1670.[9] Approximate diameter: 9 inches. Site 4. About 1628–1640.[10] Source and date as nos. 1 and 2.

4. Dish, tin glazed on its upper surface and decorated in simplified bird-on-rock style in polychrome colors—blue, green, and orange. The back is covered with a thick greenish yellow glaze probably comparable to that used for nos. 1–3, while the body is yellow, rather poorly bonded, and contains a few red ochre inclusions. The small footring is of uneven shape, being undercut at one side and square at the other, and is pierced by a single round but tapering hole. Large trivet marks are visible on the lower petals of the orange flowers, indicating that the tripod spacer was of similar size to those visible between nos.

---

1. Tait (1961), 24–25, Figs. 22–27.
2. Grohne (n.d.), p. 123, pl. 83. The fragments are undated.
3. De Jonge (1947), p. 74, pl. 45.
4. Another virtually identical dish base was recovered by Francis Celoria in excavations in the vicinity of Vine Lane in 1965. This fragment is presently unpublished. See also Pl. 39 and Fig. VIIIa.
5. For additional discussion, see pp. 38–43.
6. Tait (1960), 37, Figs. 3 and 3b.
7. For additional discussion, see pp. 40–41.
8. Garner and Archer (1972), pl. 12.
9. Taggart (1967), p. 47, no. 96.
10. For additional discussion, see pp. 42 and 44.

1–3 and comparable to the examples illustrated in Fig. XIII, nos. 8 and 9. Diameter: 8 inches. Site not recorded.[11]

In the absence of published design parallels, dating for this dish is based only on the similarity between its shape and palette to those of no. 3 above, suggesting a manufacture date in the second quarter of the 17th century.

11. Noted as coming from an unspecified site in Tooley Street.

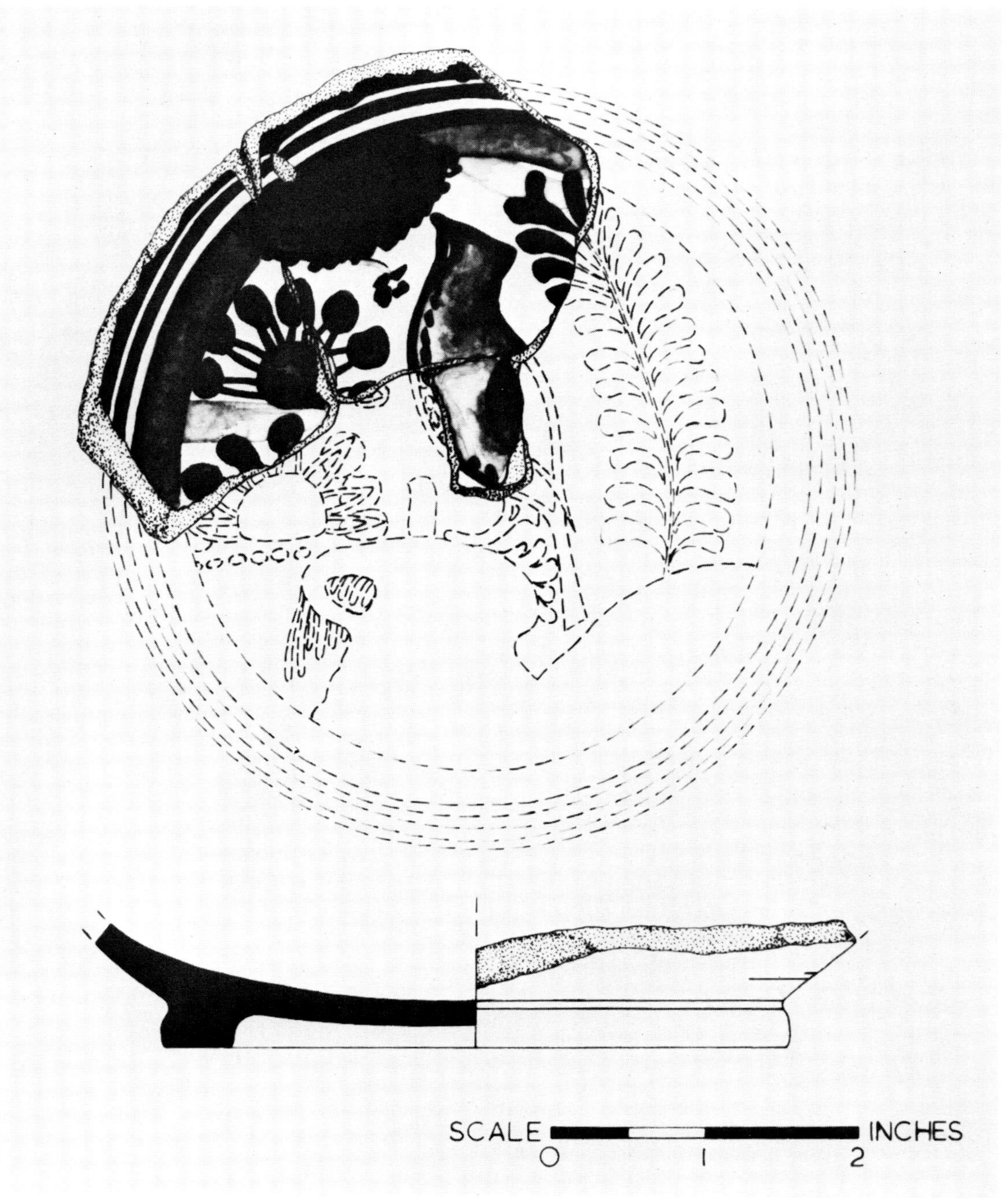

FIGURE VIII a

FIGURE VIIIa

Bowl or deep dish, base fragments only, tin glazed on the upper surface and decorated in Wan Li style, paralleling that of Fig. VIII, no. 1. The body yellow; the back is thinly lead glazed, dirty yellow in color streaked with red, the latter derived from red ochre inclusions in the soft yellow body. The footring is square cut with a small groove at the exterior junction with the base. The decoration exhibits the double-lined petals characteristic of the specimens from the Vine Lane group, but the solid blue swag at the top left seems to differ from the specimen illustrated in Fig. VIII, which may be formed from a coiled line. The beak of the bird is somewhat more stunted than that of the Vine Lane specimens. In general, however, this example is a remarkably close parallel to those in the Burnett Collection. Approximate base diameter: 4 inches. Found in a field adjacent to the Warwick River near Lee Hall, Virginia, approximately five miles upstream from Mathews Manor. Unstratified, but undoubtedly of comparable date to the example illustrated in Fig. VIII, no 1.[1] About 1628–1640.

FIGURE IX

1. Charger, yellow bodied, tin glazed on the upper surface, and boldly decorated in blue in a debased chinoiserie style, the border panels reminiscent of Fig. VIII, no. 1. The back glaze also contains some tin but is a pinkish gray in color, caused in part by the body showing through. No foot survives, but it is reasonable to deduce that it was comparable to that of no. 2 below. The decoration was one of the most common of run-of-the-mill "Southwark" designs and is paralleled in both public and private collections (see Pls. 45–47).[1] That this motif was, in fact, a product of the Vine Lane kiln site is indicated by the presence of a related badly blistered waster fragment (Pl. 49, no. 2) found along with biscuit sherds in the nearby Black Swan Yard (Site 3). These dishes were made in at least two distinct sizes as is indicated by the much larger charger base of

1. A small bowl (diameter 7 3/4 inches) with a Wan-Li style border, yellow lead-glazed on the exterior, but lacking its base and therefore its central decoration, has been found in excavations at the Kingsmill Tenement site in James City County in a context of about 1640. Virginia Research Center for Archaeology: KM.382A and 154C.

1. For additional discussion, see pp. 45–48. The example shown in Pl. 47 was illustrated in ***The Antique Dealer & Collector's Guide*** (July 1969), 52, and attributed in a dealer's advertisement to Brislington and to ca. 1680.

1.

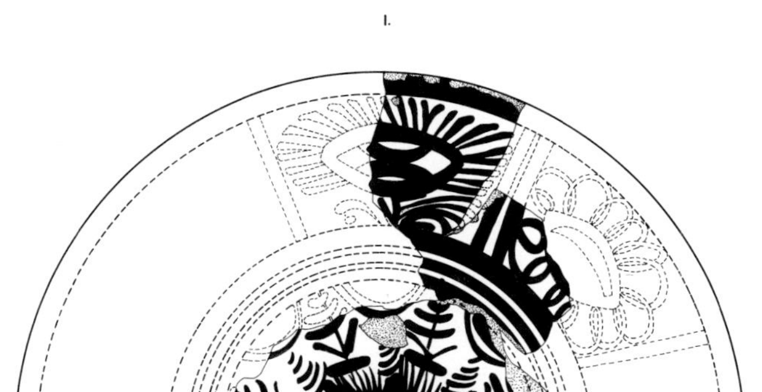

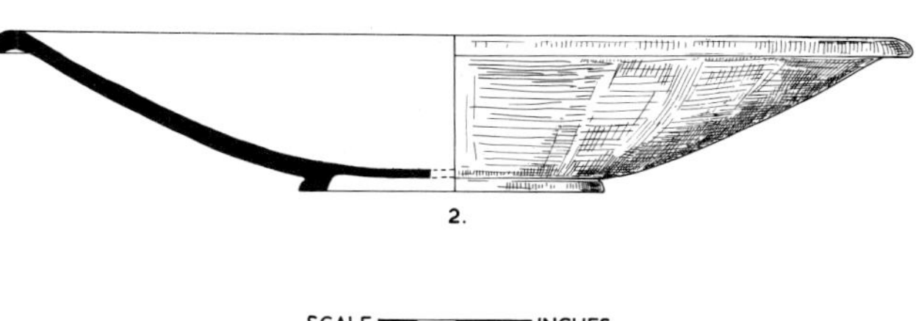

2.

FIGURE IX

comparable design shown in Pl. 49, no. 1. Unfortunately, no close dating is forthcoming for any of these pieces and no dated examples are recorded. On the basis of the previously cited border similarity with the bird-on-rock plate in the fused group (Pls. 30 and 31), a date in the second quarter of the 17th century seems reasonable, with the debasement of the original concept perhaps pointing toward the end of the period, that is, about 1640–1650. However, the charger comes from the cesspit in Black Swan Yard (Site 3) whose contents, as recorded by Sir David Burnett, range from the 1630s to at least 1680.[2] Diameter: 12 1/2 inches.

2. Dish, slightly smaller and deeper than the above, but otherwise comparable. The blue decoration is less intense, but this is almost certainly the product of a lower kiln temperature, as is the friability of the body and the poor bonding of the back glaze. The base is extremely thin in the middle and the yellow ware contains large inclusions of red ochre. Diameter: 11 3/4 inches. Site 3. About 1640–1650.

FIGURE X

1. (and Pl. 49, no. 6). Dish, tin glazed on the upper surface and decorated with a floral design in blue, green, yellow, pale orange, and purple. The back glaze would appear to contain some tin, but the entire surface is so badly blackened by soil staining that the original color cannot be determined conclusively. The body is relatively hard and is yellow at the surfaces and markedly pink in the core. The clay contains a number of red ochre inclusions, some of them of large size. The footring is square cut and is pierced by a single round hole having no relationship to the way in which this floral dish would have been suspended. The rim differs from all other specimens in the Burnett Collection by being upturned and sharply grooved on the upper surface; furthermore, the decoration is more colorful and the glaze more brilliant than any of the other drawn plates and dishes, all of which factors point to this dish not being a product of the Southwark kilns.[1] On the other hand, the presence of the red ochre inclusions may suggest a comparable body composition, and all the colors used in the decoration are represented (if in more muted tones) among the indisputably Southwark fragments. The winglike leaf decoration (infilled in green and orange) at the rim and below the blue, orange, and yellow flower is paralleled by the decoration of the hexagonal floor tile shown in Fig. II, no. 8.[2] Note, too, that the "fishhook" fronds are comparable to those on the dish shown in Pl. 43 and to two more in the Burnett Collection, Fig. XI, nos. 1 and 2. Both the palette and the style of decoration are Italianate in feeling and point to a relatively early date for this dish, perhaps in the period 1625–1645. However, it was found along with another polychrome dish or bowl of possibly later date[3] at a location described as being "about 30 yards from the kiln site" in Vine Lane (Site 4). Probably Netherlandish. Approximate diameter: 10 7/8 inches. About 1600–1640.

2. (and Pl. 49, no. 5). Dish or charger base, tin glazed on the upper face and decorated with a central tulip design in weak blue, and with a border of the same color, apparently ornamented in a broad chinoiserie design in the manner of Fig. VIII, no. 1, and Fig. IX, no. 1.

---

2. Neither the size nor the stratigraphy of the pit is on record, and some doubts must exist as to whether the early and later 17th-century artifacts were deposited at one and the same time. Other illustrated items reputedly from the Black Swan Yard cesspit are as follows: Fig. XI, nos. 1–8; Fig. XIII, nos. 1–5; and Fig. XV, nos. 1–8.

---

1. A very close parallel for the shape, the style of painting, and some elements of the design are illustrated in Rackham (1926), pl. 42, a fragmentary plate now in the Victoria and Albert Museum, but found in Amsterdam.

2. This tile is of an earlier type and need not be a product of the Southwark kilns. Similar lozengelike leaf decoration occurs on a plate in the Museum of London collections (pl. 44), and is attributed by Rackham to "the last years of the sixteenth century at the earliest." Ibid., p. 112. A pharmaceutical drug jar in the collection of the Norwich Castle Museum includes similar elements in its polychrome decoration, and was recovered from an archaeological context attributable to ca. 1640. Height 5 5/16 inches. Site 215N, deposit 33.

3. See Pl. 49, no. 7. This pomegranate design occurs, according to Garner (1948), p. 7, "on a number of chargers dated from 1634 onwards."

1.
2.
3.
4.
5.
6.
COLOR KEY
DARK BLUE
LIGHT BLUE
GREEN
PURPLE
ORANGE
YELLOW
SCALE
INCHES
0
1
2

FIGURE X

Three tripod marks, matching the size of intact trivets in the collection, heavily scar the surface. The back glaze contains no tin, is curiously blistered, and has failed to adhere to the body; very little now survives. The ware is yellow at the surfaces and pale pink in the core, and contains a few red ochre inclusions. The footring is unusually small for such a dish, is undercut on the inside, and has no hole through it. Foot diameter: 3 9/16 inches. Site not recorded. About 1650–1665.

3. Dish or charger base, tin glazed on the upper face and thickly yellow glazed on the back, the body hard and a pale yellow. The geometric decoration is executed in two shades of blue, with a single band and a central disk in a celadon green. Foot diameter: 4 3/4 inches. Site 6. About 1650.

4. Dish fragment, tin glazed on both sides, very matt, the blue decoration poorly painted, smeared, and very weak, suggestive of improper firing. The ware is pink with occasional white and red ochre inclusions. Found during river wall excavations at St. Olave's Wharf "among large quantities of Bellarmine fragments." Approximate diameter: 11 1/2 inches. Site 7. About 1625–1650.

5. Dish rim fragment, tin glazed on the upper face and thinly lead glazed on the back, the yellowish glaze streaked with red from the iron oxide inclusions in the poorly wedged body. The geometric decoration is executed in blue and purple, the latter confined to the outer elements of the interlocking arcs and to a secondary role in the central motif. Approximate diameter: 9 1/2 inches. Site 6. No firm dating evidence is available, but manufacture in the period ca. 1640–1675 seems likely.[4]

6. Bowl, waster fragment, tin glazed on both sides, the interior glaze pitted to the point where the vessel must have been rejected. The geometric decoration is executed in blue, orange, and green, the latter confined (on this sherd) to a single band low on the wall and the orange to the inner elements of the interlocking arcs. The body is pink throughout. Diameter: 9 1/4 inches. Site not recorded. About 1645–1680.[5]

FIGURE XI

1. Dish of small size, tin glazed on both sides, the yellow body soft and lacking the usual red ochre inclusions, the base slightly raised within the square cut footring. The polychrome decoration is in blue, orange, green, and yellow, this last very vivid, but run, and used to outline the compartments of the design, the rim blue dashed. The principal decorative element is an oak-leaf device in the upper right segment. Another sherd, almost certainly from the same dish, shows that the design is geometric, dividing the circle into a cross of four rectangles each possessing a green leaf ornament at the inner edge and an orange flower above, while each of the four triangles contains a blue oak leaf. Approximate diameter: 8 inches. Reportedly from the cesspit in Black Swan Yard (Site 3), although the dish is seemingly of a much

4. The interlocking-arced chain is a relatively common border ornament, but remains extremely hard to date. Honey (1949), pl. 78b, attributed his illustrated example to the North Netherlands and to the "late sixteenth or early seventeenth century." De Jonge (1947), p. 64, pl. 38, shows a more angular version attributed to Rotterdam and to the early 17th century. Another example from Tooley Street and now in the Museum of London (A.28171) was illustrated by Rackham (1926), p. 108, pl. 50c, but is not dated. The chain or arabesque border design on yet another in the Ashmolean Museum is attributed by Rackham to a date not "much earlier than 1600." Ibid., p. 113 and pl. 22a. See n. 5.

5. This fragment is illustrated in Noël Hume (1966a), p. 50, Fig. 10, no. 3, and is there used to augment fragments of a dish or charger and a plate rim sherd from Tutter's Neck, the former in a deposit of the first decade of the 18th century and the latter from a pit of about 1740. Also illustrated in the same photograph is an incomplete plate decorated with a comparable chain border found in Dutch Limburg, whose central pomegranate design closely resembles the London Museum's Tooley Street fragment (see n. 4 above). The Tutter's Neck charger and plate are also illustrated in Fig. 18 (nos. 10 and 11, p. 65) of the report cited above. These important sherds clearly demonstrated that even if the chain decoration began in the 16th century, it continued on dishes at least to the 17th century and on plates and wash basins until the early 18th century.

1.
2.
3.
4.
5.
6.
7.
8.
COLOR KEY
DARK BLUE
LIGHT BLUE
GREEN
YELLOW
ORANGE
SCALE
1
2
INCHES

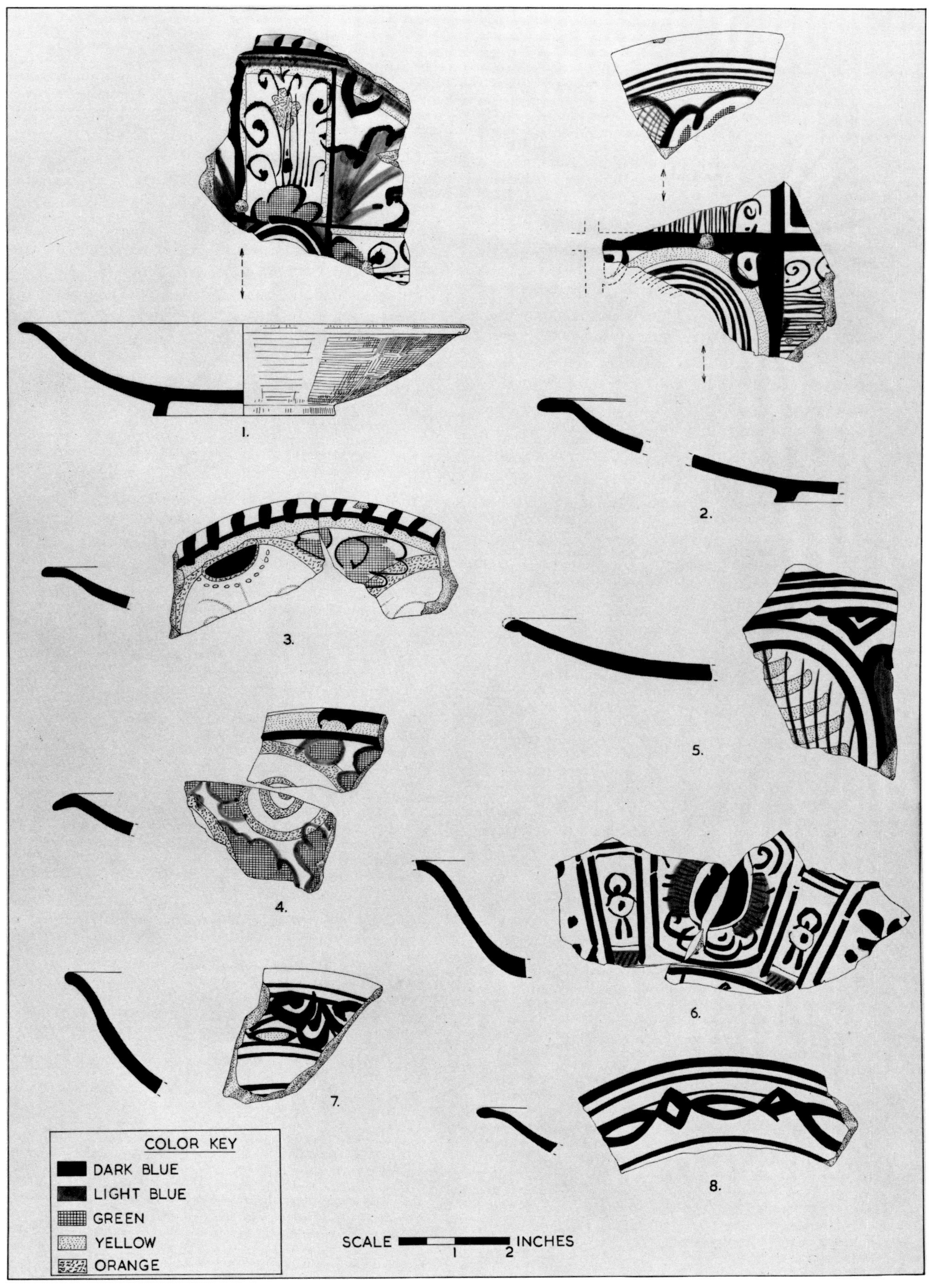

FIGURE XI

earlier date than many of the objects from that deposit.[1] About 1640–1660.

2. Dish fragments, tin glazed on both sides (but the back more yellow), with polychrome decoration rather similar to that of no. 1. The yellow body contains a few large red ochre particles, and the slightly spread footring is partially pierced by a single conical hole sealed by glaze within the foot. The decoration is geometrically divided and employs a palette of pale blue and yellow (in bands at the rim and around the central pinwheel or concentric blue rings), with green leaves and orange splashed onto the "fishhook" fronds. Approximate diameter: 10 7/8 inches. One fragment is recorded as coming from the cesspit in Black Swan Yard (Site 3), but the other is marked as having been found "nearby." About 1640–1660.

3. Dish rim with unusually angular profile, tin glazed on both sides and decorated with a blue dash edge and large orange but unusually delicately drawn pomegranates between which are green leaves outlined in blue. The yellow body is poorly wedged and contains many small red ochre inclusions. Approximate diameter: 10 inches. Site 5. About 1640–1655.[2]

4. Dish represented by two nonjoining rim and wall sherds, the rim markedly downturned, and the body pink throughout, tin glazed on the upper surface and only thinly and transparently lead glazed on the back. The polychrome decoration comprises a broad yellow band at the rim above a narrow blue line, leaf motifs in green outlined in blue, and spiral elements in orange. Both the leaves and the spirals are in muted colors that are almost Near Eastern or Hispanic in character. However, this unusual coloring probably results from temperature or atmospheric conditions in the kiln. Approximate diameter: 9 1/4 inches. Site 3. About 1635–1655.[3]

5. Charger or large dish, body sherd only, tin glazed on both sides, and the back grooved below the missing rim; the body hard, yellow, and with a few red ochre inclusions. The polychrome decoration is in blue and orange and represents London painting at its boldest, if not its most ambitious. Site 5. About 1640–1670.[4]

6. Bowl, wall fragments only, tin glazed on both sides, very thickly on the back and appearing pinkish in the ridges; the body yellow with many red ochre inclusions. The decoration is in typical Wan Li style, although the treatment of the tassels suggests that the porcelain prototype dated late in the period.[5] Approximate diameter: 10 inches. Site 5. About 1620–1645.

7. Bowl of unusual form and small size, thickly tin glazed on the inside; what little glaze there is on the back seems to have been acquired from atmospheric association with other items in the kiln rather than from deliberate lead glazing; the body pale pinkish buff and exhibiting no inclusions. The dead white glaze of the interior with its

---

1. Although not divided down the center, the oak or vine leaf element belongs to that Renaissance class. Unfortunately, however, the motif had a long life beginning (among published examples) with a dish in the Victoria and Albert Museum dated 1614 (see Bedford [1966], p. 28); followed by another better known specimen dated 1620 in the Glaisher Collection, No. 1394 (see Rackham [1935], I, p. 179, II, pl. 91); (see also Downman [1919], facing p. 50); and by a series of simplified "oak leaf" plates attributed to the last years of the 17th century (see Taggart [1967], p. 47, no. 95). The scroll-ended leaves flanking the orange flower are closely paralleled by the rim ornament of a basin dated 1639 in the Glaisher Collection, No. 144. See Rackham (1935), I, p. 179, II, pl. 93A. Archaeological dating for the "noughts-and crosses" divisions is provided by an example from a 1650–1660 deposit at Potters Bar. See Ashdown (1970), 97, Fig. 1, no. 13.

2. A polychrome dish dated 1648 with pomegranates treated with comparably dotted detail in the blossom end is included in the Glaisher Collection, No. 1407. Rackham (1935), I, p. 180, II, pl. 92B. It should be noted that although the fragments *appear* to join, the space between the two fruits is uncommonly small, and it is possible that these are not joining sherds.

3. The design is reminiscent of a leaf-decorated polychrome dish in the Glaisher Collection, No. 1402, which Rackham dates to "about 1640." Ibid., I, p. 179, II, pl. 95B.

4. A charger fragment of rather similar style has been found at Carter's Grove plantation in James City County, Virginia, in a context of about 1640. See Pl. 24.

5. A porcelain parallel for the decoration is described by Volker as a "Sino-Japanese transition type" and a "Hizen interpretation of Wan Li." See Volker (1954), p. 241 and pl. 26.

brilliant blue decoration sets this sherd apart from the rest of the collection. One lozenge-like element of the upper wall decoration is infilled with yellow. Approximate diameter: 7 inches. Site 6. About 1670–1700.

8. Dish rim, unusually concave on the upper perimeter, tin glazed on the upper surface (the back glaze of composition uncertain due to discoloration in the ground), the body pink and so poorly wedged that it has split along seams of red ochre. The chain decoration in blue may be compared with examples shown in Fig. X, nos. 4–6; and Fig. XIV, no. 1.[6] Approximate diameter: 9 inches. Site 3. About 1670–1690.

6. See Fig. X, n. 5.

FIGURE XII

FIGURE XII

1. (and Pl. 38A and B). Dish or bowl base, tin glazed on both sides and decorated and inscribed in blue, the body hard, yellow, and with no visible inclusions. The footring is V-shaped, slightly undercut inside, and has no suspension hole through the surviving segment. The upper surface is decorated in an elaborate version of the Wan Li bird-on-rock motif. This example belongs to the two bird group,[1] having one bird below and another partially concealed behind the rock. The design also includes a bowlegged moth that occurs on other specimens in this group. Also surviving from the Southwark prototype (Fig. VIII, no. 1, and Fig. VIIIa) is the flower with the double-lined petals, but here the flower at left is inverted,[2] although there is another of the more common vertically radiating type behind and below the standing bird. The total design differs from the earlier dated examples in that it has become much busier, and in that additional floral elements have been introduced, notably the "snowflake" flower that occurs thrice on this relatively small fragment.

   The back is decorated with broad zig-zag and straight lines derived from the underside ornament found on much Wan Li Chinese porcelain and is inscribed within the footring with a three-initial cipher E C S over the date 1651.[3] This is the only dated specimen in the Burnett Collection and is unquestionably the single most important piece.[4] Foot diameter: 2 5/8 inches. Site not recorded.

---

1. Tait (1961), 37, Fig. 3b (dated 1628); Museum of London, No. A6807 (dated 1630), see p. 37; Garner and Archer (1972), pl. 8B (dated 1631); Taggart (1967), p. 44, no. 75 (dated 1632); Rackham (1935), II, pls. 82 B and C (dated 1633); Bedford (1966), p. 7 (dated 1632).
2. Examples of these flowers occur in the "sky" area of the Victoria and Albert Museum charger, C59-1961, attributed to 1630–1645. See Pl. 33.
3. The three-initial cipher cannot be identified, but it should be read from bottom left to top, with the spouse's initial second: e.g., Edward and Sarah Chambers.
4. It is also the latest date so far recorded for the bird-on-rock motif in this ca. 1630 Wan Li style.

2. (and Pl. 51). Plate, tin glazed on both sides, and decorated on the upper surface in blue; the body yellow and lacking any visible inclusions; the footring small and V-shaped; the wall considerably thicker than either the base or the rim. The shape is most closely paralleled by Garner's Type E, which he attributes to "Lambeth and Bristol, 1710–1750,"[5] although there is no other reason to place this example anywhere near that date bracket. The thickness and pinkish tone of the glaze point to a manufacture date in the 17th century.

   The armorial design has been tentatively attributed to the Worshipful Company of Leathersellers, but this conclusion is difficult to support. Every description of the arms of that company from 1505 onward describes the animals as "thre Roes,"[6] "three Roe Bucks,"[7] or "3 bucks."[8] Those shown on this plate, both in the arms and on the crest, are without horns, and regardless of the fact that the arms are badly painted, it is unthinkable that the artist would have known so little about bucks as to leave out the antlers. Furthermore, the bucks on Leathersellers' arms are variously described as "coward" (which is hard to envisage when no buck had a tail long enough to pass between its legs), "regardant," or "trippant regardant." The beasts shown on this plate are passant. It is much more likely, therefore, that they are meant to be hinds and thus may relate to the familes of Brown, Weare, or Flowerdue, although the latter bears "three hinds trip-

---

5. Garner and Archer (1972), p. 81.
6. John Bromley and Heather Child, *The Armorial Bearings of the Guilds of London* (London, 1960), pp. 156–157.
7. Randle Holme, *An Academie or Store House of Armory & Blazon,* II (London, 1905), from an unpublished manuscript prepared for printing in Chester in 1682.
8. Nathaniel Bailey, *The Universal Etymological English Dictionary,* 3rd ed., II (London, 1737), n.p. Two London delftware cups dated 1660 bear the correct rendering of the Leathersellers' Company's roebucks, proving that although the painters might omit such details as crests or mottoes, they would not have been likely to mistake the bucks for hinds. One of the cups was sold at Sotheby's on July 24, 1956, where it was illustrated in the sale catalogue (item no. 68), and was bought by the Leathersellers' Company; the other is in the collection of the British Museum. Tilley (1968a), 129, Fig. 13.

See page 46. ▶

INCHES 1 2 3

pant," that is, walking, looking toward the dexter side, with three paws on the ground and one raised.[9] On the plate, all four are on the ground.

It cannot be proved that this plate is a Southwark product, for no armorial wasters have been found on any of the kiln sites. It should be noted, too, that fragments of armorial but plain-rimmed plates very much of this character (although always with the helms more competently delineated) are to be seen in the Rijksmuseum at Amsterdam and there attributed to ca. 1635–1650.[10] Approximate diameter: 8 3/4 inches Site 6. About 1650–1680.

3. Plate or dish base, tin glazed on the upper surface and greenish yellow lead glazed on the back; the body pink, poorly wedged, and exceedingly thin at the outer edge; the footring sloping internally so that only the outer edge touches the ground, and the junction softened by excessive deposits of glaze; no suspension hole. The plate is decorated on the upper surface with a checkered pattern in blue, each square containing a broad blue stroke crossed by another in orange. Foot diameter: 2 7/8 inches. Site not recorded. About 1620–1640.

4. Porringer base, tin glazed on the upper or interior surface, and yellow lead glazed on the back; the body pink and the footring square cut. The upper surface is decorated in blue with groups of triple radiating lines around a central pinwheel spiral. The glaze became so heavily pitted in firing (exposing the body beneath) that this sherd is almost certainly a waster.[11] Foot diameter: 2 3/4 inches. Site 6. About 1630–1660.

5. Plate or dish base, tin glazed on the upper surface and with poorly adhering yellowish lead glaze on the back; the body soft, yellow, and with a few red ochre inclusions; the footring heavy and roughly shaped and pierced by a single small round hole.[12] The tin glazing is of good quality, and the blue

---

9. J. W. Papworth, *An Alphabetical Dictionary of Coats of Arms Belonging to Families in Great Britain and Ireland . . .* (Baltimore, 1965 [reprint of 1784 ed.]), p. 156. Flowerdue is a relatively unusual name and therefore it is interesting (if not pertinent) to note that Temperance Flowerdewe came to Virginia in 1608 aboard the *Falcon*, married Sir George Yeardley, governor of the colony, and thus gave her name to Flowerdew Hundred, a thousand-acre tract on the south side of the James River. This in itself does not suggest a reason for a Southwark potter to be making plates for the Flowerdue family. It is a seemingly curious coincidence, nonetheless, that Sir George Yeardley owned "lands and tenements in Southwark" left to him in the 1603 will of his father, Ralph Yeardley, citizen and merchant tailor of London. He still owned property there in 1616 when the will of his brother-in-law, Edward Irbie (February 27, 1616/17), stated that "I will that my executrix shall pay unto my brother in law George Yardlie now being in Virginia, upon condition that he do make, execute and perform unto my said son Edward and his heirs, such assurances of the said great messuage called the Horne situte [situated] in Southwark aforesaid to the use of my said son Edward." In 1624 Flowerdew Hundred was sold to Abraham Peirsey of Virginia, whose widow, Frances West Peirsey, would, in 1627, marry Captain Samuel Mathews of Mathews Manor—where the initial discoveries of Southwark delftware prompted this study of the Burnett Collection. Intriguing though this circle of research may be, it cannot be proven that the "three hinds" plate was made for a member of Temperance Flowerdewe's family. For the genealogical and historical sources cited above, see *Tyler's Quarterly Historical and Genealogical Magazine*, II (October 1920), 115–130.

It may or may not be a coincidence that Rocque's map of 1746 and the revised Morden and Lea map illustrating the 1755 edition of Stow's *Survey* show "Horn Y." and "Horn's Yard" between Stoney Lane and Vine Yard only a direct distance of about 75 yards from the supposed Wilhelm kiln site (see Pl. 2A, location "D"). If Horn Yard was adjacent to the "great messuage called the Horne," then Sir George Yeardley's property lay but a stone's throw from Christian Wilhelm's. It may also be noted that the same maps show Flower de Luce Court and Flower de Luce Yard leading off the south side of Tooley Street less than 400 yards to the west. One may wonder whether this indicates the presence of Flowerdews living in this part of St. Olave's Parish.

10. De Jonge (1947), p. 94, pl. 56 (dated 1638), p. 95, pl. 57 (attributed to ca. 1640–1650). Michael Archer has suggested that because the plate shape is one hitherto attributed by Garner to 1710–1750 (Garner and Archer [1972], p. 81, example E), it may date much later than the decoration suggests. It remains my contention, however, that the thickness and color of the glaze sets this specimen apart from the later plates of this type.

11. This fragment is closely paralleled by a porringer from a garderobe at Dover Castle and believed to have been deposited during the Civil War, i.e., around the middle of the 17th century. The wall decoration of interlocking arcs and multiple encircling lines in groups of three and four of the Dover Castle porringer is a close parallel for the Burnett example shown in Fig. XIV, no. 1. See Mynard (1969), 35, Fig. 10, no. 7.

12. It is the hole that points to this fragment belonging to a plate, rather than to a porringer or bowl.

◂ *See page 48.*

painting brilliant in color and comprising chevron motifs of varying thickness around a broad blue circle enclosing a narrower central pinwheel spiral. Well-defined trivet marks scar the glaze. Foot diameter: 2 7/8 inches. Site not recorded. About 1630–1660.

6. Saucer base, tin glazed on both sides; the body yellow and relatively hard.[13] The foot is drawn down and appears to grow out of the wall and is characteristically concave. The upper surface is decorated in blue with groups of lines of decreasing length in the manner of many of the more simply decorated apothecaries' jars and pots. These devices surround a circle within which is a three-initial cipher reading R $\overset{O}{♀}$ M.[14] Foot diameter: 1 7/8 inches. Site not recorded. Probably about 1650–1675.

7. Porringer base fragment, tin glazed on the upper surface and with a bright yellow lead glaze on the back; the body yellow to pink in the core and with red ochre inclusions. The upper or interior surface is decorated in blue in a geometric pattern of grouped arcs within two or more encircling bands. From its shape, thickness, and decoration, this fragment almost certainly came from a porringer comparable to that illustrated in Fig. XIV, no. 1.[15] Foot diameter: 2 5/8 inches. Site 6. About 1640–1670.

8. Plate base, tin glazed on the upper surface and with pink to yellow lead glaze on the back; the body pink with red ochre inclusions; the footring sloping inward at the ground edge, and with a groove at its junction with the wall. The base is unusually thick and appears to sag within the footring. The decoration of the upper surface is in blue and comprises a series of circles of varying width and color density, the central group overlaid by a radiating pattern of hooked lines to create the multiple petals of a stylized flower. The glaze has run away from the body at one point and piled up around the hole to a thickness of 1/8 inch. This is almost certainly a waster. Nevertheless, it should be remembered that the design was one of the most common in the Netherlands, where it is usually attributed to Rotterdam.[16] (See Pl. 43.) Foot diameter: 3 7/16 inches. Site not recorded. About 1610–1660.

9. Small saucer, tin glazed on the upper surface and yellow lead glazed on the back; the yellow body soft and with large red ochre inclusions; the footring small and concave. The decoration is in blue and so roughly executed that it might truly be described as "slap dash." The glaze is marred by a large trivet stilt scar. Foot diameter: 1 3/4 inches. Site 6. About 1640–1680.

10. Miniature vase or perfume flask base fragment; pale blue tin glaze inside and out; the body thick, hard, and pinkish yellow with no visible inclusions. The slightly raised base is virtually unglazed. The chinoiserie decoration is delineated and washed in two tones of blue, both of which had run in the kiln, although not enough to cause the vase to be discarded.[17] Base diameter: 1 3/8 inches. Site 6. About 1680–1700.

11. Jug or vase base of pedestal form, tin glazed inside and out, and heavily pitted and blistered on the interior of the base; the body

---

13. For a discussion of saucer usage in the 17th century, see p. 50, n. 17.

14. See n. 3 above.

15. See n. 11 above and Cotter (1958), pl. 82, upper, for a comparable example.

16. De Jonge (1947), p. 61, pl. 34, p. 63, pls. 36 and 37. Grohne (n.d.), p. 121, pls. 79 and 80, there described as "early Dutch faience." A fragmentary plate found in a context attributed to the "middle, or second quarter, of the 17th century" was reported by Addyman and Biddle (1965), 117, Fig. 17, no. A2/3. Another possibly significant specimen is recorded by Bloice (1971), 132, Fig. 57, no. 58. The color or colors employed are not stated, but the inference is that the sherd is deduced to be a product of this factory whose operation is not known to have begun before 1680. It should be noted that this stylized floral design incorporating either a central spiral or concentric circles continued (or reappeared) on English delftware manufactured at Lambeth and elsewhere as late as the mid-18th century. See Victoria and Albert Museum, C27-1925. However, the Norfolk House specimen has an outer encircling band and thus much more closely resembles the Burnett Collction waster. An intact dish in the Victoria and Albert Museum (C850-1920), diameter 10 1/2 inches, closely parallels the line spacing and tones of the Burnett sherd, while employing both yellow and orange in its outer decoration. The dish is attributed to London and to the "early 17th century."

17. For a close parallel but with figures outlined in purple, see Ray (1968), p. 192, no. 120, and Fig. 61, tentatively attributed to Lambeth and to the late 17th century.

yellow but pink on the base surface, relatively hard, and with a few red ochre inclusions. The slightly rising base exhibits swirled "pulling" marks similar to those found on some of the biscuit ointment pots. The blue-painted decoration is of uncertain character save that the ladderlike motif resembles that of a jug discarded in about 1510 and found at Gateway House in London (Pl. 3). This parallel is of Italianate form and may well be an example of the Faenza ware that reached England in the 15th and 16th centuries as forerunners of the Netherlandish products that were to supersede the Italian trade in the latter century.[18] There is reason to believe that the Burnett fragment may be an Italian (or an early Antwerp) specimen and is therefore one of the small number of undeniably imported examples included in the collection.[19] Base diameter: 3 13/16 inches. Site 5. About 1480–1520.

12. Small vessel of uncertain form, perhaps a miniature vase, with one or possibly two round-sectioned handles with scroll terminals at the lower extremities; tin glazed inside and out; the body yellow, relatively hard, and with only occasional and very small red ochre inclusions. Approximate girth diameter: 2 1/2 inches. Site 5. The thickness of the glaze and the style of the handle terminal, coupled with the heavy cordon below the flaring mouth, suggest a date in the period 1650–1720.[20]

FIGURE XIII

1. Porringer base, tin glazed on both upper and lower faces; the body soft, very pale yellow, and with small red ochre inclusions; the footring broad, shallow, and slightly everted. The back glaze is thin and adheres poorly. The upper or interior decoration is in blue, the basal area bisected, and the resulting quadrants decorated with concentric arcs. The wall decoration was probably akin to that shown in Fig. XIV, no. 1. Foot diameter: 2 11/16 inches. Site 3. About 1640–1660.

2. Saucer base of a type comparable to no. 6; tin glazed on the upper surface, greenish yellow glazed on the back; the body soft and pale yellow with small red ochre inclusions; the foot straight at the exterior and concave within. The decoration is in blue and crudely composed from groups of relatively straight dashes.[1] Foot diameter: 1 13/16 inches. Site 3. About 1640–1660.

3. Saucer fragment, tin glazed on the upper surface, and with a yellow lead glaze on the back; the body yellow and with small red ochre inclusions; the foot comparable to that of no. 2, except that the thinness at the crown of the concavity has made the bottom extremely thin. The blue decoration comprises a series of straight lines radiating from a central dot; too little of the rim design survives for it to be identified with certainty, but probably diagonally blue dashed.[2] Foot diameter: 1 13/16 inches. Site 3. About 1650–1670.

4. Dish or very shallow bowl, tin glazed on both faces; the body yellow and with a few small red ochre inclusions; the footring V-shaped. The blue decoration owes something to the Chinese rock motif but also includes flowers that are European in character. Diameter: 8 1/4 inches. Site 5. About 1680–1700.

---

18. Museum of London, 23045, E.R. 161C. For a parallel see Rackham (1952), p. 27B, attributed to the early 16th century.

19. A close parallel for both the decoration and the shape (i.e., the pedestal foot and the sharply undercut base edge) is combined in two pinch-mouthed Italian (Faenza) jugs in the Victoria and Albert Museum; an example having the ladderlike decoration in blue is catalogued as having been found at Orvieto in Italy (C114-1914). Both jugs are attributed to the second half of the 15th century.

20. See Pl. 26 and discussion on p. 34.

1. A porringer with somewhat comparable decoration has been found in an undated context at Jamestown, Virginia; see Cotter (1958), pl. 82, upper. For a close type and decoration parallel, see Hurst and Golson (1955), 67, Fig. 15, no. 24. The fragment is identified as Dutch, but no supporting evidence is cited. The shape is similar to that of Fig. XIII, no. 3, save that the Norwich foot is expanded into a footring and is grooved at its exterior junction with the wall.

2. A saucer with a rim of this type has been found in an undatable context at Jamestown, Virginia; see Cotter (1958), p. 184, pl. 82, upper right.

5. Fluted or lobed dish, wall fragments only; thickly tin glazed on both faces; the body hard, yellow, and with no visible inclusions. The glaze is unusually white, almost comparable in tone to that of 19th-century ironstone china.[3] Approximate diameter: 9 inches. Site 5. About 1650–1690.

6. Saucer, tin glazed on both faces; the body hard, yellow, and with occasional red ochre inclusions; the foot straight and gently concave within. A triangular scar at the edge of the foot might have resulted from contact with a broken sagger peg. There are trivet scars (1 11/16-inch span) on the interior. The

3. For a fluted dish of rather similar type (but with the lobes of two alternating widths to create a Tudor rose form) dated 1651, see Garner and Archer (1972), pl. 28B. Another dish having fewer lobes of larger but equal widths, painted in blue and inscribed M.E. 1669, was illustrated in *Country Life,* CXXXVIII (October 14, 1965), 956.

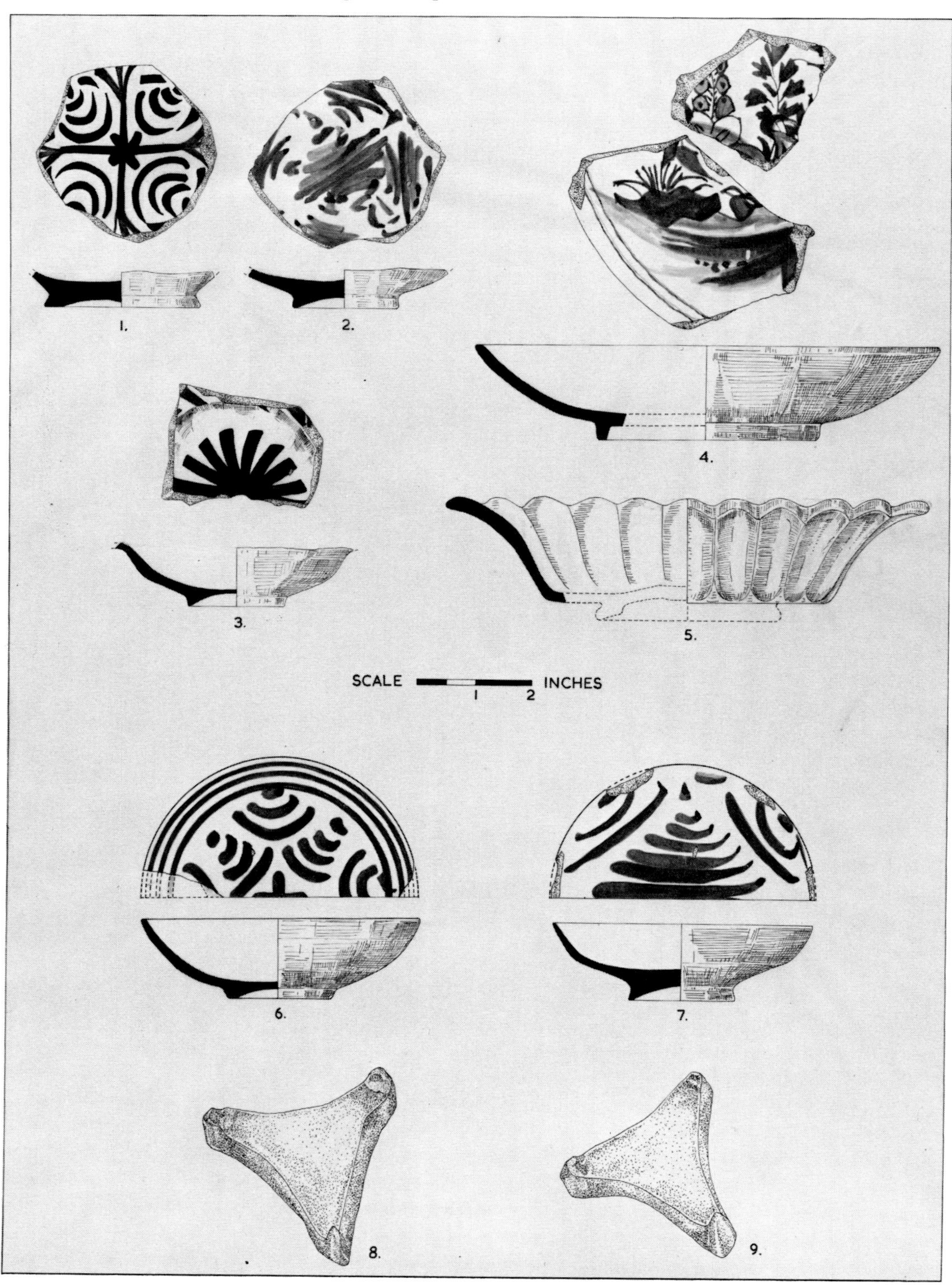

FIGURE XIII

blue decoration is of simple character, three bands encircling groups of arcs of two sizes around a central cross. Diameter: 4 13/16 inches. Site not recorded. About 1650.

7. Saucer, virtually complete, tin glazed on both faces; the body yellow and with few red ochre inclusions, but one large enough to protrude through the glaze on the upper surface. The foot is similar to that of no. 2 save that the exterior wall is slightly spread and the concavity somewhat deeper. The decoration is in pale blue, made up from a series of relatively straight lines of diminishing length arranged in a diamond, and framed by four groups of concentric arcs. Three trivet scars are clearly visible, the trivet having a spread of 1 3/4 inches.[4] Diameter: 4 9/16 inches. Site 6. About 1650.

8. Trivet, biscuit, the ware hard and pink, but with an intermittent yellow surface in the manner of much of the biscuit waste products. The small pointed feet were pinched by hand after the triangular shape had been cut from a flat, tilelike sheet of clay.[5] Span: 2 1/2 inches. Site 2. 17th century.

9. Trivet, biscuit, the ware soft, pale yellow, and with many small red ochre inclusions; the only intact foot more crudely shaped than those of no. 8. Span: 2 1/2 inches. Site 2. 17th century.

FIGURE XIV

1. Porringer handle and wall fragment, tin glazed internally and decorated in blue; the exterior coated with a yellowish lead glaze of uneven thickness; the body yellow and with no visible inclusions. The interior wall is decorated with three bands above a zone of chain decoration formed from interlocking arcs, with four bands below it.[1] The interior base design cannot be determined, but it would appear to be geometric in character (see Fig. XIII, no. 1). The handle is decorated in blue using a triple-lined "crow's-foot" technique reminiscent of the porringer base shown in Fig. XII, no. 4. The piercing of the handle comprises two crescents below a circular hole, the crescents largely obscured by redeposited clay. From beneath, all three holes appear circular. The crudely cut and angular lobing of the handle edge is believed to be an early characteristic.[2] Approximate diameter: 5 inches. Site not recorded.[3] About 1640–1670.

2. Porringer wall fragment and part of handle, tin glazed both inside and out, polychrome decorated with central pinwheel motif and

---

4. It should be noted that the trivets used between saucers were not of the "crow's foot" type represented in the Burnett Collection, but were solid triangular pads pinched up into sharp prunts at each corner. The evidence for this is provided by a saucer waster in the British Museum (with decoration very similar to that of no. 7) that still has its 1 3/8-inch equilateral triangle pad attached to its foot (Pl. 56, left). This important specimen was found in Tooley Street in 1907. See p. 68, n. 2. British Museum No. 1907, 10-14, 7.

5. For a discussion of trivet sizes and dating, see pp. 53–54.

---

1. The term porringer is here used to describe any shallow bowl with a single, flat handle projecting horizontally from the side. The popular and more dramatic designation of "bleeding bowl" cannot be supported when bowls of this type are found so frequently on domestic sites. In describing two examples initialed and dated A ∘ H 1673, L. L. Lipski (1968), 149, has expressed surprise that two identically "customized" bowls should exist "because" he says, "reason tells us that only one should have been made because it was a special order." That might be true if A. H. was ordering a bleeding bowl, but if he was wanting porringers, he might have ordered a dozen. In short, porringers should only be called bleeding bowls when they are graduated on the inside to indicate the quantity extracted. Even then, however, contemporary usage (1696) termed them "Blood porringers." Wills (1967), 443. It should further be noted that English delftware porringers are not documented as occurring (as do pewter and silver examples) with two handles, although the wine cups listed in 1696 may have been smaller porringer-type vessels with two handles. Ibid. Three double-handed porringers dated 1686, illustrated by Garner (1948), pl. 12, have since been recognized as Dutch. Consequently, it is dangerously misleading for archaeologists to reconstruct a second handle when they find but one. See Mynard (1969), 35, Fig. 10, nos. 5 and 7. Evidence that Netherlandish porringers commonly had two handles is provided by several 16th- and 17th-century examples illustrated by Boschma (1971), pp. 30–33, pls. 11–13 and 17.

2. Note that all items lacking site identification come from locations on the north side of Tooley Street.

3. The most complete of the delftware porringers from Jamestown has wall decoration of this type. Unfortunately, it is an unstratified item. See Cotter (1958), p. 184, pl. 82, upper right. Another example was found in a context of 1652–1656 on the St. Nicholas's Almshouses site in Bristol. Barton (1964), 200–201, no. 9.

1.
2.
3.
4.
5.
6.
7.
8.
COLOR KEY
DARK BLUE
LIGHT BLUE
ORANGE
YELLOW
SCALE
INCHES
1
2

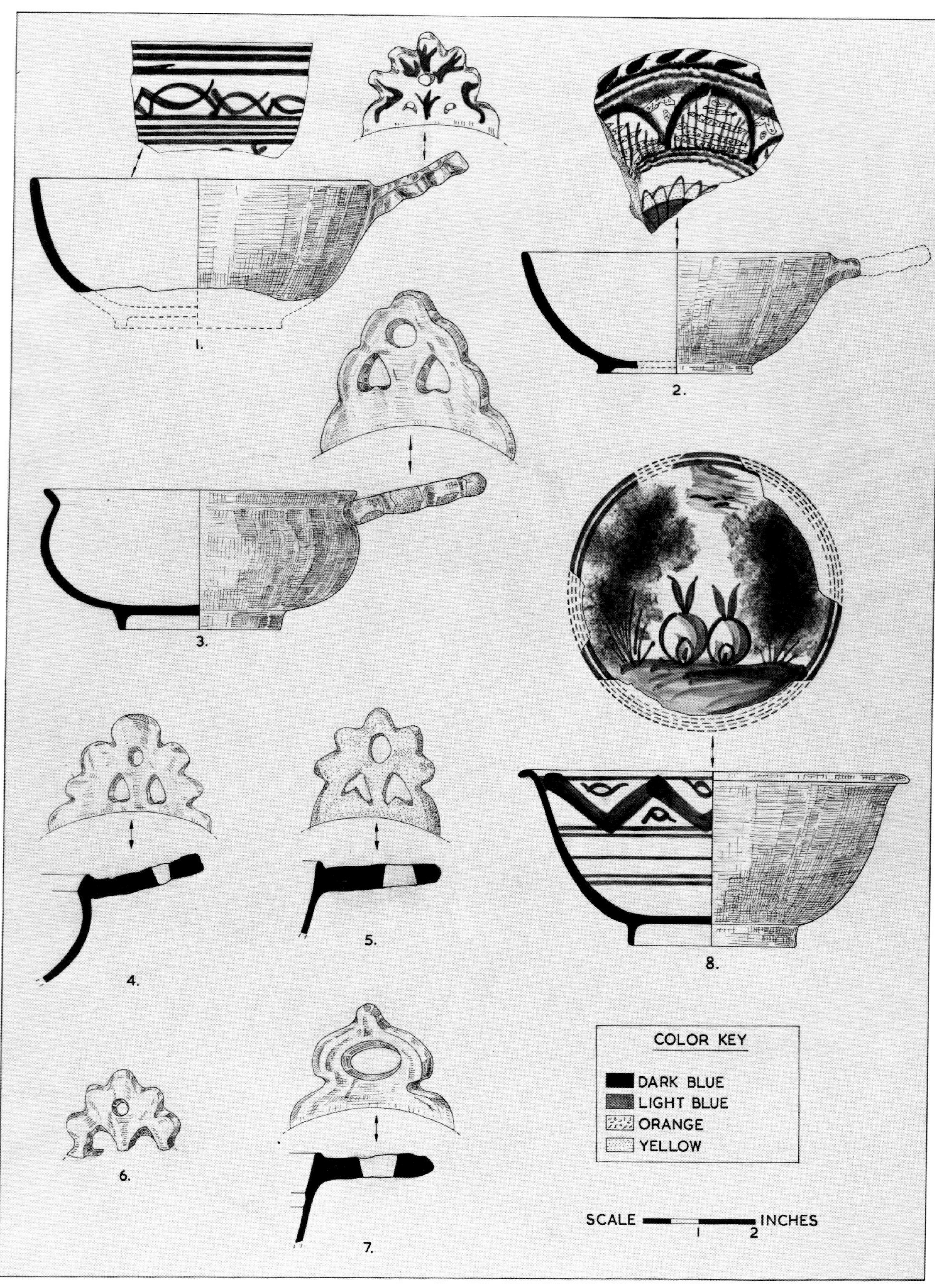

FIGURE XIV

wall decoration comprising a series of blue arcs "barred" with narrow blue lines, crossed with orange stripes, and with dotted orange chevrons between, the zone enclosed between triple blue bands. A bright yellow band encircles the central blue pinwheel and overlies the ends of the radiating "petals." The rim is blue dashed and the remaining handle fragment is a bright green. The exterior glaze is of uneven thickness and a greenish gray, marred by an irregular patch of cobalt-tinted white glaze as used on the interior. The base within the square cut footring is unglazed, the body yellow and containing no inclusions. Insufficient handle survives to indicate its piercing. Height: 2 1/8 inches. Site not recorded. About 1635–1650.

3. Porringer of shallow, bulbous form, with large and heavy handle, everted lip, white glazed inside and out, heavily crazed over all, and pinkish at the edges, the body yellow and without inclusions. The footring is square cut and the base rises slightly internally.[4] The handle is a good example of the fully developed seven-lobed form pierced with two hearts and a single circular hole.[5] Bowl height: 2 1/2 inches. Site not recorded. About 1680–1710.

4. Porringer wall and handle fragment of type similar to, but smaller than, no. 3 above; white tin glazed inside and out, heavily crazed but lacking the pinkish tint of no. 3; the body yellow and without inclusions. The closest dated parallel is provided by an example in the Colonial Williamsburg Collection marked 1698 and decorated in an importantly debased version of the Wan Li bird-on-rock design.[6] Approximate diameter: 6 inches. Site not recorded. About 1680–1710.

5. Porringer handle, yellow-surfaced biscuit pink in the core; five rather than the usual seven lobes; two heart-shaped holes and one circular hole. The example differs from all the other examples in that the three holes were cut from beneath and therefore are much larger on the underside. The wall of the bowl is straight and not everted as are the later specimens described above (nos. 3 and 4). The irregular treatment of the five handle lobes might be considered a development of the type demonstrated by no. 1. Approximate diameter: 5 1/4 inches. Site not recorded. About 1650–1670.

6. Porringer handle, plain white tin glazed overall, hard yellow body; smaller than any of the others; pierced by two heart-shaped holes and one circular hole, all cut from above. Maximum surviving width: 2 inches. Site not recorded. About 1670–1700.

7. Porringer handle and wall fragment, the essentially oval handle clipped at either side to create a single oval lobe with a nipple terminal; the oval pierced by one large hole of corresponding shape and cut from above. The body yellow and without inclusions; thick white tin glazed overall, slightly pink cast and with very little crazing. The bowl rim is straight in the manner of the early

---

4. The bowl shape occurs in silver by 1678 (*Country Life*, CLI [April 27, 1972], suppl., 44), but it is doubtful whether it was adopted by delftware potters until several years later.

5. The origins of the double heart and round hole handle design are thought to be metallic, i.e., in silver and pewter. However, it occurs in its fully developed five (rather than seven) lobed form by 1662, as is demonstrated by an example thus dated and decorated in polychrome with the figures of a countryman and his wife. The bowl has a straight rim but is decorated around the walls with two zones of impressed bosses convex on the interior. See Berry (1933), p. 23, no. 29 and pl. XVIIB. There are three more porringers with this bowl shape, but only one with the hearts and round hole handle, and that, although decorated with a portrait of Charles II, is undated. See Grigaut (1954), p. 17, no. 18. The others are both dated and both are in the Colonial Williamsburg Collection. One has lost its handle but is dated 1672 (53.974) and is important in that it provides the latest known date for the bowl style. The other is dated 1660 and is decorated with a full-length portrait of Charles II in polychrome, but its handle differs from all other examples by being made up from four S-bent rolls of clay to create a much lighter but still heartlike handle design (illustrated in Sotheby's sale catalogue, March 24, 1959, p. 25, no. 98). The impressed boss technique seems to have begun on plates and platters (Pls. 28 and 34) and later to have been popular on white posset pots and candlesticks (see p. 72, n. 4).

As noted above (n. 1), three Dutch versions of the heart-pierced porringer handle were mistakenly published by Garner (1948), pl. 12, as English. Dated 1686, these differ from the usual London version in that they are pierced by three radiating heart-shaped holes to create a fretted floral motif.

6. Dated specimens are rare, but an example with this style of handle and marked "Mary Miller 1727" was illustrated in Christie's ceramic sale catalogue for March 9, 1970, p. 7, no. 10. A blue line around the wall slightly above the girth might support a "Blood porringer" identification for this example.

examples represented by nos. 1, 2, and 5. There is a decorated example of the same shape in the collection of Mr. Louis Lipski dated 1673,[7] and another in the Birmingham Museum and Art Gallery decorated with a portrait of James II and dated 1686.[8] The latter's bowl has an everted rim in the manner of nos. 3 and 4, and seems to represent an evolutionary step in the development, or rather the decline, of this handle form.[9] Approximate diameter: 5 inches. Site not recorded. About 1665–1685.

8. Bowl with relatively straight wall, small everted rim, and straight square cut footring, slightly blue-tinted white tin glaze overall, decorated in blue on the inside. Specks of blue unintentionally dot the exterior, and there is a piece of what appears to be a sagger peg beneath the surviving rim fragment. The central motif of two departing rabbits may have been taken from a tile design.[10] The flanking bushes are sponged rather than painted, although the ground color is brushed, as is the sky with its three stylized birds. The wall of the bowl is ornamented with a double line above the base design, then a single line followed by two more lines, and a chevron-decorated zone (with "A" motifs between) and a single line above. No parallels for this design have been found, but the bowl is of a shape that can be attributed to the late 17th century. Height: 3 1/16 inches. Site 6. About 1680–1700.

FIGURE XV

1. Pitcher or handled bottle; base, lower wall, and handle terminal fragments only; tin glazed inside and out, and decorated in blue with chinoiserie motif of uncertain form but involving rocks and "grasses." The body is thin, very yellow, and without inclusions. The glaze has the high gloss characteristic of Netherlandish products, and part of a star or cross mark in blue on the base suggests a similar origin. The handle is not shown in profile, its placement being such that to do so the surviving decoration would be obscured. The rat-tail style handle terminal is enclosed within a thin blue line and the handle itself seems to have been blue dashed. De Jonge shows two bottles that may be of this type, although with handles commencing at the shoulder rather than at the lower wall; these he attributes to the late 17th century.[1] Approximate base diameter: 2 3/4 inches. Site 3.[2] Probably Dutch. About 1680–1700.

2. Porringer wall and handle fragments; the standard yellow biscuit coated with an opaque blue glaze inside and out, and decorated in the so-called "bleu persan" style of Nevers, with white tin glaze splashed on the surface, the latter becoming bluish gray through prefiring contact with the blue covering glaze.[3] The bowl rim is everted in the manner of Fig. XIV, no. 4, and the handle

---

7. Lipski (1968), 149 and pl. 152.

8. Garner and Archer (1972), pl. 32B.

9. Another example having a much larger oval hole that transforms the handle into a loop with a lug is illustrated by Bedford (1966), p. 26. Although the porringer is undated, it is decorated in Nevers "bleu persan" style and so can be attributed to the last decades of the 17th century (see Fig. XV, no. 2). It is important to note, however, that the Bedford specimen has a straight rim in the style of Fig. XIV, no. 7, suggesting that it belongs to the beginning rather than the end of "bleu persan's" popularity, i.e., about 1680. The British Museum possesses a comparable white glazed handle fragment found in Tooley Street in 1907 (see p. 68, n. 2). No. 1907, 10-14, 19.

10. Although no such rabbit-decorated delft tiles have been found, the comparable treatment of sheep and other domestic animals is relatively common. For example, see Korf (1964), pl. 15, upper right.

---

1. De Jonge (1947), p. 215, pl. 187, p. 215, pl. 188. There is also a small Dutch delftware "milk jug" of rather similar form in the Glaisher Collection (Rackham [1935], I, 341, no. 2717, II, p. 209) that has its handle anchored lower on the wall. This example is attributed to the early 18th century.

2. The objects illustrated in Fig. XV are all allegedly from a brick-lined cesspit in Black Swan Yard. However, the porringer (no. 2) has one piece marked as coming from that location and another joining sherd indicated as having been found at Battle Bridge House (Site 6), which clearly indicates that the collection has suffered some mishandling since it was assembled.

3. The blue ground color is generally assumed to contain a tin oxide opacifier, but it seemed that this might be unnecessary, for the cobalt-colored lead glaze used in "Littler's blue" and in decorating Rhenish stonewares contains no tin. Furthermore, it might be expected that the tin would reduce the brilliance of the blue. Miss

was pierced by two hearts in the same style. A third circular hole can reasonably be assumed. No dated English examples of this Nevers technique are recorded, but specimens decorated in late Ming style indicate that the blue glazed ware was popular in the late 17th century.[4] Archaeological evidence generally seems to support such dating, although examples in the Ming style have been found in contexts dating as late as the mid-18th century.[5] Approximate bowl diameter: 5 1/4 inches. Site 3. About 1680–1700.

3. Lid rim and flange fragment, white tin glazed overall, markedly pink in crevices, and the glaze thick and bubbled; the body yellow and without inclusions. Such lids were used as covers for the straight-sided or bag-shaped posset pots of the third quarter of the 17th century.[6] Approximate rim diameter: 7 3/4 inches. Site 3. About 1650–1675.

4. Bowl or flower pot, originally with pedestal foot, tin glazed overall, decorated in blue with alternating floral and late Ming style landscape panels, the body soft, yellow, and without inclusions. The dramatic flaring of the rim indicates that this bowl did not have handles. In the absence of an obviously English parallel, and in view of the strength of the blue decoration, a Dutch origin cannot be ruled out. Approximate rim diameter: 9 3/4 inches. Site 3. About 1680–1700.

5. Ointment pot rim and wall fragment, white tin glazed, the body hard and yellow. The shape is akin to that shown in Fig. IV, no. 6, and can be attributed to the second half of the 17th century. Approximate diameter: 2 1/2 inches. Site 3. About 1650–1680.

6–8. Tobacco pipe bowls of a type generally attributed to the third quarter of the 17th century. Stem hole diameters are 9/64 inches, 7/64 inches, and 7/64 inches respectively. The three pipes represent the range of bowl variations in a group of ten, the rest being comparable to no. 7 and having similar stem hole measurements. Using the Bindford formula,[7] the mean date for the group should be 1656.37, but based as it is on far too small a sample, this dating for the contents of the Black Swan Yard cesspit is palpably awry. Site 3. About 1650–1680.

Arlene Palmer, assistant curator at the Henry Francis du Pont Winterthur Museum, very kindly undertook to run a Kevex spectrometer test on three specimens in the Winterthur Collection using a typical English white-ground delftware plate as a control, an English blue-ground delftware example with a white chinoiserie motif, and a French blue-ground Nevers specimen. The test showed that the English "bleu persan" contained as much tin in its glaze as did the white-grounded control specimen. The Nevers example, however, showed only a trace of tin, indicating that it possessed an essentially cobalt-stained lead glaze. It is possible that further testing may establish this difference as a means of distinguishing between French and English "bleu persan" specimens.

4. See Fig. XIV, n. 9. A "rope" handled flower vase was found in London, Eastcheap, in 1949 in a context of about 1680–1710 and was published in *The Illustrated London News* (October 8, 1949), 8. Similar but unstratified handle fragments have been found at Yorktown, Virginia, and at the Chiswell site in Williamsburg. A saucer in what may be termed reverse Nevers (i.e., blue splashed on white) was found in a context of about 1702–1710 at Tutter's Neck, Virginia. Noël Hume (1966a), pp. 65–66, Fig. 18, no. 8. A porringer decorated with similar splashed white on blue glaze, but with its handles pierced by a single heart-shaped hole, was illustrated in Sotheby's ceramic sale catalogue for October 15, 1959. Another similarly glazed and handled specimen, but with a straight-sided bowl akin to those shown in Fig. XIV, nos. 5 and 7, was illustrated in *The Connoisseur,* CL (June 1962), 131. The latter example presumably belongs to the beginning of the "bleu persan" range, i.e., about 1680.

5. A so-called relish dish akin to Garner and Archer (1972), pl. 49B, right, has been found at the Chiswell site in Williamsburg (6941, E.R. 1569G-2H) in a context of about 1750.

6. Garner and Archer (1972), pl. 26B, an example in the Glaisher Collection (No. 1319) dated 1651. There is in the British Museum a straight-sided posset pot decorated with the standard bird-on-rock motif and dated 1632 below one handle and on the inside of the lid. Hobson (1903), p. 140, no. E.101. The prevalence of decorated posset pots with lids in the later years of the 17th century suggests that most of the decorated *and* plain white posset pots surviving from it were originally supplied with lids. This was probably true even of the small white pot shown in Pl. 8. For another plain white posset pot having a lid with a broad rim comparable to the fragment discussed here, see *Antique Collector,* XXXVI (December 1965–January 1966), xi.

7. This dating formula is summarized by Noël Hume (1970), pp. 299–301. The bowl type is shown in its chronological context ibid., p. 303, Fig. 97, no. 11. See also Oswald (1975), pp. 40–41, type 17, about 1640–1670.

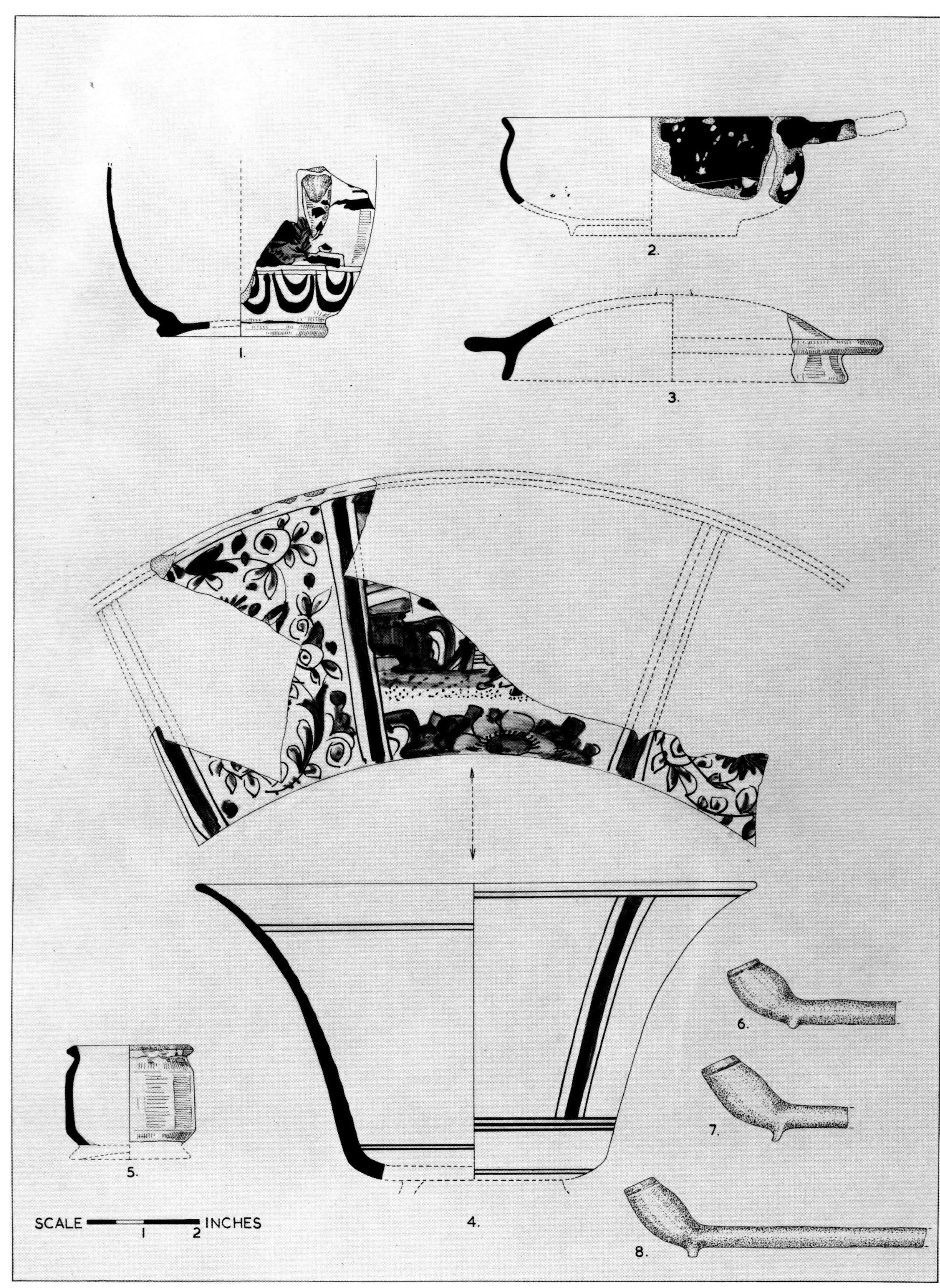

FIGURE XV

FIGURE XVI

1. Chocolate cup or capuchine,[1] foot and lower wall fragments only; tin glazed overall, the white ground markedly pink and suggestive of an early date; the body yellow and without inclusions. The foot is slightly spread and there is a pronounced ridge at the girth, a feature borrowed from contemporary silver forms. The blue decoration above the ridge is of uncertain character; below it is a repeating chain motif built from hooks and swags. Encircling the top of the foot are three blue lines, all of them defused in firing. Foot diameter: 1 5/8 inches. Site 6. About 1685–1710.[2]

2. Tea bowl, blue tinted, white tin glazed overall, the body yellow to buff. The lip is slightly everted,[3] the wall very thin, and the base and footring relatively thick. This last feature is peculiar to the specimen, for the collection includes another example identically decorated whose foot is delicately V-shaped and whose base is of paper thinness. Both cups are decorated in blue on the outside with four alternating floral panels, with narrow chevron-painted vertical ribbons between. Inside, the bases are painted with a rosette surrounded by swags and alternating "crow's feet" and G-shaped curlicues. Below the interior lip is a thick chain or stylized garland motif.[4] Height: 2 7/8 inches. Site 6. About 1690–1725.

3. Tea bowl of type similar to the above, the tin glaze comparably tinted, but the footring more sharply cut and the base raised within it. The blue decoration of birds and flowers is derived from Wan Li porcelain, and there is a slightly larger but otherwise identical flower on the interior base. On the exterior base, however, there is a painter's mark in the shape of an "N" or a "2." The interior rim design does not survive. Foot diameter: 1 7/16 inches. Site 6. About 1700–1725.

4. Bowl or large cup, tin glazed overall, the body yellow and without inclusions. The strikingly brilliant blue decoration is Islamic in style and is created from blues of three degrees of intensity. There is a wide blue band around the interior lip and traces of what may have been a star design on the interior base. A fragment of an identical cup has been found in James City County, Virginia, in a context of about 1690–1710, but it is of such poor execution that it might be mistaken for a waster.[5] Portuguese.[6] Approximate diameter: 3 1/2 inches. Site 6. About 1660–1685.

5. Bowl usually described as a slop basin,[7] thick tin glaze overall, decorated in poly-

---

1. The term is derived from the ca. 1690 trade card of Nottingham stoneware potter James Morley. See Lewis (1956), pl. 85.

2. A close parallel for the shape is provided by a polychrome-decorated example in the Burnap Collection and there attributed on unspecified evidence to "ca. 1710–1720." See Taggart (1967), p. 53, no. 138. For a Scottish silver example of this general shape dated 1695, see Judith Banister, "Some Unusual Sporting Silver," *Country Life,* CXXXVI (August 6, 1964), 331, pl. 4. For another related cup of 1705, see ibid., CLIII (February 8, 1973), 39. A plate with comparable "hook-and-swag" decoration serving as a fence in a chinoiserie design is dated 1689 and is in the Victoria and Albert Museum (C.21-1963).

3. The everted lip sets these delicate, porcelain-copying tea bowls apart from most delftware cups of this period, for their rims are usually straight.

4. Decoration of similar character is to be seen on the marly of a plate dated 1689 in the Victoria and Albert Museum (C.21-1963).

5. Pettus site, Virginia Research Center for Archaeology Collection: KM.58A.

6. Evidence for the Portuguese origin of this bowl has been provided by Mr. R. J. Charleston, who has in his private collection a small covered bowl decorated in similar style and also with the arms of Portugal. To the top of its broken finial, the bowl and cover measure 4 3/4 inches in height. A photograph is on file at the Victoria and Albert Museum (Neg. no. Y.645). A rather similarly painted plate, although more clearly influenced by Ming porcelain, has been found in a mid-17th-century garderobe deposit at Ballyhack Castle in Ireland. Michael Archer has described the plate as representing "the first time that Portuguese delftware has been certainly identified from these islands [the British Isles] though a few sherds from the large Plymouth series have been suspected as such." Mr. Archer attributes the Ballyhack plate to the mid-17th century while Mr. Charleston places his bowl somewhat earlier in the same century. However, the shape of the Burnett Collection bowl (and, of course, that of the Virginia example) suggests a date no earlier than the third quarter of the 17th century. Fanning (1975), 106–107, Fig. 2, no. 5, and pl. IV, no. 1.

7. Bowls of this size are common on tavern sites and are to be seen in convivial paintings indicating that they were used as containers for liquor. See Oswald (1975), p. 31, pl. II, no. 3, for a conversation piece by Joseph Highmore, *Mr. Oldham and his friends,* dated 1740.

1.
2.
3.
4.
5.
6.
7.
8.
9.
10.
11.
COLOR KEY
DARK BLUE
LIGHT BLUE
RED
GREEN
SCALE
1
2
INCHES

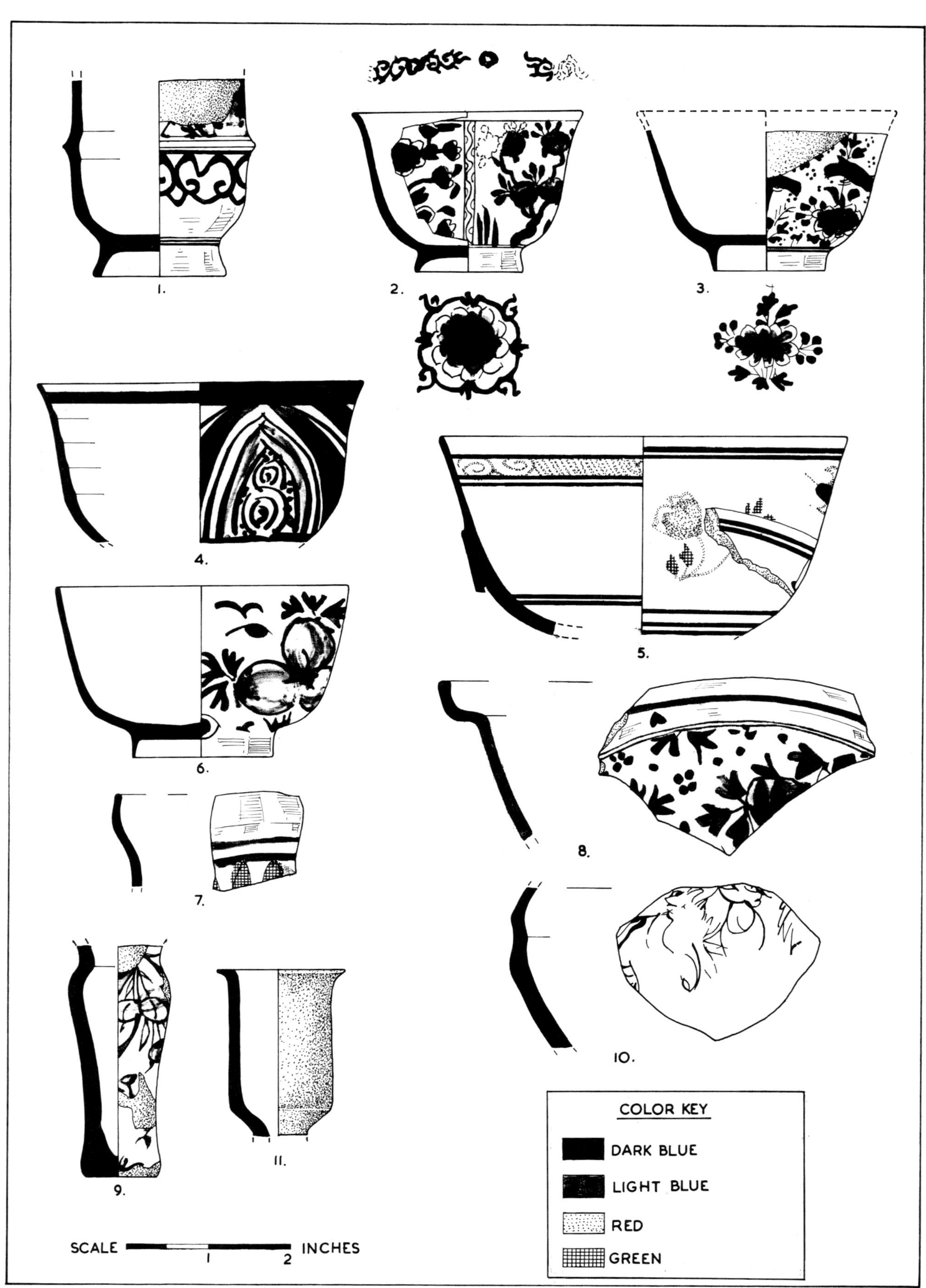

FIGURE XVI

chrome, and with part of an identical bowl adhering to the wall, making this specimen an indisputable waster. The exterior is decorated with simply executed flowers in what may be termed a very sticky red, in turn overlaid with green leaves.[8] The rim and lower wall are emphasized by groups of blue lines. Similar lines occur on the interior, and below the rim enclose a zone of red swirls and stripes. The thin body is of good quality, yellow, but not very hard. Approximate diameter: 4 5/8 inches. Site 6. About 1720–1740.

6. Large tea bowl, extremely poorly glazed over a buff body, yet the glaze appearing pinkish in thin areas and a greenish gray where it is thick and pooled. Much of the glaze has drifted up both the footring and the body suggesting that the cup was fired in an inverted position. However, there is no indication of sagger adherence at the rim, and the foot surface is unglazed, suggesting that kiln particles had been filed from the foot—the usual explanation for the absence of glaze on footrings. The crude fruit-and-frond decoration is pale blue and slightly blistered, suggesting that it, too, had been adversely affected by the cup's sojourn in the glost oven.[9] A probable waster.[10] Height: 2 inches. Site not recorded. About 1720–1740.

7. Flower pot, rim sherd only, thickly tin glazed and polychrome decorated, the body yellow and very granular in the fractures. The high gloss and the unusual treatment of the green leaves, outlined in manganese below two gray blue lines, suggest a possible Dutch origin for this specimen. Although it is impossible to be certain of the shape, it is likely that the vessel was pedestal footed.[11] Approximate rim diameter: 3 1/2 inches. Site not recorded. About 1710–1740.

8. Bowl with offset and shelved rim, thick white tin glaze overall, the body a pale yellow; decorated on the exterior only in very pale blue with a fruit-and-frond design similar to that used on no. 6. The brushwork is poor, but its stipple decoration around the fruit is clearly derived from a Chinese original. Such bowls were fitted with lids and were probably used for toilet purposes.[12] They are more common archaeologically than in museum collections. Approximate rim diameter: 7 1/4 inches. Site not recorded. About 1715–1740.

9. Perfume flask, thick white tin glaze overall, decorated with floral devices in pale blue; the body hard, granular in the fractures, and surprisingly thick. The base is so small that this flask could not stand and therefore cannot have been part of a miniature garniture. The rim is missing but seems to have been slightly everted. Surviving height: 2 11/16 inches. From a site in the vicinity of St. Olave's church. Probably late 17th to early 18th century.

10. Flask or bottle, body sherd only; thick white glaze on the outside but only a pool of glaze over part of the interior—suggesting a narrow-necked vessel not easily glazed internally. The flask was markedly ribbed at its girth and decorated with a dark blue and spidery rendering of the full-cheeked grotesque known to collectors as the "Pipe-

---

8. The rich sealing-wax red is usually considered to be the product of a secondary firing. But being overlaid by the green, one must conclude either that both colors (and thus virtually all this bowl's decoration) were applied in a post-glazing firing or that only one glost firing was necessary.

9. A plate with the fruit-and-frond motif dated 1698 is in the collection of the Victoria and Albert Museum (C.90-1931).

10. It is evident from examining much British pottery exported to America that items legitimately claimed as wasters when found on kiln sites must not be so construed elsewhere. Although this bowl would, by all reasonable standards, be considered a reject, potters were not averse to shipping "seconds" for sale to indiscriminating markets in rural or colonial areas where customers either gladly accepted second-rate goods at prices they could afford, or were too far-flung to lodge effective complaints.

11. For a much larger English version of this general type (about 1700), see Bedford (1966), p. 8; for a mid-18th-century example, see Garner and Archer (1972), pl. 97. This small sherd is illustrated to draw a distinction between vases with everted and shelved rims and bowls having similar rim forms, e.g., Fig. XVI, no. 8

12. Unstratified examples have been found in Williamsburg excavations, and there are several lid fragments in the collections; none, however, pierced as is the only published example. See Archer (1973), p. 37, no. 87. Decorated in polychrome, the author describes it as a "flower bowl" and attributes it to a date around 1730. It seems likely, however, that bowls of this type held flowers in a slightly unconventional manner, serving as containers for aromatic lavender or potpourri.

smoker,"[13] and usually attributable to the period 1650–1660.[14] These blowing profiles are normally seen at either end of drug jar labels, but in this case two heads appear to be drawn back to back.[15] Approximate girth diameter: 3 1/4 inches. Site 5. About 1630–1660.

11. Socket for a candlestick of late 17th- or 18th-century style;[16] pale pink biscuit; therefore unfinished and an extremely important diagnostic item. The wall is thick and the rim thickened, square cut, and slightly flaring. Socket height: 1 7/8 inches. Site not recorded. About 1675–1750.[17]

FIGURE XVII

1. Drug jar of albarello form, grayish white tin glaze inside and out, the body yellow at the unglazed rim, but buff to pink under the glaze. The wall is slightly more concave in the midsection than are those of any of the obviously Southwark examples in the Burnett Collection, and the decoration is more Italianate. The principal design is composed from rectangular panels outlined and diagonally crossed in blue, the resulting triangles partially filled by inner solid triangles built from three graduated stripes, those at top and bottom in blue and those at the sides in manganese purple. The panels are separated by two vertical blue lines with a broad yellow stripe between. Above, the panels are topped by two horizontal blue lines, a broad purple band, and two more blue lines; below, the purple band is flanked by single blue lines. At the shoulder and above the base are zones decorated with blue dots between horizontal blue lines. Probably of Antwerp manufacture. Approximate shoulder diameter: 4 3/4 inches. Site 6. About 1570–1610.

2. Drug jar of cylindrical form, very thinly grayish white, tin glazed inside and out, the exterior polychrome decoration so faint as to be almost invisible; the body yellow, soft, and with no visible inclusions. The glaze condition suggests that this may be a waster. The unusual flaring foot is undercut so that the outer edge does not touch the ground, and the base has the curious arced pulling mark encountered on several biscuit specimens. The lower wall is decorated with four broad purple bands, and the central body zone is occupied by a broad but pale blue chain design. Base diameter: 4 9/16 inches. Site not recorded. About 1640–1680.[1]

3. Drug jar of albarello type, base and lower wall fragments only, grayish white tin glaze inside and out, pink in spots on the inside base possibly drawn from red ochre in-

---

13. The so-called "pipe-smoker" occurs in a variety of forms, all of them seemingly developed from blowing cherubs of the kind one finds on early nautical charts. In some cases the cheeks are no longer inflated and the blown air has become an elongated tongue that somewhat resembles a lion's tail. It is this that has been described as a pipe. The illustrated example, although incomplete, is therefore important in that it shows the head in its full-blown form.

14. Crellin (1969), pp. 17–18, pls. 10 and 12.

15. The British Museum possesses an oviform mug painted in blue with the name IOHN LEMAN and the date 1634 enclosed within a panel terminating in similarly "blowing" grotesque heads. See Hobson (1903), p. 133, item E 37. It is possible, therefore, that the Leman mug is a better indication of the date of the Burnett Collection fragment than are the previously cited drug jars. There are also less obvious relationships with the open-mouthed and long-tongued profiles decorating the Victoria and Albert Museum's polychrome-painted mug inscribed ANN CHAPMAN ANNO 1642. (No. 1107-1853.) See Archer (1973), p. 19 and pl. 64, no. 22.

16. Because only the socket survives, it is possible that it was intended to be part of the dual-purpose lid for a delftware foodwarmer. See Bedford (1966), p. 39.

17. Garner and Archer (1972), pl. 75B, attributed to Liverpool and to about 1750. This example is in the Colonial Williamsburg Collection (1964-443) and is one of the very few recorded specimens of an 18th-century English delftware candlestick. One might expect the excavated socket form to have been borrowed from silver, but very few metal sockets of the 18th century are without sculptured ornament. In the absence of the stem, it is possible that this candleholder was copied from a much earlier 17th-century type. See, for example, *Antiques,* XCII (December 1967), 814, bearing the London date letter for 1679.

1. On the evidence of comparably shaped polychrome-decorated ointment pots, e.g., Pl. 12, right, and Fig. V, no. 1, the unusual foot shape suggests an early date. The pale blue chain decoration, on the other hand, is of a type that persisted well through the 18th century, although generally on much broader jars and with blue rather than purple flanking bands. There are two more non-waster examples of good color in the collection, neither of which possesses the raised foot. One is otherwise of comparable proportions, but the other had been wider than it was tall, with a base diameter of approximately 5 3/4 inches. Both are from Site 6 and presumably of similar date.

1.
2.
4.
3.
5.
6.
8.
7.
COLOR KEY
DARK BLUE
LIGHT BLUE
PURPLE
YELLOW
RED
GREEN
SCALE
1
2
INCHES

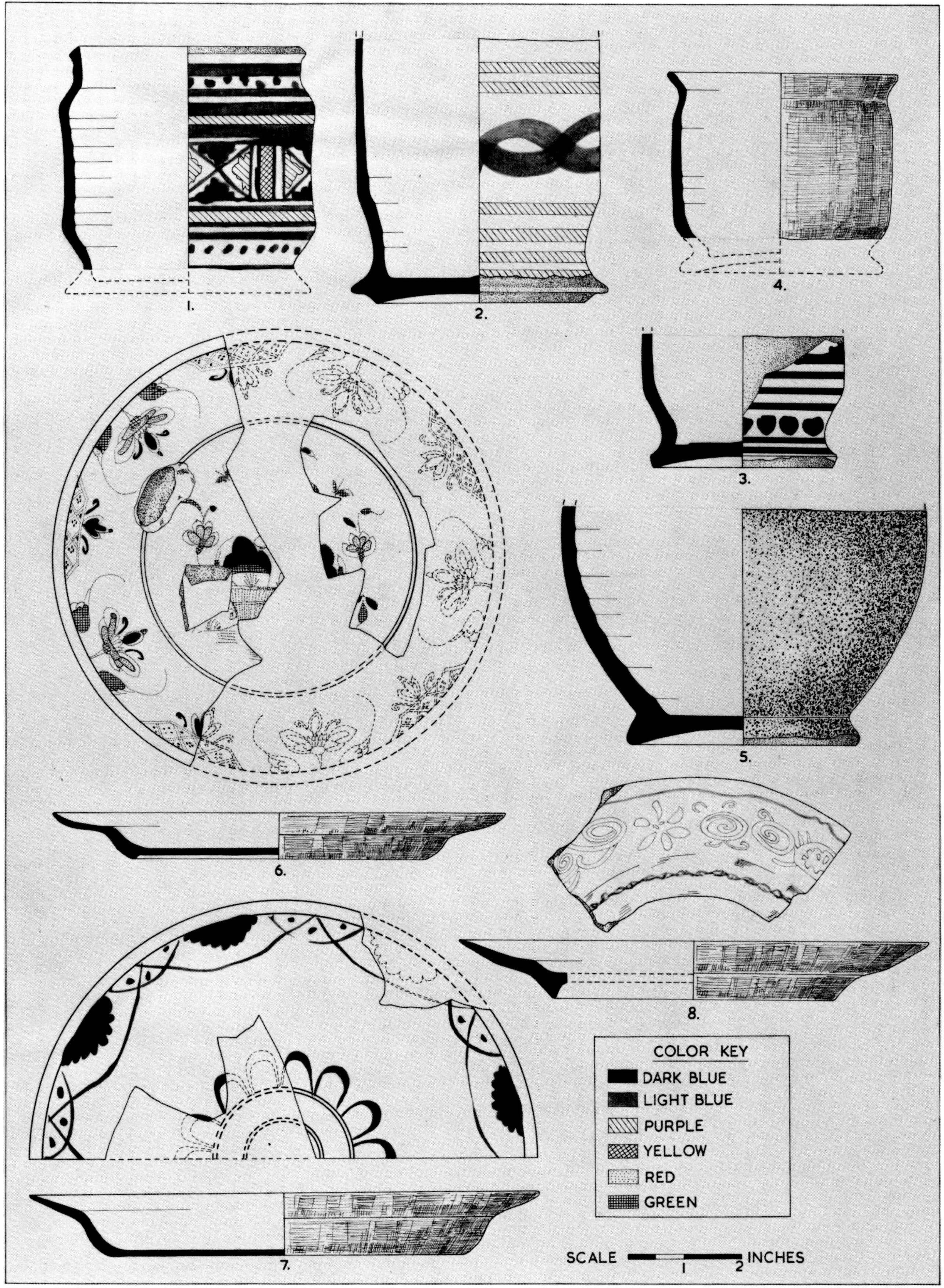

FIGURE XVII

clusions in the soft yellow body.[2] The latter is toned to a pale pink on the unglazed underside of a slightly rising base. The exterior is decorated in a bright blue, with two bands above the foot and three more above a row of dots; the wall decorated with the beginning of a graduated three-line triangle in the style of Pl. 12 and Fig. V, nos. 1–3. It is extremely likely that this jar was also decorated with triangles in orange. Base diameter: 3 1/4 inches. Site not recorded. About 1612–1640.

4. Ointment pot of larger than average size, rim and wall fragment only, white tin glaze with pinkish cast overall, the body hard, granular, and yellow; wall markedly ribbed externally. Approximate rim diameter: 4 inches. Site not recorded. About 1670–1710.

5. Bottle or pitcher of large size and bulbous form, base and lower wall fragment only, white tin glazed internally and with powdered manganese stipple on the outside; the body soft, yellow, and with a few small red ochre inclusions. The interior glaze is broadly crazed, but that of the exterior is not. The foot is slightly expanded and raised within. Base diameter: 3 15/16 inches. Site not recorded. About 1640–1675.[3]

6. Plate; the overall tin glaze a greenish blue rather than the cold pinkish white characteristic of earlier specimens; polychrome decorated, and the body a pale yellow with no visible inclusions. The glaze has pooled away from the wall in so large a patch that this plate must be a waster, and therefore provides important evidence of continued potting in St. Olave Parish in the second quarter of the 18th century.[4] The central basket of flowers motif comes orginally from Chinese porcelain but is common on French faiënce. The diaper pattern of the marly is executed in red and blue, as are the alternating flowers, although with the addition of yellow. Green is used in the winglike leaves flanking the flowers, and the entire palette is employed in the central design.[5] The plate has its base raised within the wall and belongs to Garner's shape D, which he ascribes to a post-1730 date.[6] The marly is slightly dished (an effect accentuated by the pooling of glaze on the underside), and is also marred by a large sagger peg mark around which the glaze has gathered. For intact examples of this plate decoration see Pls. 52–54, but note that the central design is encircled by a chainlike motif whereas the excavated example bears only two thin blue lines that Garner has claimed to be a Lambeth characteristic.[7] Diameter: 7 7/8 inches. Site 6. About 1730–1750.

7. Plate; the thick overall tin glaze a greenish blue, polychrome decorated; the body hard, granular, and yellow. The shape belongs to Garner's type B, which he attributes to Lambeth and to a date range of 1690–1780.[8] The marly is narrow, slightly upturned, and marred by heavy sagger peg scars; the base has no footring. The marly decoration comprises a purple outer line and a pattern of crudely executed swags, dots, and clustered "petals" in blue. The central motif is lost but was surrounded by concentric circles in purple within radiating blue swags. A matching rim fragment has been found at Lambeth.[9] Diameter: 9 inches. Site 6. About 1725–1750.

---

2. A slightly more angular jar of this type is included among the biscuit specimens. See Fig. III, no. 12.

3. A manganese-stippled jug of comparable size and dated 1673 is included in the Burnap Collection (Taggart [1956], p. 99, no. 98), but its wall slopes gently outward to the shoulder, whereas the Burnett example seems to have been more globular. Although no manganese-decorated delftware bottles of this size appear to have been published, the Burnap Collection includes a purple-stippled bottle 7 11/16 inches in height, evidence, therefore, that such decoration did occur on bottles. Ibid., p. 45, no. 84, attributed to 1660–1672. Another example 8 3/4 inches in height was auctioned at Sotheby's on September 30, 1975, and in the catalogue (p. 8, no. 31) was attributed to the first half of the 17th century.

4. Where the glaze has run, the redeposited pool is much whiter than elsewhere, and the greenish blue cast has separated into a transparent lead glaze pushed ahead and away from the flowing tin.

5. For further design discussion, see p. 49.

6. Garner and Archer (1972), p. 81.

7. Garner (1937), p. 53.

8. Garner and Archer (1972), p. 81.

9. Garner (1937), facing p. 57, pl. XIIa, row 3, no. 1.

8. Plate; the overall tin glaze a bluish green, the body yellow and granular. The shape is Garner's type D,[10] the marly somewhat upturned, and the base raised within the wall. The rim is scarred by the removal of a large sagger peg. The marly is decorated with an outer single blue line that has run badly in firing, but the broad area within the circle is decorated in "bianco supra bianco" copying better quality Chinese porcelain. The technique of applying white decoration to a tinted "white" background is attributed to Lambeth, Bristol, and Liverpool. However, this pattern of crudely painted white flowers and spirals is closely paralleled by an example dated 1747 in the Robert Hill Warren Collection at Oxford and there attributed to Lambeth.[11] The Oxford specimen, although matching in its white design, differs in that it lacks the Burnett specimen's outer blue line or its chainlike ring at the base of the wall, the exact character of which was obscured when the color ran in the kiln. Approximate diameter: 7 3/4 inches. Site not recorded. About 1745–1760.

FIGURE XVIII

1. Chamber pot base and wall fragment; hard, tight-grained yellow biscuit. The absence of ochre inclusions points to a date no earlier than the second half of the 17th century; at the same time the vessel's bag shape, low shoulder cordon (indicating a shallow form), and vestigial, everted, and rolled up foot all place this example among the earliest recorded chamber pot forms in delftware. Base diameter: 6 7/16 inches. Site 5. About 1650–1675.[1]

10. Garner and Archer (1972), p. 81.

11. Ray (1968), pl. 80, no. 152. A large part of a plate with a comparable border has been found at Lambeth; see Garner (1937), facing p. 57, pl. XVa. As neither the Garner specimen nor that in the Burnett Collection can claim to be wasters, it is impossible to be sure which was made where.

2. Chamber pot; thick white tin glaze inside and out, but unglazed on the base save for small spots visible only under a magnifying glass. The body glaze has a pinkish cast and is heavily crazed, and the body itself is hard, granular, and yellow. The rim is everted and slightly thickened, there is a heavy shoulder cordon that is really an undercut shelf, the lower wall curves into a short square cut foot, and the lower handle terminal is folded up upon itself. Height: 4 11/16 inches. Site not recorded. About 1675–1725.

3. Chamber pot; thick white tin glaze inside and out, less pink than no. 1, and glazed on the base. The body is less hard and a paler yellow. The rim is everted and slightly downbent, and the shoulder cordon less pronounced than that of no. 1. The glaze is pitted and pooled in places, but not sufficiently for the pot to have been rejected. No handle survives. Height: 4 13/16 inches. Site not recorded. About 1675–1725.

4–9. Chamber pot rim and wall fragments illustrating the range of shapes represented. The thick pinkish white glaze of no. 5, marred only by a few widely spaced crazing lines, suggests that this is one of the earliest in the group, that is, about 1670–1700. The latest is no. 9, its horizontally everted rim and bluish gray glaze setting it apart from the rest and suggesting a date in the mid-18th century.[2] No. 8 has a greenish cast to its glaze, a

1. Although no dated delftware chamber pots are recorded, this example's bag-shaped body form closely resembles that of two dated posset pots, one dated 1651 (*Country Life*, CLVI [November 14, 1974], 1434, pl. 1), and the other dated 1661 (Crellin [1969], p. 211, pl. 353). The Burnett Collection includes another biscuit basal sherd having a comparable foot, but the ware paler in color and less hard fired. Base diameter approximately 6 1/4 inches. Site 5. About 1650–1675.

2. These chamber pots become taller as they get later, the cordon disappears, the rims are less authoritatively everted, and by the mid-18th century the glaze is usually a bluish gray. For a transitional example discarded in about 1730, see Noël Hume (1958), 162. For another of this type, along with an example of a mid-18th-century form, see Noël Hume (1962), pp. 205 and 207, Fig. 26, nos. 5 and 6, both interred around 1772. For a general review of ceramic chamber pot shapes, see Celoria (1968).

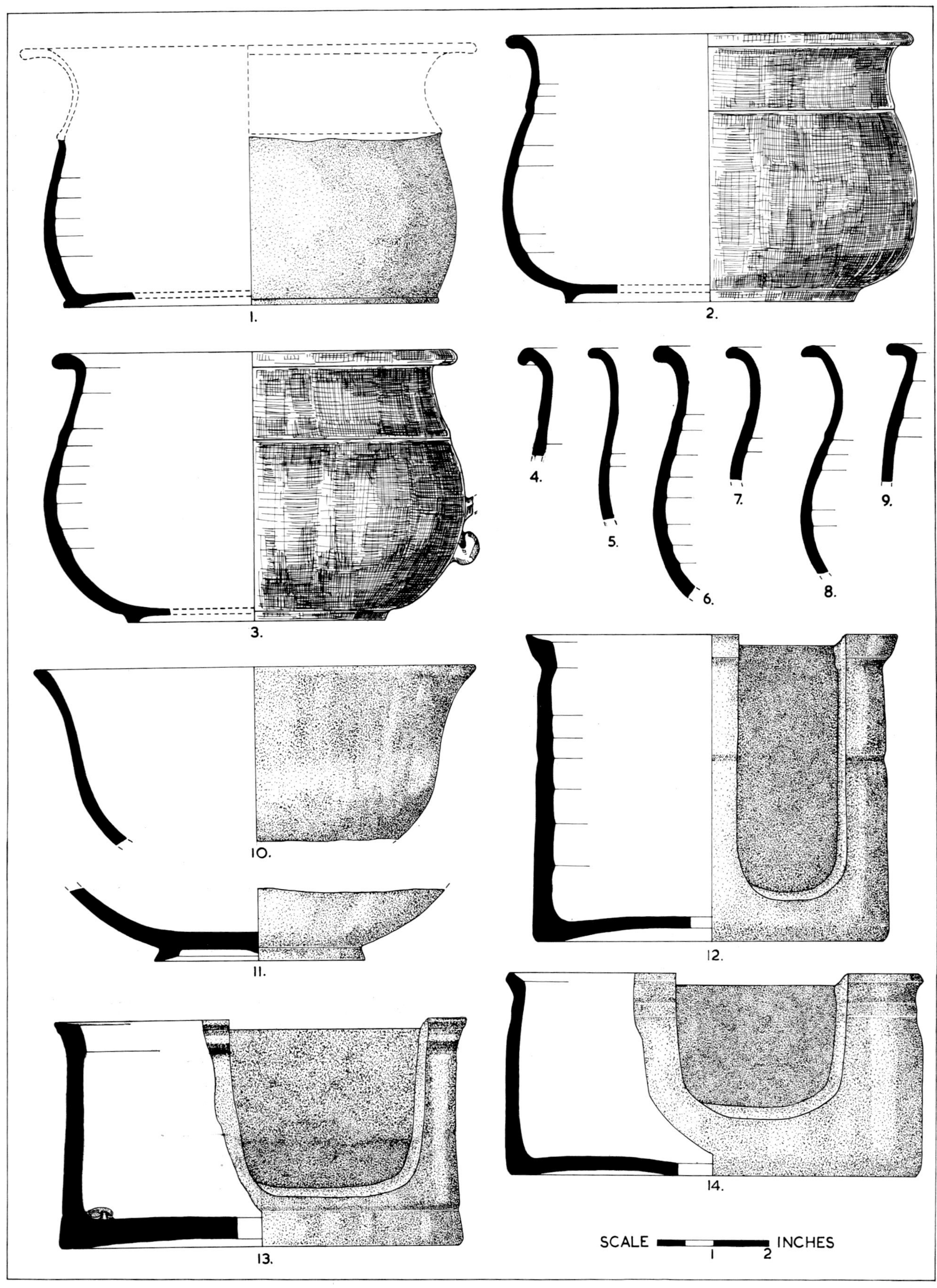

FIGURE XVIII

feature encountered in contexts of about 1720–1740.

10. Bowl; rim and wall fragment, hard biscuit, yellow on the outside but pinkish in the core, a gray line dividing the two but too deep in the ware to be considered evidence of slip. The core exhibits small red ochre and sand particles. The rim is thickened and flaring rather than everted, indicative of an earlier date than the bowl shown in Fig. XIV, no. 8. The profile is much more akin to that of Fig. XI, no. 6, and so is suggestive of a date in the second quarter of the 17th century. The fine quality of both clay and potting is believed to be misleadingly indicative of a later date.[3] Approximate rim diameter: 8 inches. Site 5. About 1630–1660.

11. Bowl or charger base, the former suggested by the relatively small footring, the absence of a suspension hole, and the curvature of the exterior wall. The extreme thickness of this biscuit specimen is such that the exterior and interior profiles suggest different vessel shapes. The body is a patchy pink and yellow, but generally pink in section with inclusions of yellow clay and red ochre, the latter protruding from both the interior and exterior surfaces. Foot diameter: 3 3/4 inches. Site 2. About 1612–1660.

12. Sagger of cylindrical form, the wall having a probably unintentional external groove above the midsection and a rim slightly thickened, offset, and grooved on the top creating a shape reminiscent of 17th-century stoneware butter jars. A slot approximately 1 3/4 inches wide has been cut from the rim to within 3/8 inch of the floor, and there is a trace of a central hole in the base.[4] The yellow body is poorly wedged and contains many inclusions of both pale yellow clay and red ochre. The surface is extremely friable and retains traces of yellow lead glaze inside and pinkish tin glaze on the underside of the base. Diameter: 6 5/16 inches; height: 5 3/8 inches. Site 2. 17th century.[5]

13. Sagger of short cylindrical form, the wall leaning slightly inward to the rim, which is flattened and gently everted as the result of pressure between forefinger and thumb. A 3 1/2-inch-wide slot was cut through the wall when the pot was in leather-hard condition. There is also an irregular central hole in the base 1 1/16 inches in diameter. The body, although exhibiting several large red ochre inclusions, is otherwise comparable to that used in the manufacture of quality delftware—unlike the poorly wedged fabrics employed for nos. 12 and 14. The interior to one side of the opening is coated with a very thin pinkish glaze; on the other side of the opening there are patches of thick tin glaze that appear greenish in the pools, imbedded in one of which is part of the rim from a small delftware drug jar. Patches of thin pinkish glaze are concentrated toward the base center, and the thicker tin glaze is present in the central hole and in the basal fracture. Diameter: 7 1/8 inches; height: 4 inches. Site 2. 17th century.

14. Sagger of short cylindrical form comparable to no. 12 but shorter; the yellow body poorly wedged and veined with ochre bearing clay; the surface extremely friable and partially glazed on the inside with an unintentional coating that varies from opaque white to transparent pink. Approximate diameter: 6 3/4 inches; height: 3 1/2 inches. Site 2. 17th century.

---

3. There is another biscuit bowl fragment of similar shape from the same location. This example is pink-bodied but contains massive yellow inclusions along with occasional flecks of red ochre. The potting is coarse, with the exterior surface ridged and scratched with what at first appears to have been a narrow smoothing board but which is more likely to have been the result of a scarred thumb. Similar although less distinct grooving is visible on the exterior surface of the illustrated specimen, indicating, in spite of the totally different bodies, that both bowls were the work of the same man. Second bowl, rim diameter approximately 9 3/8 inches. Site 5. About 1630–1660. The shape of both bowls is best paralleled by an example from Oxford (see Pl. 49), and by another with similar decoration from Colchester (Blake, Hurst, and Corant [1961], 7, Fig. 32, no. 33), and it is on the basis of the design of these bowls that the biscuit specimens are dated.

4. The base of this example is fractured close to the center, but the clay being so poorly bonded, it is difficult to be certain that what appears to be a deliberate central hole is really that. However, the collection also includes a fragment of a smaller sagger of comparable type (diameter 5 inches) which does retain its intentionally cut central hole. It is reasonable to conclude, therefore, that all such 17th-century saggers were pierced in this way.

5. Saggers of these 17th-century types have also been found in excavations at Norfolk House, Lambeth, showing that they are not peculiar to Southwark sites. See Bloice (1971), 118, Fig. 52, nos. 1 and 2.

Conclusions

THE delftware fragments discussed and illustrated on the foregoing pages are of great importance in broadening our knowledge of the range of shapes and decorative designs employed by London potters in the seventeenth century. Comparisons between that material and the products of excavations in Virginia make it clear that, at least from the 1640s onward, a full range of London delftware was reaching households in the colony. The large quantities of waste products represented by the Burnett Collection, by the material recovered in more recent excavations from neighboring Montague Close, as well as by the 1965 test digging in "Potts Fields" north of St. Olave's church, all indicate that production was extensive and capable of serving markets beyond the environs of London.

The Thamesside delftware potters' and their backers' business relationship with the Virginia Company and associates actually in the colony makes it clear that Virginia was the recipient of Southwark products. Although these may still be visually indistinguishable from wares produced contemporaneously in the Netherlands, it is reasonable to deduce that the vast majority of the specimens found in Virginia are of London, rather than of Dutch, manufacture. If that premise is accepted, it follows that the factories on the south bank of the Thames were indeed able to produce much more than was needed in the metropolis alone. It is fair to assume, therefore, that specimens found in England that match designs and shapes now proved to have been made in Southwark are more likely to be London products than Netherlandish imports. Consequently, delftwares found in England matching waster examples from Southwark kiln sites must be *proved* to be Dutch rather than English—not the other way round as has hitherto been the case. In short, the burden of proof henceforth rests with those who wish to identify the wares as imports.[1]

In spite of Sir David Burnett's belief that foundations flanking Vine Lane to the east were those of pottery kilns, there is insufficient evidence from the distribution records provided by his collection to confirm the presence of a kiln in that location. The distribution chart (see Appendix I) shows that most of the tile fragments come from Area 7 close to the river, and most of the biscuit dishes from Area 2 adjacent to the "kilns" beside Vine Lane. Beyond that there is little identifiable pattern, and it is entirely possible that even the tile and dish associations are the product of offsite dumping rather than indications of kiln proximity. The documentary evidence points strongly to the Pickleherring kilns being located south of Still Stairs and north of Potts Fields (see asterisked location, Pl. 2A), but there is no such documentation for kilns in the Vine Lane or Black Swan Yard areas whence came most of the Burnett Collection. That kiln waste was widely distributed has been revealed by the discovery of quantities of early eighteenth-century delftware and brown stoneware kiln waste used in filling gulleys and employed as yard metalling east of Gravel Lane (Bankside power station site), and by similar wares being used to compact the river foreshore east of Queenhithe Dock on the north shore. Further supportive evidence has been found in Virginia where, in the second quarter of the eighteenth century, stoneware and lead-glazed earthenwares were used as street metalling by Yorktown pothouse owner William Rogers when serving the town as surveyor of its landings, streets, and causeways.[2]

Although the Burnett Collection includes several items that are palpably not of Southwark manufacture, it is fair to conclude that all that reasonably could be, in fact are. There is small chance that waste products included in the collection come from the Montague Close kilns, for those were in another parish, and in the seventeenth century parish boundaries were much more important than they are today. It may be contended, therefore, that the illustrated waster and related material is the product of potters working in the parish of St. Olave. Beyond that one dare not go.

As for the eighteenth-century material, the few irrefutable wasters do not come from a site established by documentary evidence to have been occupied by a potter. Once again, therefore, one can say only that the sherds illustrate some

1. See p. 16, n. 35.

2. C. Malcolm Watkins and Ivor Noël Hume, "The 'Poor Potter' of Yorktown," *United States National Museum Bulletin* 249, Contributions from the Museum of History and Technology, Paper 54 (Washington, D. C.: Smithsonian Institution, 1968), 82.

of the shapes and designs manufactured in St. Olave's Parish. More broadly speaking, however, the claim can reasonably be made that all the English pieces in the collection dating prior to the mid-eighteenth century are more likely to be Southwark products rather than those of Lambeth, Rotherhithe, or Wapping. Furthermore, there is no likelihood at all that any of them had been brought from Bristol or Liverpool.

APPENDIX I
Distribution of Kiln Waste

	Plate or Figure Number	Biscuit	Glaze Damaged	Site
TILES	9.1		x	7
	2		x	7
	3		x	7
	4		x	1
	5	x*		4
	I.1		x	7
	II.1		x	7
	2		x	7
	3		x	7
	6		x	7
	9		x	7
	10	x		4
OINTMENT POTS and DRUG JARS	III.1	x		–
	2	x		–
	3	x		–
OINTMENT POTS and DRUG JARS	III.4	x		–
	5	x		–
	6	x		4
	7	x		–
	8	x		–
	9	x		–
	10	x		4
	11	x		6
	12	x		4
	13	x		7
	14	x		4
	15	x		–
	IV.1		x	–
	8		x	–
	11		x	–
	13		x	4
	20		x	–
	V.3		x	–
	XVII.2		x	–
	–	x(8)		2
	–	x		6
	–	x(2)		1

For key, see page 107.

	Plate or Figure Number	Biscuit	Glaze Damaged	Site
CUPS, MUGS, CANS, and JUGS	18.L	x*		1
	22.R	x*		7
	VI.1	x		1
	2	x		5
	3	x		5
	4	x		1
	5	x		7
	6	x		7
	7	x		–
	8	x		1
	9	x		5
	10	x		7
CHARGERS, DISHES, PLATTERS, and PLATES	30-31		x*	4
	40		x*	4
	49.2		x	5
	VII.5	x		2
	6	x		2
	7	x		2
	8	x		2
	9	x		–
	10	x		2
CHARGERS, DISHES, PLATTERS, and PLATES	VII.11	x		2
	12	x		2
	VIII.1		x	4
	2		x	4
	3		x	4
	XI.4		x	6
	8		x	–
	XVII.6		x	6
	XVIII.11	x		2
	–	x(4)		1
	–	x(2)		7
	–	x(24)		2
CANDLESTICKS	VI.16	x		4
	XVI.11	x		–
SALTS	VI.14	x		4
	15	x		4
VASES	VI.17	x		5
	18	x		1
	–	x		1
	–	x		6
BOWLS and PORRINGERS	VI.12	x		5
	13	x		5
	XIV.5	x		–
	XVI.5		x	6
	6		x	–
	XVIII.10	x		5
	11	x		2
CHAMBER POTS	XVIII.1	x		5

	Plate or Figure Number	Biscuit	Glaze Damaged	Site
SAGGERS	XVIII.12	x		2
	13	x		2
	14	x		2
	–	x(7)		2
	–	x		3
TRIVETS	XIII.8	x		2
	9	x		2
	–	x(3)		2
	–	x(2)		7

* Indicates pictorial duplication.
(1) Indicates numbers of sherds not illustrated.
Site Identification (for locations, see Pls. 2A and 2B).

1. Possible kiln location.
2. Deposit of biscuit fragments.
3. Cesspit, Black Swan Yard.
4. Trench in Vine Lane.
5. Butter Factory site (Black Swan Yard).
6. Battle Bridge House site.
7. St. Olave's Wharf.

Where no site number is shown, it is known only that the item comes from a location on the north side of Tooley Street between Battle Bridge House and St. Olave's church.

Appendix II Norwich and Aldgate: The Pickleherring Precursors

MOST of what little is known about the first delftware potters to set up in business at Norwich is derived from the much quoted statement by John Stow that "about the year 1567, Jaspar Andries and Jacob Janson, Potters, came away from Antwerp, to avoid the Persecution there, and settled themselves in Norwich; where they followed their Trade, making Gally Paving Tiles, and Vessels for Apothecaries and others, very artificially."[1] Stow went on to say that "Anno 1570 they moved to London" and petitioned Queen Elizabeth for permission to set up in business there, claiming that "they were the first which brought in and exercised the said Sciences in this Realm." That claim cannot necessarily be taken at face value, for it was de rigueur for any applicants for licenses or patronage to claim preeminence in their calling. As noted earlier (p. 3), Andries's father had been invited to work in England as a maker of painted earthenware in the reign of Henry VIII, although he did not in fact do so.

Stow notwithstanding, there is no firm evidence that Jasper Andries moved to London; on the contrary, he was in Colchester in 1571 and is said to have been back in Norwich a year later. Little is known about Andries beyond the fact that both he and his wife, Anne, came from Brabant and that both were aged twenty-eight in 1571.[2] While in Norwich, Andries was admonished for leading a drunken life and was told to pull himself together.[3] It is conceivable that his drinking problem later caused Andries to leave Norfolk, for in her study of London records Rhoda Edwards has found that a Jesper Androse was living in the Thamesside village of Lambeth in 1576. The parish register of St. Mary's, Lambeth, shows that this man's son Jasper was baptised on July 12, 1577, and buried the next day, and that another son, John, was buried on December 25 of the following year.[4] Jesper (or Jasper) Androse's trade is not cited, and there is therefore nothing to indicate that he was a potter or that he came from Norwich.

The activities of Jacob Janson (who changed his name to Johnson when he moved to London) in Norwich are even less defined than those of Andries, for as Rhoda Edwards has noted, Janson's name is not listed in the 1568 roll of aliens resident in Norwich—although Andries's does appear.[5] Indeed, Janson's name does not even figure in the surviving text of the joint petition to

---

1. Stow, *Survey of the Cities of London and Westminster,* II, 6th ed., p. 327.

2. Edwards (1974), 31.
3. Ibid.
4. Ibid.
5. Ibid., 77.

the queen, there being a hole in the paper where the second partner was originally identified. Attached to the petition, however, is an attestation dated 1570 and provided by the Dutch Church in Norwich that names "Jacobum Joannis" and "Casparum Andreae."[6] It was John Stow, therefore, who identified Joannis as Janson, and there is little doubt that he was the Jacob Johnson named as living within Aldgate Ward in the 1571 list of aliens then resident in London. He was identified as follows: "Jacob Johnson Pott Maker and Margerye his wife, came into England about iii 1/2 years ago, for religion, and one of the Douche church and borne in Flaunders."[7] A three and one-half year sojourn in England tallies reasonably well with the Andries and Janson petition of ca. 1570, which states that they had been in the country "almoaste three yeares."[8]

Artifactual evidence from Norwich is more tantalizing than telling, but by no means without significance. Both salvage and controlled excavations by the staff of the Norwich Museum and the Norwich Archaeological Unit from time to time have unearthed biscuit fragments of "Vessels for potycaries and other[s]" that might parallel the contents of "the chest withe their handyworke" presented to the queen by Andries and Janson along with their petition.[9] Most of the unfinished delftware sherds were found in 1948 during excavations carried out by Mr. E. M. Jope on the corner of Ber Street and Thorn Lane, a site which the present director of the Norwich Archaeological Survey, Alan Carter, believes to have been the location of the Andries and Janson pothouse. Mr. Jope's fragments were not available for study, but the Norwich Castle Museum has very kindly supplied drawings which show that by and large the wares are thicker and less skillfully thrown than are comparable London products. A few representative fragments are shown in Fig. XIX (A–E), and although most of them appear anomalous in one way or another, there is nothing about them that clearly identifies them as being of sixteenth-century date. None of the ointment pot and drug jar sherds drawn by the Norwich Museum exhibits the waisted albarello profile characteristic of such wares in the Tudor period (for example, Fig. XIX, no. 5). There is, however, one wall sherd from a glazed and polychrome-decorated drug jar akin to a specimen in the Burnett Collection (Fig. XVII, no. 1) which I have attributed to Antwerp and to ca. 1570–1610. The thickness of the Norwich fragment may be evidence enough to associate it with the Ber Street–Thorn Lane biscuit sherds, but the Norwich Museum's drawing does not indicate that it is a waster. As most of the early delftware found in the town is assumed to be Netherlandish (until firm evidence to the contrary can be presented), Mr. Jope's unstratified glazed fragments must therefore be treated with caution.

While in Norwich in November 1975 I was privileged to examine most of the early delftwares from recent excavations in the town, but only two items, a small bottle and a mug of early seventeenth-century type, seemed anomalous, both painted by the same hand in a design that smacked neither of London nor the Netherlands.[10] These vessels could perhaps have been local products, although not necessarily as early as the third quarter of the sixteenth century. I also saw a biscuit drug jar base sherd from another Ber Street site, and although it had to be a local product, there was nothing in its shape to place it appreciably earlier than drug jars from Southwark.[11] The same could also be said of a drug jar rim sherd from the vicinity of St. Benedict's Gate at Norwich, a site a considerable distance from Thorn Lane.[12] Slender and inconclusive though the evidence is, one cannot ignore the possibility that there were other delftware potters working in Norwich after Janson moved to London in 1570 or 1571.

Alan Carter has explored the surviving documentary records (which are incomplete in the late sixteenth century) and can find no subsequent references to potting within the city limits prior to the mid-seventeenth century. However, ceramic historian Anthony Ray has stated that after moving to Colchester in 1571, Jasper An-

6. Ibid. The original petition is in the collection of the British Museum, Lansdowne MSS 12, fols. 131–132.

7. Information kindly supplied by Mr. J. P. M. Latham, citing R. E. G. Kirk and Ernest F. Kirk, eds., "Return of Aliens dwelling in the City and Suburbs of London," Pt. II, 1571–1597, *Huguenot Society Publications,* X (Aberdeen, 1902), 66.

8. Lansdowne MSS 12, fols. 131–132.

9. Ibid.

10. Recovered from salvage archaeology on a building site in St. Stephen's Street. Misc. Acc. 117.952.

11. Norwich Museum, Acc. No. 702.964.

12. Norwich Museum, Acc. No. 63.952.

dries returned to Norwich the following year. "He may have stayed in Norwich," Ray adds, "for it is recorded that a pottery there went bankrupt in 1698, which may have been the one he had originally established."[13] Mr. Ray does not document this information, nor does he identify the bankrupt factory as having made delftware. In the absence of much more substantial evidence, it would be unwise to link Andries in 1571 to an unidentified factory more than a century later, simply because they happened to be in the same town. Furthermore, Janson and Andries were not the only alien potters resident in Norwich after 1568, for in that year the roll also included George Andree, potter.[14] Was he, one may ask, a relative of Jasper Andries, and did he have his own factory? These are but two of countless tantalizing questions that remain to be resolved before the place of Norwich in the English delftware industry can be seen in its proper perspective. The fragments so far recovered only demonstrate that archaeological answers may yet be forthcoming; but this in itself is a major step in the right direction.

The petition of Andries and Janson requested permission to settle in London and to secure the authority to sell and transport their wares free of customs duties for the period of twenty years. However, the records show that a prior application was already signed or under review. A consortium of Lincolnshire and Northamptonshire businessmen had requested the right to import foreign craftsmen to establish new trades in England, among them "the arte and science of baken of erthen vessell and other erthen woorke after the manner of Turkye Italye Spayne and Netherlond with purtraict and coloures."[15] There can be no doubt that these men, Richard Bertie, Thomas Cecil, Francis Harrington, and Edmund Hall, were planning to manufacture tin-enameled earthenware (maiolica) to compete with the wares then imported from the Mediterranean, from the Iberian peninsula, and from the Netherlands. There is no evidence, however, that they did in fact set up any factories for making delftware, although, as Rhoda Edwards has pointed out, it is possible that they helped Janson get started at Aldgate where no small number of Flemish potters gathered in the 1570s.[16] The absence of any surviving documents dealing specifically with Janson's venture leaves the door open for his having operated under the patent granted to Bertie and his partners.

By the summer of 1571, Jacob Johnson was established at the Sign of the Rose in the precinct of Chrychurche (St. Katherine Creechurch).[17] This was identified in 1576 as being "The Late Duke's Place," referring to Thomas Howard, duke of Norfolk, who acquired the property through his marriage to the daughter of Sir Thomas Audley who had died there in 1544.[18] Until the Reformation the land had been occupied by the Holy Trinity Priory founded in A.D. 1108 by Matilda, wife of Henry I. The priory land embraced an area enclosed by the modern Aldgate Street, part of Leadenhall Street, Creechurch Lane, Bury Street, Bevis Marks, and Duke Street. Although in the late seventeenth century the street running parallel to the inside (west side) of the medieval city wall was identified as Duke's Place, that name was previously applied to the entire precinct of the priory. When John Rocque's map was

---

13. Ray (1968), p. 34. This conclusion is stated even more firmly by Archer (1973), p. 6: "The Norwich pottery is known to have been in existence until about 1698." But here again, documentation for that conclusion is omitted. In reviewing this problem, Alan Carter has kindly provided the following information: He states that "in a selective check on a wide range of documents [he] has found no further references to potting within the City limits until the mid-17th century. Nothing is known of the two potters (Richard Childerhouse and William Prike *fl* 1651–58) then named; it is presumed, however that like a group of six early 18th century potters (Richard Lawes, Thomas Royle, Benjamin Lewis, Henry Minns, Obadiah Silcock, and Blackwell Dixon *fl* 1706–24), they were producing local red wares. None of the men's property was inventoried at death, and wills survive for only two of them. Beyond the fact that Thomas Royle (who died in 1713) originated in Staffordshire, the wills are as uninformative about the men's trade as Jacob Johnson's." Mr. Carter adds that "no trace of the 1698 bankruptcy has been found so far." Personal communication, January 22, 1976.

14. Edwards (1974), 77, citing W. J. C. Moens, ed., "The Walloons and their Church at Norwich, their History and Registers 1562–1832," *Huguenot Society Publications,* I (Lymington, 1887–1888), 207.

15. Edwards (1974), 8, quoting Patent Roll C. 66/1062, P.R.O.

16. They included Martin Taye of Flanders, a "painter of Pottes"; another decorator, John Bowger of Antwerp, potter John Aman of Brabant; and John Fott and William Tande, both Flemish potters who had moved to Aldgate's Creechurch parish from Sandwich. All these men are listed in the 1571 "Return of Aliens dwelling in the City and Suburbs of London." See n. 7. above.

17. A corruption of Christ Church.

18. [Anon.], *The City of London* (London: The Times Publishing Co., 1927), p. 41.

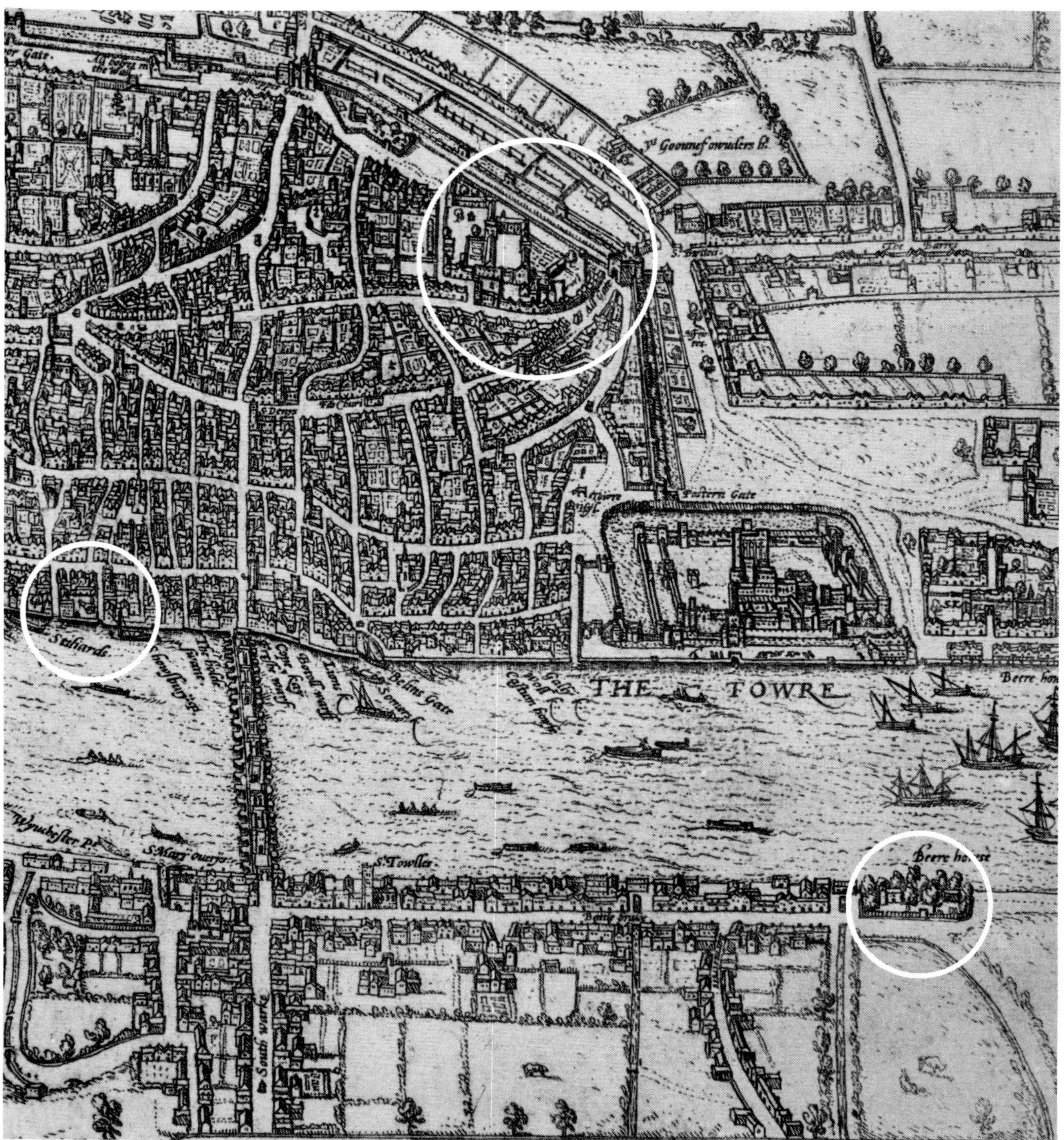

Plate 57.
A detail from G. Braun's and F. Hogenberg's Londinum Feracissimi Angliae Regni Metropolis, *first published in 1572 in a German atlas of major European cities titled* Civitates Orbis Terrarum. *Circled are Creechurch Parish (Aldgate), the approximate location of Samuel Sotherne's Steelyard warehouse, and the "Beere house" site adjacent to Pickle Herring Street. The open space below the beer house later became Potts Fields. The cows grazing in the field in this Elizabethan map may have led to the area's being termed "the Farm" as recently as the 1950s. At Aldgate the bastioned city wall is clearly visible, as is the ditch beyond it. Aldgate pump is shown standing alone at the junction of Fenchurch and Leadenhall streets immediately west of the gate. It is important to note that although the map was printed in 1572, it was probably drawn twenty years earlier and so does not accurately depict the amount of building that had subsequently gone on in the Creechurch area.*

published in 1746,[19] the street called Duke's Place had disappeared (along with the city wall) and had been replaced by a much narrower road called Shoemakers' Row, and the name Duke's Place had been given to a court to the west opening into Mitre Street. Today called Mitre Square, this Duke's Place also led into a much larger open space identified as Duke's Place Court on William Morgan's map of 1682. However, on Wenceslaus Hollar's map showing the extent of the Great Fire of 1666 (which stopped short of the Aldgate area) one large open square is shown and marked as "Dukes Palace."[20] This must be assumed to refer to the house built there by Sir Thomas Audley after he pulled down the Holy Trinity Priory.

The point of all this is that in Jacob Johnson's time Duke's Place defined a much larger area than is indicated by seventeenth-century and later maps, thus making it extremely difficult to locate the house known as the Sign of the Rose. It was last identified in John Strype's *An Accurate Edition of Stow's Survey of London* (1720) wherein he described the parish boundaries of St. Katherine Creechurch and included the statement "So on into the Street to the Pump and Westward on to the Sign of the Rose, sometime the Dwelling House of one Thomas Shepheard."[21] Unfortunately, Strype gave no names for the streets bordering the parish, and so all that can be deduced is that Thomas Shepheard's house (née Johnson's) stood to the west of Aldgate pump (Pl. 57). That structure appears on several early maps a few yards to the east of the junction of Leadenhall and Fenchurch streets, a distance in excess of 135 yards from the medieval city gate. The pump is a similar distance from the site of the Roman and later bastion known to archaeologists as "Bastion No. 6," to the east of which ran the medieval city ditch from whose filling came the Aldgate delftware waste products illustrated in Fig. XIX.

The ditch dug to protect the walled city on its landward sides had originally been seventy feet wide, but by the mid-sixteenth century it had become so filled with refuse that it was little more than a narrow open sewer winding its way through the garbage. Nevertheless, it continued to be shown on maps drawn as late as the second quarter of the seventeenth century. By 1681, however, when William Morgan's map was issued,[22] the ditch had been built over in many areas, although the Roman and medieval wall still survived; indeed, bastions nos. 6 and 7 are clearly identified. Here, then, is the dilemma. If Jacob Johnson lived and had his pothouse at the Sign of the Rose (and always supposing that this was the same dwelling that Strype placed west of Aldgate pump), it would have been a major undertaking to carry his kiln waste across two streets, past one city block, over the wall, and into the ditch. It should be noted that this sector of the wall survived into the eighteenth century, and the absence of any artifacts of that date from the ditch layers in which the delftware sherds were found precludes the possibility of their having been brought in with fill from somewhere else at a much later date. There is, however, no proof that this did not occur during Johnson's working life at Aldgate or in the years shortly thereafter.

The sherds recovered in the course of Peter Marsden's excavations on behalf of Guildhall Museum (now the Museum of London) came from four closely related deposits: Excavation Register numbers 1352, 1353, 1354, and 1355. The first of these contained one kiln trivet, the second nineteen biscuit sherds (plus two sagger fragments), the third two biscuit sherds, and the fourth three. There is no visible indication that the biscuit fragments are of differing dates or the products of more than one factory, but, like the Norwich evidence, there is also little to indicate that most of these unfinished wares are any earlier than are those from the Southwark sites. The exceptions are a small albarello-shaped ointment pot (Fig. XIX, no. 5) which unquestionably has a sixteenth-century appearance, and two mug or jug bases (Fig. XIX, nos. 10 and 11). The archaeological dating of the four groups is loose at best, for the majority of the ceramics are coarse, lead-glazed earthenwares whose generally Flemish character could place several of them anywhere between the second quarter of the sixteenth century and the mid-seventeenth century. Similarly vague conclusions were reached in 1948

19. Rocque, *A Plan of the Cities of London and Westminster.*

20. Wenceslaus Hollar, *A Map or Groundplot of the Citty of London and the Suburbes thereof* . . . (London, 1666), engraved by John Overton; reprinted in Philippa Glaville, *London in Maps* (London: The Connoisseur, 1972), pp. 92–93.

21. 1755 ed., p. 399. Information kindly supplied by Mr. J. P. M. Latham.

22. William Morgan, *London, Westminster and Southwark Accurately Surveyed* (London, 1681–1682).

when material from excavations across the city ditch close to its northwestern extremity (Cripplegate Buildings) prompted Adrian Oswald to date comparable ceramics between 1550 and 1640.[23]

The delftware from the ditch at Bastion No. 6 clearly demonstrates that layers E.R. 1353–1355 cannot represent an undisturbed chronology of ditch fill, for the lowest level (E.R. 1355) includes glazed fragments ranging in date from ca. 1525 to 1685, and which, if taken at their face value, would therefore place the Aldgate factory in the last quarter of the seventeenth century. Although this was palpably not so, it is more difficult to preclude the possibility that the biscuit sherds stem from a pothouse in operation well into the first half of the century. Again, this may not be so; but in the absence of more archaeological evidence it cannot be ruled out.

Just as the thickness of the majority of the Norwich fragments, coupled with some technical anomalies (e.g., Fig. XIX, C and D), set them apart from the London biscuit wares, so there are foot variations that distinguish the Aldgate group from Pickleherring wares in the Burnett Collection. The problem is that these are purely manipulatory differences so minor that they may represent the idiosyncracies of different throwers rather than evolutionary design characteristics. On the purely visual evidence of body composition, hardness, color, and the appearance of the adhering unfired glaze, there is no way to distinguish between Aldgate and Pickleherring biscuit fragments. Furthermore, the previously discussed nitric acid test also fails to identify any chemical differences.[24]

The principal characteristic suggesting a common origin—and perhaps a common date—for several of the Aldgate fragments is a sharpness of their bases, which turn slightly upward and outward on both pharmaceutical vessels and other hollow wares (Fig. XIX, nos. 2–4, 9, 10, 11, and 16).[25] Unfortunately, the last of them, no. 16, demonstrates the frailty of this reasoning, for there can be no doubt that this is a base fragment from an IHS vase of the type shown in Pls. 3 and 4, which, because of their essentially Catholic iconography, must predate the Reformation.[26] Furthermore, in spite of the fact that a surprising number of these vessels have been found in London, their Netherlandish origin cannot be questioned. When Bernard Rackham discussed them, he noted that a significant number had been found in London on sites of religious houses.[27] The Aldgate fragment is yet another, having been found "over the wall" from the Holy Trinity Priory. This house of the Augustinian Order was also known as Christ Church Priory, and therefore vases bearing the IHS (Jesus) device would have been particularly appropriate to it.

The same archaeological deposit (E.R. 1355) also contained another fragment from a jug of comparable "IHS" shape, with decoration closely akin to the vase shown in Pl. 3 (left), but with the addition of a vertical orange stripe. With these two Flemish or Netherlandish vases of the pre-Reformation era included in the group, one must immediately question the evidence of any glazed fragments that cannot be unequivocally identified as wasters—and none can. At the other end of the date range are two sherds unlikely to date before the 1640s. One belongs to a plate or dish of the classic Pickleherring class represented by those illustrated in Pls. 45 and 46 (and tin glazed on the back), and the other is a small sherd from a plate decorated in chinoiserie style that may date as late as the 1680s. The top layer (E.R. 1352) contained no biscuit fragments, and in spite of the presence of a possible anomalous trivet and several mid- to late seventeenth-century delftware sherds (see p. 107, n. 18), it can safely be ignored.

Regardless of all the foregoing expressions of caution and the presentation of negative evidence, a case can be made to tie several vessels already in museum collections to an Aldgate source—if not necessarily to Jacob Johnson. The previously discussed base or foot idiosyncracy exhibited by biscuit drug jar and mug (or jug) fragments in the Aldgate group is paralleled on a mug in the Fitzwilliam Museum. Although this has been attributed to Christian Wilhelm, there is no real support for that conclusion other than the fact that the vessel appears to be "early" and has an undated silver mount of generally Elizabethan

23. Hurst and Golson (1955), 82, n. 53.

24. See p. 16, n. 35.

25. This basal characteristic is not common to all the Aldgate hollow wares, as Fig. XIX, nos. 6–8, demonstrate.

26. Rackham (1926), p. 99. The antiquity of these IHS vases is shown in a page from an illuminated book of hours written in about 1480 for Maximillian I, archduke of Austria. Ibid., pl. 2 and p. 97.

27. Ibid., p. 99.

Plate 58.
A silver-mounted maiolica jug decorated in Islamic style and possessing a foot remarkably similar to the Aldgate biscuit fragment shown in Fig. XIX, no. 10. The jug has hitherto been dated ca. 1620, and attributed to Christian Wilhelm. Height: 6 1/4 inches. Fitzwilliam Museum, Glaisher Collection: 1291.

appearance, factors that could just as well promote an Aldgate origin (Pl. 58).[28] The mug is decorated in a design loosely Islamic in character, as is that of another jug in the Museum of London which has been tentatively attributed to Aldgate.[29] That specimen unfortunately does not have a base that parallels the Aldgate sherds. In addition, a jug in the Braintree Museum, attributed by Michael Archer to the second half of the sixteenth century, has a lower body shape akin to that of two of the Aldgate fragments (Fig. XIX, nos. 10 and 11).[30] Finally, there is a single,glazed plate rim fragment among the Aldgate sherds (Fig. XIX, no. 14) decorated in Urbino style, whose body is consistent with that of the biscuit pieces, suggesting that Mediterranean-style decoration was produced at an Aldgate factory.

Only one other glazed fragment speaks out on behalf of the so-called "Aldgate Potter," a base sherd richly painted in polychrome: blue, orange, and bright yellow (Fig. XIX, no. 13). The body is pinkish in color, as are virtually all the Aldgate biscuit sherds, and the square cut foot is almost identical to that of the group's only biscuit plate (Fig. XIX, no. 12). This small piece of evidence suggests that Aldgate painters were capable of creating brilliant colors while using a relatively thin but totally concealing tin glaze, which, incidentally, was also applied to the underside of the specimen. It should be noted, however, that three other sherds from Stratum E.R. 1355 exhibit the thin and yellowish back glaze typical of most of the specimens in the Burnett Collection. There is, however, no evidence that these three sherds were made at an Aldgate factory.

Jacob Johnson died in 1593 and in his will was described as a "merchant dwelling in Dukes Place within the City of London." Later, in defining the legacy to his second wife, Oyken [van] Popping, the will referred to "the moveable goodes and merchandizes which at this presente, and at the time of my decease are and shall be in the house The Rose in Dukes Place aforesaid, wherein my said Wyfe hath her trade of merchandize."[31] No mention is made of Johnson's trade as a potter or of any tools or products relating to it. Nevertheless, for more than twenty years Johnson was resident at the Rose and may have sold pottery there—even if he made it outside the city walls. In that time vast quantities of delftware could have been produced and (if the Southwark kilns are typical) equally vast quantities of kiln waste should have been generated. Ironically, however, only one intact specimen has so far been credited to Aldgate, and that was made at least seven years after Johnson's death. A plate in the Museum of London's collection (see Pl. 27) is inscribed THE • ROSE • IS • RED • THE • LEAVES • ARE • GRENE • GOD • SAVE • ELIZABETH • OVR • QVENE • and is dated 1600 (or 1602). This is the earliest recorded delftware specimen having an inscription in English, and as its date precedes any known South-

28. Tait (1961), 26–27, pl. 31. See also p. 106, n. 11.

29. Garner and Archer (1972), pl. 2A.

30. Archer (1973), p. 13, no. 3, p. 57, no. 3.

31. Transcript of the 1593 will of "Jacobi Janssen" kindly provided by Mr. J. P. M. Latham, from the original at Somerset House.

wark manufactory by more than a decade, the plate's Aldgate origin seems reasonably assured. Although the inscription appears at first reading to be purely patriotic, there is a possibility that it has a double meaning and advertises the red and green emblem of the Johnson family shop in Aldgate.

Johnson's widow was still in residence in Duke's Place in 1594,[32] and we know from his will that he left three sons and two daughters, but there is no record that any of them took over the pottery business, if, indeed, the family still had it. There is no knowing what became of the potters and painters who had joined Johnson in Dukes Place in 1571,[33] but Christian Bonharincke, whose name was not recorded among them, was living there in 1617 and was listed in the roll of aliens as having been in England for forty years. Another alien potter identified only as Peter was recorded as being a resident in Dukes Place as late as 1621.[34] If pottery-making continued in the vicinity of Aldgate through the first quarter of the seventeenth century, then we are faced with as yet insurmountable difficulties when trying to associate the handful of fragments from the ditch at Bastion No. 6 with Johnson or attempting to arrive at any close dates within the documentarily established brackets of 1570–1621. The archaeological stratigraphy cannot do it, nor can the evidence of the fragments themselves.

In conclusion, mention must be made of a mercer named Samuel Sotherne who, in 1620, was charged with infringing the patent of Hugh Cressey of the Montague Close factory in Southwark by luring away workers to operate furnaces Sotherne had constructed for the firing of "divers great quantities of paving tyles."[35] Cressey brought suit after raiding Sotherne's warehouse at the "Stilyard" on Thames Street near London Bridge (Pl. 57). Rhoda Edwards has stated that the site of Sotherne's pothouse is not known other than that it was in Middlesex on the north side of the river.[36] It is tempting, however, to recall that in 1840 the London antiquary Charles Roach Smith obtained a delftware kiln trivet from an unspecified site in Thames Street.[37] If that item of kiln furniture came from the Steelyard, it could suggest that Samuel Sotherne had something more than a warehouse in this location.

It can be argued, however, that by 1620 permission would not have been granted to set up a pothouse almost in the center of the City's densely populated riverside sector. The same might have been expected of potters resident in Aldgate, a factor that explains the movement away from the City, first to Southwark, and later to Rotherhithe, Greenwich, and Lambeth on the south bank, and to Hermitage Dock, Wapping, on the north. This last has sometimes been claimed to have been the direct descendant of the Aldgate factory, but as far as is known, it was not started until the 1660s by one John Campion, a pewterer, later in partnership with master potter William Knight, who continued to operate the factory into the early eighteenth century (Pl. 1).[38] In 1724 Henry Holding, a potter from Montague Close, took over its management, and the pothouse remained in operation at least as late as 1767,[39] thus providing archaeologists and collectors with one more headache, namely the appearance of the wares of another London factory in operation for a hundred years, none of whose products have so far been identified! That such ignorance can surround so late an enterprise makes it small wonder that so little is known about the lives and products of Norwich and Aldgate potters working almost two centuries earlier.

---

32. Edwards (1974), 78. See also Kirk and Kirk, eds., "Return of Aliens," *Huguenot Society Publications,* II (1902), 468.

33. See n. 16 above.

34. Edwards (1974), 94. See also Kirk and Kirk, eds., "Return of Aliens dwelling in the City and Suburbs of London," Pt. III, 1598–1625, *Huguenot Society Publications,* X (Aberdeen, 1907), 249.

35. Edwards (1974), 104, citing Chancery Proceedings C. 3/305/47, P.R.O.

36. Ibid.

37. See p. 54, n. 6.

38. Edwards (1974), p. 15. It is an interesting coincidence that the supposed Norwich (Andries) kiln site is adjacent to Ber Street and that John Knight lived at the corner of Nightingale Lane and Burr Street near Hermitage Dock. Alan Carter states that the Norwich name is derived from Bergestreet, i.e., hill street. The word "burr," however, is cited in the *Oxford English Dictionary* (among several other interpretations) as meaning "a partly fused mass of brick; a clinker." It is possible, therefore, that the Hermitage location may have previously been associated with brickmaking.

39. *The Compleat Compting House Companion* (London, 1763) lists Messers. Addison & Abernethy of Hermitage Street, Wapping, as makers of white earthenware, and Henry Kent's *The Directory* for 1767 cites Abernethy & Livie, Potters, at the same address. There is, however, as yet no proof that these partners were the successors of Henry Holding.

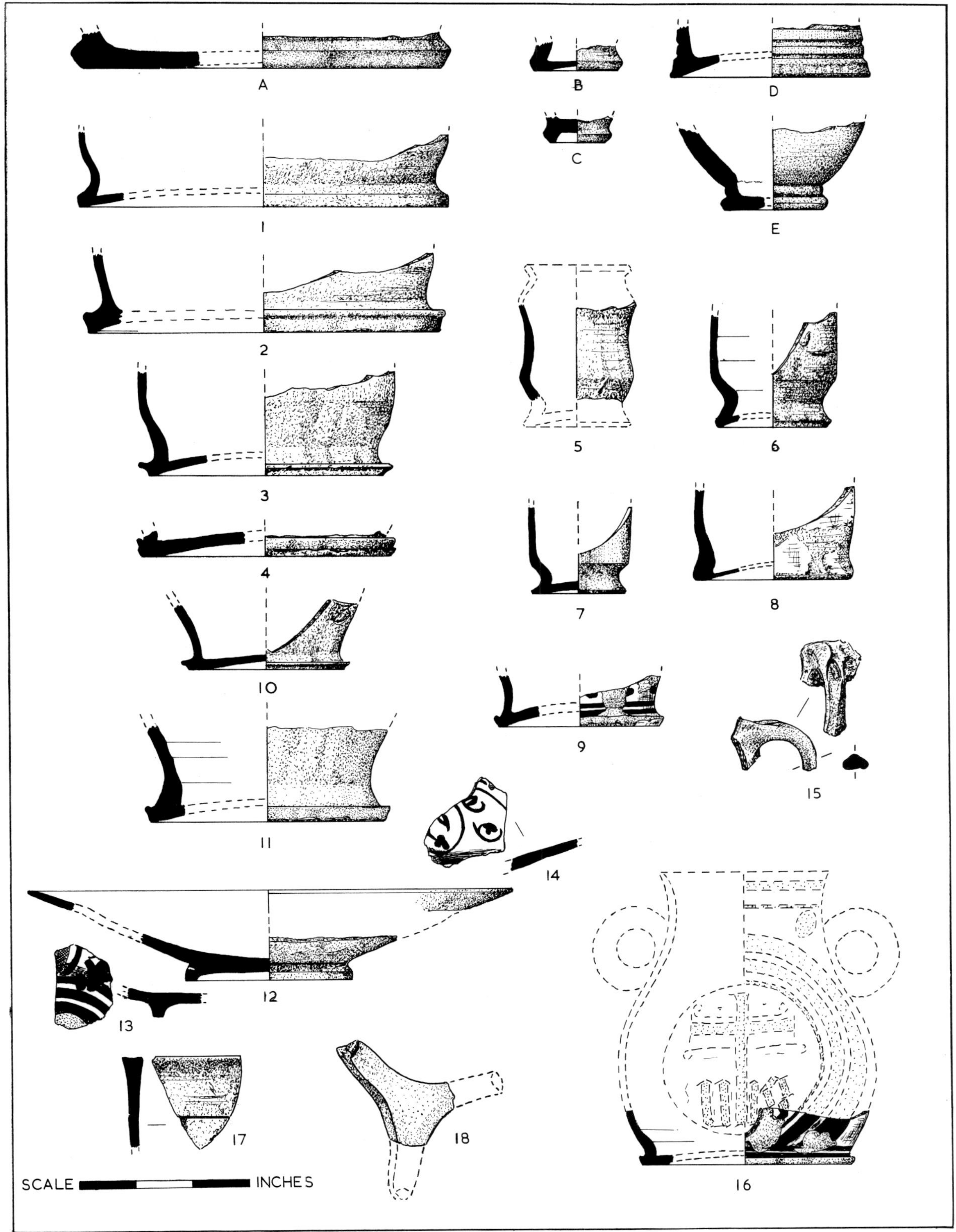

FIGURE XIX

FIGURE XIX

Fragments A to E were found in 1948 on a site at the junction of Ber Street and Thorn Lane in Norwich,[1] but because the sherds are not available for study, knowledge of them is derived only from drawings kindly supplied by Mr. William Milligan of the Norwich Museum. Fragments 1 to 18 are from the upper filling of London's city ditch adjacent to Bastion No. 6, northwest of Aldgate, and were generously loaned to the writer by the Museum of London.

1. Acc. No. 202.948 (d).

NORWICH

A. Pharmaceutical drug jar base; biscuit. Base diameter: approx. 5 3/4 inches. Post-1568.

B. Ointment pot base, very thick in the lower wall and unusually rounded; biscuit.[2] Base diameter: 1 11/16 inches. Post-1568.

C. Ointment pot base very thick in the base, which is markedly raised within the foot. This is a rare and possibly unique characteristic among English delftware ointment pots of the late 16th and 17th centuries.[3] Biscuit. Base diameter: 1 1/4 inches. Post-1568.

D. Lower wall and base of mug, the wall decorated with sharply defined grooves, features setting it apart from any known English earthenware mugs of the late Tudor or early Stuart periods.[4] Biscuit. Base diameter: 3 9/16 inches. Post-1568, possibly as late as the 18th century.

E. Mug or bottle, lower wall and basal fragment; biscuit. The wall is extremely thick and clumsily potted, and the padlike base is divided from it by an equally clumsy cordon.[5] Surviving maximum diameter: 3 5/16 inches. Post-1568.

ALDGATE

1. Pharmaceutical drug jar base; biscuit, body yellow outside and pink within, with red ochre inclusions. The base is everted and square cut. Base diameter: approx. 6 1/2 inches. E.R. 1353. Post-1571.

2. Pharmaceutical drug jar base; biscuit, the body pink and pale yellowish pink on the exterior surface, yellow clay inclusions. The base is everted and projects into a slightly upswept ridge. Base diameter: approx. 6 3/8 inches. E.R. 1353. Post-1571.

3. Pharmaceutical drug jar base; biscuit, the body pink and pale yellow on the exterior surface, small yellow clay inclusions. The base is everted and outswept into a sharp ridge, the base markedly raised. Greatest surviving wall diameter: 4 1/2 inches. E.R. 1353. Post-1571.

4. Pharmaceutical drug jar base; biscuit, the body pink but pale yellow on both exterior and interior surfaces. The base has been tooled upward to create a groove between it and the wall, a development of the foot style demonstrated by nos. 2 and 3 above. Base diameter: 4 1/2 inches. E.R. 1355. Post-1571.

5. Ointment pot wall fragment; biscuit, essentially yellowish buff throughout, but with slight pinkish tone in the core where the sherd thickens at its lowest extremity. The pot was of albarello form, and is the only example of its class that exhibits characteristics indicative of a pre-1600 date.[6] Estimated height: 2 3/4 inches. E.R. 1353. 1571–1600.

6. Ointment pot base and wall fragment; biscuit, pinkish buff, a few white inclusions, but yellow on the exterior. The base is fairly sharply cut and exhibits no throwing details to distinguish the pot from others well represented in the Pickleherring material.[7] Body diameter: approx. 2 1/4 inches. E.R. 1353. 1571–1645.

7. Ointment pot base and lower wall; biscuit, pink in the core but yellowish buff on the surfaces both inside and out, save in the bottom where the pink extends almost to the edges. There are a few yellow clay and red ochre inclusions, also pulling marks on the base. Traces of unfired tin glaze remain on the outside, but there is no evidence of decoration. The shape is akin to that of no. 6

---

2. For the usual range of ointment pot base shapes in the early 17th century, see Figs. III and IV.

3. See n. 2. above.

4. For examples of straight-sided English delftware mugs or cans of the 17th century, see Pls. 6, 7, 22, 23, and 37. The Norwich fragment is unlike delftware mug forms of any period and is, instead, much more akin to the brown, and white saltglazed stonewares of the 18th century.

5. The shape and surviving measurements are approximately paralleled by the Pickleherring biscuit example shown in Fig. VI, no. 7, which is attributed to ca. 1630–1650. See also p. 68, n. 5. Similarly shaped mugs occur in lead-glazed earthenware, sometimes in brown tortoiseshell and often with vertical scored lines or quartz-chip rustication. See *Catalogue of the Guildhall Museum* (London, 1908), pl. LXX, no. 11. These are usually attributed to the first 40 years of the 17th century.

6. For a shape parallel, see Garner and Archer (1972), pl. 2B. The authors attributed this 2 3/8-inch high example to London and to the early 17th century.

7. See Fig. III, nos. 1 and 2, Fig. IV, nos. 1–3, and Pl. 12.

and similar to many Southwark examples.[8] Body diameter: 1 13/16 inches. E.R. 1353. 1571–1645.

8. Ointment pot base and lower wall fragment, the former very thin and the latter much too thick; biscuit, yellowish buff on the exterior but pink inside and in the core, a few white clay and red ochre inclusions. The exterior and base retain unfired tin glaze but no indication of decoration. The sherd is anomalous in that it is extremely weak both in the roundness of the base and the lack of angle in the lower wall. The pot is quite unlike any of the known variations recorded as dating from the early 17th century, and were it not for its alleged association with a Tudor potter, one might be tempted to date it in the second half of the 17th century.[9] Base diameter: 2 7/8 inches. E.R. 1353. Post-1571.

9. Base fragment of small drug jar (or large ointment pot), tin glazed inside and out, and decorated with two narrow blue bands above the base and with small, widely spaced blue dashes above. The body is yellow on all exposed faces and slightly pink in the core. Red ochre inclusions are visible in the section. The base is delicate and tooled slightly upward in a miniature version of no. 4. The glaze and decoration have spotted and pooled in the firing, but these blemishes are not sufficient to class the sherd as a waster.[10] Base diameter: 3 inches. E.R. 1353. 1571–1650.

10. Base fragment of jug or large mug; biscuit, yellowish buff on the outside, but pink inside and through the core, which exhibits numerous small white clay inclusions. The base spreads into a sharp flange similar in character to that of no. 3, and is largely pink on the underside. The closest parallel is provided by a jug in the Glaisher Collection that copies the general shape of Rhenish stonewares and is closely allied to the so-called Malling jugs (Pl. 58).[11] It seems reasonable to suggest that this jug is, in fact, an Aldgate product, and thus a clue to the intended appearance of the biscuit vessel. Base diameter: 3 1/16 inches. E.R. 1353. 1571–1620.

11. Lower wall and base fragment from a jug of similar character to no. 10, but of larger size, biscuit, pink inside and out, but buff in the core where the wall is thickest. There is unfired glaze on the outside and adhering to the base. The treatment of the foot is akin to that of drug jar no. 4, although rather more square cut. Base diameter: approx. 4 3/8 inches. E.R. 1354. 1571–1620.[12]

12. Plate or dish base and plate rim; both are in the biscuit state and are pink throughout, with yellow clay and red ochre inclusions. There is no evidence that the sherds are from the same object, although that possibility cannot be excluded. The rim is sharper at the edge than those of any plates in the Burnett Collection, although its thickness would be considerably increased after the application of the glaze. The footring is externally square cut, if somewhat lopsided, and curves gently inward to the base within. A small suspension (?) hole has been attempted, but it has failed to extend through the footring. Dating is based on the decorative evidence of

---

8. See p. 105, n. 7.

9. It must be remembered that galleypots were among the easiest shapes to produce and therefore would have been attempted by apprentices—some of whom may have been in need of much more training. The chances that their products would end up on the waste pile should be greater than would those of the master.

10. The treatment of the foot and the color of the body make this vessel compatible with the Aldgate biscuit sherds.

11. Fitzwilliam Museum, Cambridge, Glaisher Collection, No. 1291, illustrated in Rackham (1935), I, p. 168. The jug is there said to have been decorated by the same hand that painted a charger dated 1620 (Glaisher Coll., No. 1394). That association is debatable at best, and Michael Archer (1973), p. 15, no. 8, has pointed to a close parallel for the charger in the collection of the Rijksmuseum at Amsterdam. The parallel between the basal flanges of both sherd and mug is striking, but it is not conclusive evidence of early date, for a two-handled bowl dated 1632 in the Burnap Collection (Pl. 35) possesses similar foot characteristics. In support of the Aldgate fragment's early date, attention is drawn to the way in which the body flairs outward into an almost conical form above the foot, a style that contrasts with the generally bulbous bodies of most jugs, mugs, and bottles of the first half of the 17th century (e.g., Pls. 5, 25, and 36). The conical shape has its parallel in a silver-mounted jug in the museum at Braintree, Essex (Acc. No. 311.67), which Archer considers to be English and to date from the second half of the 16th century. Archer (1973), p. 13, no. 3, p. 57, no. 3.

12. Dating is based on the argument presented in n. 11 above. Although one is tempted to put the terminal date at ca. 1600, the presence of potters at Aldgate as late as 1621 leaves too many doors ajar. Unlike most of the drug jars and ointment pots, however, the jug or mug fragments nos. 10 and 11 do present stylistic evidence in favor of a relatively early cut-off date. See Rackham (1926), pl. 47 for a jug of comparable shape dated 1562.

the similarly footed sherd no. 13 below. Diameter: approx. 8 1/2 inches. E.R. 1353. 1590–1625.

13. Foot and base fragment of plate or dish; the body pale pink and with white clay inclusions. The sherd is tin glazed on both upper and lower surfaces, but the glaze does not cover the base of the footring or the entire area within it. This back glaze has a slight bluish cast. That on the upper surface is a clean white, ornamented with rich polychrome painting in blue, yellow, and orange.[13] Insufficient decoration survives to be certain of the design, but the vivid colors point to an early date. E.R. 1353. 1590–1625.

14. Plate or dish rim fragment, the body buff with white clay inclusions, and tin glazed on both surfaces. The upper is decorated with thin pale blue foliate lines and "acorns" in a generally Urbino and even Islamic style.[14] E.R. 1353. 1570–1600.

15. Mug or jug handle; biscuit, buff on the exterior surface, but pink within. The handle is crudely formed, the clay that could not be smeared laterally to anchor the handle to the neck has been drawn up and folded back on itself creating a pair of overlapping flaps above the handle.[15] E.R. 1353. Post-1571.

16. Base and lower wall fragment from a double-handled vase decorated in two tones of blue with a cartouche containing an IHS monogram. The vessel was tin glazed inside and out, although the interior is thin and bluish in the crevices. The body is pale yellow and contains one red ochre inclusion. The foot is delicate and has been trimmed upward to create a shallow, glaze-filled trough between base and wall, in the manner of Aldgate fragments nos. 4 and 9. The conjectural reconstruction is intended only to demonstrate the character of the vessel and not to represent its actual shape.[16] Base diameter: approx. 3 13/16 inches. E.R. 1355. 1490–1538.

17. Sagger rim sherd; the body a hard pinkish red earthenware, yellow on the surfaces and containing white clay inclusions. The rim is slightly thickened, flat on the top, and there is a seemingly intentional groove one inch below it. Diameter: approx. 6 inches. E.R. 1353. Post-1571.[17]

18. Kiln trivet; pale yellow body containing small red ochre inclusions. There are wood grain marks on the otherwise smooth upper surface, contrasting with the roughness of the underside. Part of one pinched foot survives.[18] Point spread approx. 3 3/4 inches. E.R. 1352. 16th or 17th century?

---

13. The orange is unequivocally that when laid over yellow, as it is here, but in many instances the same basic color medium comes out a muddy brown.

14. For the possible significance of this sherd see p. 117; for three Netherlandish design parallels attributed to dates from the mid- to late 16th century see Boschma (1971), p. 27, nos. 2 and 4, p. 29, no. 6. See also De Jonge (1947), p. 96, pl. 58, p. 99, pl. 60.

15. Like the curious bases included in the Aldgate group, it is possible that this handle is representative of a single, idiosyncratic craftsman and may not be at all characteristic of Aldgate handles in general. Nevertheless, the fact that it differs from handles among the Pickleherring fragments makes the folded flap technique one to watch for.

16. See Pls. 3 and 4. For three more IHS vases found in London, and another secular example (also from London) with vertical orange stripes similar to a small sherd in the Aldgate group (E.R. 1355), see Rackham (1926), pls. 24 and 26. For an IHS specimen found in Brussels, see Boschma (1971), p. 29, no. 8. Another Netherlandish secular example with lozengelike leaf designs similar to Pl. 49, no. 6, and Fig. II, no. 8, is illustrated by Van Beuningen (1973), p. 113, no. 551, and is attributed to the second half of the 16th century. See also De Jonge (1947) p. 45, pl. 16. For additional details concerning the significance of the drawn fragment, see p. 116.

17. This is one of two fragments from group E.R. 1353, the other being a body sherd of similar color and equally hard. It may be important to note that the Aldgate sagger pieces are quite unlike all but one of the Burnett Collection examples, being both harder and red-bodied with buff inclusions, as opposed to the Pickleherring group's yellowish ware with red inclusions. The Burnett Collection parallel for the Aldgate body is a thin base sherd with a central hole and fired extremely hard (not illustrated). However, it comes from the Black Swan Yard cesspit (Site 3), which contained ceramics and tobacco pipes dating at least as late as ca. 1680 (see Fig. XV, nos. 1–8).

18. This, the only trivet fragment present in the Aldgate group, is much more slender and waisted than are those in the Burnett Collection (Fig. XIII, nos. 8 and 9), and thus is more closely paralleled by the Roach Smith example from Thames Street (p. 54, n. 6). However, this is not in itself a very significant dating guide, as L. L. Lipski (1969), 149, has published a comparable waisted example dated 1730 and found on the site of Bristol's Lime Kiln Lane delftware pottery. A Netherlandish example dated 1684 is illustrated by De Jonge (1947), p. 196, pl. 169, and is a relatively close shape parallel for the Burnett Collection examples cited above (see also pp. 53–54). Because the Aldgate specimen comes from a stratum that also includes a rim fragment of a plain white octagonal delftware plate (and several other seemingly mid- to late 17th-century sherds for which no Elizabethan parallels are known), a late date for the trivet cannot be ruled out. Indeed, the yellowness of the body sets it apart from the rest of the Aldgate kiln waste.

Bibliography

Addyman, P. V., and Biddle, Martin
1965 "Medieval Cambridge: Recent Finds and Excavations." *Proceedings of the Cambridge Antiquarian Society,* LVIII (1965), 74–137.

Archer, Michael
1973 *English Delftware.* Amsterdam: Rijksmuseum, 1973.

Ashdown, John H.
1970 "The Pottery and Other Finds." Contribution to K. Rutherford Davis's paper, "A Seventeenth-century Pottery Group and Associated Finds from a Well at Potters Bar." *Hertfordshire Archaeology,* II (1970), 88–104.

Barton, K. J.
1964 "The Excavation of a Medieval Bastion at St. Nicholas's Almshouses, King Street, Bristol." *Medieval Archaeology,* VIII (1964), 184–212.

Bedford, John
1966 *Delftware.* New York: Cassell and Company, 1966.

Berry, Francis
1933 *Wine Trade Loan Exhibition Catalogue of Drinking Vessels also Books & Documents etc. etc. etc.* London: Vintners' Hall, 1933.

Biddle, Martin; Barfield, Lawrence; and Millard, Alan
1961 "The Excavation of the Manor of the More, Rickmansworth, Hertfordshire." *The Archaeological Journal,* CXVI (1961), 186–188.

Blake, Bryan P.; Hurst, J. G.; and Grant, L. H.
1961 "Medieval and Later Pottery from Stockwell Street, Colchester." *Transactions of the Essex Archaeological Society.* 3rd Ser., I, pt. 1 (1961), 41–51.

Bloice, Brian J.
1971 "Norfolk House, Lambeth: Excavations at a Delftware Kiln Site, 1968." *Post-Medieval Archaeology,* V (1971), 99–159.

Boschma, C.
1971 *Antwerps Plateel: Tentoonstelling Fries Museum Leeuwarden, 18-12-1971 t/m 29-1-1972.* Leeuwarden, Holland: Fries Museum, 1971.

Celoria, Francis [P. Amis]
1968 "Some domestic vessels of southern Britain: a social and technological analysis." *Journal of Ceramic History,* No. 2 (1968).

Cotter, John L.
1958 *Archaeological Excavations at Jamestown.* Archaeological Research Series, No. 4. Washington, D. C.: National Park Service, 1958.

Crellin, J. K.
1969 *Medical Ceramics in the Wellcome Institute.* London: Wellcome Institute of the History of Medicine, 1969.
1970 "Medical Ceramics: Their Scope and Significance." English Ceramic Circle, *Transactions,* VII, pt. 3 (1970), 191–199.

Davies, Isabel
1969 "Seventeenth-century delftware potters in St. Olave's Parish, Southwark." *Surrey Archaeological Collections,* LXVI (1969), 11–31.

Dawson, Graham J.
1970 "London: Southwark, Montague Close." *Post-Medieval Archaeology,* IV (1970), 183–184.
1971 "Montague Close, Part 2." *The London Archaeologist* (summer 1971), 250–251.

Dawson, Graham J., and Edwards, Rhoda
1973 "The Montague Close Delftware Factory Prior to 1969." Surrey Archaeological Society, *Research Volume I* (1973), 47–62.

De Jonge, C. H.
1947 *Oud Nederlandsche Majolica en Delftsch Aardewerk.* The Hague: Martinus Nijhoff, 1947.

Downman, Edward Andrews
1919 *Blue Dash Chargers.* London: T. Werner Laurie Ltd., 1919.

Edwards, Rhoda
1974 "London Potters circa 1570–1710." *Journal of Ceramic History,* No. 6 (1974).

Ellis, Aytoun
1952 *Three Hundred Years of London River: The Hay's Wharf Story 1651–1951.* London: The Bodley Head, 1952.

Fanning, T., and Hurst, J. G.
1975 "A Mid Seventeenth-Century Pottery Group and Other Objects from Ballyhack Castle, Co. Wexford." *Proceedings of the Royal Irish Academy,* LXXV, Sec. C (1975), 103–118.

Garner, F. H.
1937 "Lambeth Earthenware." English Ceramic Circle, *Transactions,* No. 4 (1937), 43–66.
1948 *English Delftware.* London: Faber and Faber, 1948.

Garner, F. H., and Archer, Michael
1972 *English Delftware.* 2nd rev. ed. London: Faber and Faber, 1972.

Glaisher, J. W. L.
1914 *Burlington Fine Arts Club Exhibition of Early English Earthenware.* London: Burlington Fine Arts Club, 1914.

Grigaut, Paul L., comp.
1954 *English Pottery and Porcelain 1300–1850.* Detroit: Detroit Institute of Arts, 1954.

Grohne, Ernst
n.d. *Tongefasse in Bremen Seit Dem Mittelalter.* Bremen: Arthur Geist, n.d.

Harrington, J. C.
1962 *Search for the Cittie of Ralegh.* Archeological Research Series, No. 6. Washington, D. C.: National Park Service, 1962.

Hobson, R. L.
1903 *Catalogue of the Collection of English Pottery in the Department of British and Medieval Antiquities and Ethnography of the British Museum.* London: British Museum, 1903.

Hodgkin, John Eliot, and Hodgkin, Edith

1891 *Examples of Early English Pottery Named, Dated, and Inscribed.* London: Privately printed by Cassell and Co. Ltd., 1891.

Holme, Randle

1905 *An Academie or Store House of Armory & Blazon.* Pt. II. London: Roxburghe Club, 1905.

Honey, William B.

1949 *European Ceramic Art.* London: Faber and Faber, 1949.

1952 *English Pottery and Porcelain.* London: Faber and Faber, 1952; first published in 1933.

Hughes, G. Bernard

1957 "Old English Spout-Pots." *Country Life,* CXXI (January 17, 1957), 98–99.

Hurst, J. G., and Golson, J.

1955 "Excavations at St. Benedict's Gates, Norwich, 1951 and 1953." *Norfolk Archaeology,* XXXI, pt. 1 (1955), 4–112.

Jewitt, Llewellynn

1878 *Ceramic Art of Great Britain.* 2 vols. London: Virtue and Co., 1878.

Korf, Dingeman

1964 *Dutch Tiles.* New York: Universe Books, Inc., n.d.; Dutch ed., 1964.

Lane, Arthur

1960 *A Guide to the Collection of Tiles.* Victoria and Albert Museum. 2nd ed. London: H. M. Stationery Office, 1960.

Lewis, Griselda

1956 *A Picture History of English Pottery.* London: Hulton Press, 1956.

Lipski, L. L.

1969 "Dated English Delftware." English Ceramic Circle, *Transactions,* VII, pt. 2 (1969), 144–150.

Mactaggart, Malcolm

1959 "English Delft Adam and Eve Chargers." *The Connoisseur Year Book, 1959.* London: The Connoisseur, 1959.

Mankowitz, Wolf, and Haggar, Reginald G.

1957 *The Concise Encyclopedia of English Pottery and Porcelain.* London: Andre Deutsch, 1957.

Mountford, A. R., and Celoria, F.

1968 "Some Examples of Sources in the History of 17th Century Ceramics." *Journal of Ceramic History,* No. 1 (1968).

Mynard, D. C.

1969 "A Group of Post-Medieval Pottery from Dover Castle." *Post-Medieval Archaeology,* III (1969), 31–46.

Noël Hume, I.

1956 *Treasure in the Thames.* London: Frederick Muller, 1956.

1958 "Relics from the Wine Trade's Own Church." *The Wine and Spirit Trade Record.* (February 17, 1958), 158–164.

1962 "Excavations at Rosewell, Gloucester County, Virginia, 1957–1959." *United States National Museum Bulletin 225.* Contributions from the Museum of History and Technology. Paper 18. Washington, D. C.: Smithsonian Institution (1962), 153–229.

1966a "Excavations at Tutter's Neck in James City County, Virginia." *United States National Museum Bulletin 249.* Contributions from the Museum of History and Technology. Paper 53. Washington, D. C.: Smithsonian Institution (1966 and 1968), 29–72.

1966b "Mathews Manor: Preview of a Major Archaeological Discovery." *Antiques,* XC (December 1966), 832–836.

1968 "Excavations at Clay Bank in Gloucester County, Virginia, 1962–1963." *United States National Museum Bulletin 249.* Contributions from the Museum of History and Technology. Papers 52–54. Washington, D. C.: Smithsonian Institution (1966 and 1968), 1–28.

1970 *A Guide to Artifacts of Colonial America.* New York: Alfred A. Knopf, 1970.

Oswald, Adrian

1950 "London Stoneware Pottery, Recent Excavations at Bankside." *The Connoisseur,* CXXVI (December 1970), 183–185.

1975 *Clay Pipes for the Archaeologist.* Oxford: British Archaeological Reports, 1975.

Parkinson, Michael R.

1969 *The Incomparable Art, English Pottery from the Thomas Greg Collection.* Manchester: City Art Gallery, 1969.

Rackham, Bernard

1926 *Early Netherlands Maiolica.* London: G. Bles, 1926.

1935 *Catalogue of the Glaisher Collection of Pottery & Porcelain in the Fitzwilliam Museum Cambridge.* 2 vols. Cambridge: Cambridge University Press, 1935.

1952 *Italian Maiolica.* London: Faber and Faber, 1952.

Rackham, Bernard, and Read, Herbert

1924 *English Pottery.* New York: Charles Scribner's Sons, 1924.

Ray, Anthony

1968 *English Delftware Pottery in the Robert Hall Warren Collection, Ashmolean Museum, Oxford.* London: Faber and Faber, 1968.

Solon, L. M.

1886 *The Art of the Old English Potter.* New York: D. Appleton and Co., 1886.

Taggart, Ross E.

1967 *The Frank P. and Harriet C. Burnap Collection of English Pottery in the William Rockhill Nelson Gallery.* rev. ed. Kansas City: Nelson Gallery–Atkins Museum, 1967.

Tait, Hugh
1960 "Southwark (Alias Lambeth) Delftware and the Potter, Christian Wilhelm." Pt. 1. *The Connoisseur,* CXLVI (September 1960, U. S. ed.), 36–42.
1961 "Southwark (Alias Lambeth) Delftware and the Potter, Christian Wilhelm." Pt. 2. *The Connoisseur,* CXLVII (March 1961), 22–30.

Tilley, Frank
1967a "London City Company Arms on English Delftware." Pt. 1. *The Antique Collector,* XXXVIII (June 1967), 121–129.
1967b "London City Company Arms on English Delftware." Pt. 2. *The Antique Collector,* XXXVIII (December 1967), 265–271.
1968a "London City Company Arms on English Delftware." Pt. 3. *The Antique Collector,* XXXIX (June 1968), 125–130.
1968b "London City Company Arms on English Delftware." Pt. 4. *The Antique Collector,* XXXIX (December 1968), 279–283.
1969a "London City Company Arms on English Delftware." Pt. 5. *The Antique Collector,* XL (June 1969), 136–138.
1969b "The 'AW' Master-Salt." *The Antique Collector,* XL (April–May 1969), 80–81.

Van Beuningen, H. J. E.
1973 *Verdraaid Goed Gedraaid.* Rotterdam: Museum Boymans–van Beuningen, 1973.

Volker, T.
1954 *Porcelain and the Dutch East India Company.* Leiden: E. J. Brill, 1954.

Wills, Geoffrey
1967 "English Pottery in 1696: An Unpublished Document." *Apollo,* LXXXV (June 1967), 436–443.
1969 *English Pottery and Porcelain.* Garden City, N. Y.: Doubleday and Co., 1969.

INDEX